AN INDIAN JOURNAL

AN INDIAN
JOURNAL

NORA SCOTT

Edited by
John Radford

The Radcliffe Press
London · New York

Published in 1994 by
The Radcliffe Press
45 Bloomsbury Square
London WC1A 2HY

175 Fifth Avenue
New York
NY 10010

In the United States of America
and Canada distributed by
St Martin's Press
175 Fifth Avenue
New York
NY 10010

A full CIP record for this book is available from the British Library

Library of Congress catalog card number: 93–60691
A full CIP record is available from the Library of Congress

ISBN 1–85043–776–9

Copy-edited and laser-set by Selro Publishing Services, Oxford
Printed and bound in Great Britain by WBC Ltd, Bridgend, Mid Glamorgan

Contents

List of Illustrations

*All illustrations of Indian scenes are reproduced
from original paintings by Nora Scott*

Glossary of Indian Words

amah	a female native servant, nursemaid; usually *ayah* in India
ayah	
begum	a term, or title, used of a well-born Muhammadan lady
betel	the betel leaf, called *pan*, was wrapped round the betel nut and condiments, and offered to visitors. The whole is called *pan supari* (the leaf and the nut)
bheestie	Muhammadan water-carrier, from the Persian for a dweller in Paradise (*bihisht* = Paradise). Kipling's Gunga Din was a *bheestie*
chaprassi	an orderly
chobdar	a mace or staff bearer, a kind of superior orderly for a senior official
dacoity	gang-robbery with violence
durbar	court, hall of audience, levee
garawallah	under-coachman (lit. horseman)
lota	small metal or earthen water vessel
maidan	large level area, a plain or parade ground
mali	gardener
massall	lamp-man or lower servant
Mohurram	the first month of the Muhammadan year, held sacred on account of the deaths of Hassan and Hussain
nawab	a term, or title, used of a Muhammadan noble

nazir	a word applied to various officials, but hard to see who are meant in Bassein
peon	an orderly
punkah	ceiling fan; a coolie pulled a rope to move a wooden beam with cloth attached
qui hai	call for a servant (lit. 'Is there anybody?')
sais/syce	groom, man in charge of a horse
shikarri	hunter, or guide through forest or jungle
sowar	rider, mounted orderly or man in the cavalry
taboot	coffin or bier, is called *taziya* in Northern India; both words are used for the models of the tombs of Hassan and Hussain, carried in procession at the *Mohurram*
tamasha	festivity, spectacle
tattoo-walla	pony-boy
toddy-wallahs	the men who climb the palm trees for toddy
tonga	light pony-trap for hire
tulsi	sweet basil, plant revered by Hindus
zenana	the women's part of the house

Notes on Some of the Proper Names Occurring in the Journal

Bella Vista	The Scotts' house in Bombay
Bell-Irving, Miss (Etta)	An artist friend of Mrs Scott
Bertha	A younger step-sister of John Scott, who came to them for a visit of some months
Conny (Constance)	The author's younger sister. In middle age she turned the papers and recollections of their father, Frederic Hill, into his autobiography. Later she wrote eight books which were well received, chiefly on women writers (Jane Austin, Fanny Burney, etc.)
Diler Jung	A Muhammadan title in Hyderabad, which means 'valiant in war'. The man's actual name was Abdul Huq
Ellen[1]	The author's elder sister, an artist who painted chiefly portraits. She illustrated most of Constance Hill's books (see above)
Ellen[2] (Nellie)	A very young woman who had come to the author in England as a kind of superior servant. In India the birth of the youngest Scott child added to her duties, and she was always there as a 'help' or extra pair

of hands. She stayed 40 years with the author (till the latter's death) and then for 20 (till her own) with that same youngest child. A whole life of devoted service to one family.

Ellaby/Ethel/Pechey

Misses Ellaby (Charlotte) and Pechey were lady doctors; evidently there was already a scheme to bring such women to India, where hardly any Indian lady would dream of seeing a male doctor. Ethel (Miss Dewar) lived with Miss Pechey, and became a great friend of the author whom she would help to entertain Indians.

Sir Jamsetjee Jeejeebhoy

A leading Parsee gentleman. The enterprising and philanthropic Parsee community was an asset to Bombay out of all proportion to its size. Less inhibited by custom and religion than Hindus or Muhammadans, they were a help in social relations

Joseph

The Scott's English-speaking servant

Kumranessa

A Muhammadan friend. The name indeed means 'the ladies' moon', from *qamar* (moon) and *nisa* (ladies)

Manning, Miss

An English lady who had founded societies to improve the lot of Indian women

Marian

Friend of the author, and wife of Major (later Colonel) Willoughby

Morland, Mrs (later Lady)

A lady in Bombay with a fine voice

Sakharam, Miss

Also called Rukmabai. A young Hindu who became very friendly with the author

Stokes, Mrs	A friend, and wife of Colonel Stokes
Salar Jung, Lady	Salar Jung means 'leader in war'. The reference here is apparently to a noble family in Hyderabad. Cf. Diler Jung (above)
Trayer, Monsieur	A French artist under whom Ellen Hill had studied in Paris in the 1860s. He became a friend of all the family

Editor's Note

READING and rereading my grandmother's diary has been a labour of love. The only sadness came from having to wield the scissors with so drastic a hand. The total quantity was much too great for this sort of volume.

I wish to thank my two sons for the help they have given me in different ways. Without their assistance, this book could hardly have been published.

I am also grateful to Dr Lester Crook, who has represented the publishers in all our dealings. It has been a pleasure to work with him.

John Radford
Woodbury
Devon

Preface

In the autumn of 1882 my husband was appointed to the High Court of Bombay as one of the puisne judges, and our life in Egypt — the life that had been ours for ten years — came to an end. His first legal appointment had been that of the English appeal judge on the international tribunals there. We had learnt to love Egypt, and to be interested in the various political changes that were taking place in the country, and we came away with keen regret.

In October, he went out to Bombay, but I could not join him until the following year — for with five children, one a baby, we arranged that they and I should spend that first winter in England in the good climate of Bournemouth. The following year I went out to India leaving our children in the loving care of my husband's sister and brother-in-law, Dr and Mrs Birkbeck Hill — Dr Hill being my own cousin. They lived in Berkshire in beautiful country.

I had not to wait till I reached India to greet my husband, for he had taken advantage of the vacation at the High Court and had come halfway to meet me; we met in the harbour of Alexandria. But we did not go on at once to Bombay. We stayed a week in Egypt and spent most of the time in Cairo with Lord Cromer. The reforms inaugurated before we left Egypt were being carried out with fair success. At the end of that pleasant week, seeing so many of our old friends, we said another 'goodbye' to the old country — to Cairo, Alexandria and Ramleh — the desert — the blue sea — the palm trees — the Bedouin tents — the camels — the donkeys — all vanished and instead of them appeared before us the canal, that wonderful link between the near and the distant East, and then the Red Sea and Perim and the straits of Bab-el-Mandeb, the 'exiles' gate,' as Sir Alfred Lyall christened them — and indeed they are. We sail on and on till we are nearing Bombay — and then! a

xiv

loud report — the ship is telling the good people of the city of Bombay, that great key of India, that the voyage from England is accomplished and London and Bombay have clasped hands again.

That was a wonderful night when, by moonlight, we left the great ship and came away in a little tug with the friendly agent of the P & O Company, who brought us over the harbour till we were under the lights of the Yacht Club. Soon we were on dry land and our carriage and servants are waiting for us. We drive along the low-lying ground, by the harbour, the road winding about and rising more and more as we ascend Malabar Hill — up and up — till we are on the summit and we look down on the great city below us, with its vast harbour and half circle of lights. And then — a little further — we come to some big gates, and we turn in, and we are in our own compound. We see steps and a long veranda and men in turbans smiling and salaaming, to welcome the judge sahib and his wife the 'memsahib'. Indeed to me it all seemed fairyland, it could not be real, sober, earnest. And the next day it seemed to me and my companion too that we were in a fairyland. Then came mail day — and many were the letters I had to write — to my mother, our children, my sisters and some kind relations and friends who were counting on a letter from me. But as I came to have many duties outside our home and my time was more than full, the idea occurred to me of writing at least one long letter with a history of the week's doings; and this letter might be sent first to my father and mother and to our children, and then be sent round the little circle of relations and kind friends who were much interested in our new life in India.

1

March–April 1884

Bombay life and weather, painting bullocks,
Khandalla, a party of schoolgirls

17 March 1884

MY little Ranee, at home, is 18 months old today. She was just four weeks old when her father left her, and all of us, at Hampstead, and came out here to a strange country and new work.

Yesterday we had a visit from Sir Jamsetjee Jeejeebhoy, and we had a long talk about Miss Manning's society — the Society for Promoting Female Education, and for Promoting Social Intercourse between the various races in India. Sir Jamsetjee is president, Mr West vice-president, but Mr West only consented after repeated requests to be vice-president, on condition that he was 'never asked to do anything'. The work in the High Court is so heavy that it is difficult for the judges to undertake any other regular work. Sir Jamsetjee was not very hopeful about the success of the Society here. He thinks the objects good of course, but does not think any formal society can do much in promoting friendliness. He agreed with John, that at Madras the work is easier. There is a large population of native Christians there and a large number of Indians who speak English. But he maintains that social intercourse, with Indian ladies, can only be brought about by degrees and by private efforts. There are not the same difficulties in the way of social intercourse with Parsees, but they are very much of a race apart and their number is comparatively small. Sir Jamsetjee has a large school, for Parsee children. I am to go and see it one day soon.

19 March

Last Monday, our friends, Miss Pechey and Miss Dewar, were present at a very interesting ceremony — a Hindu wedding. They were invited on this occasion as Miss Pechey knows the little bride and her family. When they arrived at the house, they were conducted upstairs, to the reception rooms, where the bride's friends were assembled. Flowers were presented to them, garlands of pink roses and sweet smelling little white flowers rather like jessamine, and queer little stiff nosegays. Then they were invited to join in an important part of the ceremony, the procession of the friends of the bride, to fetch the bridegroom. Seeing that it would be considered a great politeness to do so, they readily agreed and set off, walking with all the bride's relations, and friends, to the house of the bridegroom. Miss Pechey said they felt it very odd, and rather amusing, to be walking there, in this native procession. They were twice the size of the little slim Hindu ladies. The bride's little brothers accompanied them. The bridegroom received them at his house, where more nosegays were presented to them. Miss Pechey says the bridegroom was quite a boy. He did not seem more than 16 years old. He had a pretty embroidered robe on for his wedding, but he did not look happy, he looked rather cross, perhaps he was only bored. Then the procession returned to the house of the bride's parents, escorting the bridegroom. Miss Pechey and Miss Dewar were obliged to leave soon afterwards, so they did not see the concluding ceremonies.

Friday 21 March

Mrs Jardine and I have been painting the white bullocks this morning. They are such grand creatures; I believe these very large bullocks come from Mysore. It is difficult to keep them still, but the man in charge of them is beginning to learn that we want them to keep as much as possible in the same position; he helps us much more than he did at first. We are painting them in the compound, just below the drive, on a little plateau of grass (now very brown and withered) that overlooks the lower road (Breach Candy) and the sea. There are some rough steps down from the drive. At first the bullocks went very timidly down the steps, but now they know their way quite well.

Miss Pechey is very busy now at her consulting rooms. So many native patients have come already that I think she will soon have a very large practice. Miss Pechey's fees for visiting patients are the same as those of most of the English doctors here — ten rupees a visit (more if the place is distant), but in order that poorer patients should have the benefit of good advice, and by the wish of the committee, who appointed her, Miss Pechey charges only half that fee to those patients who go to her rooms. Yesterday an English engineer came to the rooms to ask Miss Pechey if she would see his wife. He said she could not bear the thought of going to a hospital, and yet the doctors' fees here were quite beyond him. When Miss Pechey told him it was five rupees only at her rooms, his whole face brightened up and he exclaimed, 'Then you will have a great many patients. You will make a large fortune.' The dispensary (when it is ready) will be for the very poor. The women will either pay nothing or a few pice (about a penny). From 7.00 o'clock till 9.00 Miss Pechey will be at the dispensary, from 10.00 till 12.00 at her consulting rooms. At 12.00 she goes out to see patients, from 5.00 to 6.00 o'clock she is again at her consulting rooms. Miss Pechey must have a carriage, and two if not three horses for herself. Miss Dewar is buying a victoria and horse for herself. They cannot manage with less than this. Miss Pechey said if she were to charge 'the small fees Parsee doctors do, it would not pay for coach hire.' Their house is almost ready for them, some of the servants are already there, and some furniture. The last fortnight we have had first two, then four, then five of their servants staying here; one of them was a Muhammadan, a friend of our *chobdar*'s. He has been learning to wait.

Sunday 23 March 1884

Our dinner party went off very well last night; no one seemed 'bored'. We were to be 18 and the table just held that number comfortably. After five or six guests had arrived, I saw a tall lady in white satin, coming up the room, and I looked at her wondering who she could be — feeling sure she was no one we expected. Then I recognized the gentleman following her, Mr Geary, editor of the *Bombay Gazette*. I saw then how it was; they were invited for next Saturday, the 29th, and had mistaken the day. I thought they would feel very uncomfortable if they found out their mistake, and they must discover it if no cards with their names were at their places at table. But I could not disappear and go and write the cards, and so, perplexed in my mind but smiling hypo-critically at my guests, I was wondering what I could do when I saw Miss Pechey and Miss Dewar entering. I went to meet them and asked

Miss Dewar to go and write two cards. Off went Miss Dewar directly and wrote two cards, and John managed to disappear for a minute and settle where they were to sit, and finally we all trooped in to dinner — Mr and Mrs Geary quite comfortable and innocent of their mistake. It was a pity, however, as there was the editor of the rival paper, the *Times of India*, not far off at the table from Mrs Geary; and besides being public rivals, the two editors are not very friendly, and we had especially arranged to have them on different days.

Monday 24 March

I have been out this morning for three hours paying calls. Miss Dewar, who had to call on some of the same people, came with me. We first went to Government House, Malabar Point. The house is at the extreme edge of the promontory of Malabar Hill. The south-west wind, which blows so hard in the monsoon, has bent the trees away from the sea and all up the drive these trees — Indian figs, I think — have a strange appearance and must look very weird at night. We found Miss Fergusson at home and had a pleasant visit; she was less shy than usual. One lady we called on, a nice, kindly, motherly woman, took me for Miss Pechey, and finding out her mistake when we were half through our visit, was so overcome that she could do nothing but apologize, though as she had not seen either of us before there was not anything very extraordinary in the mistake. Then we went on and ended by calling on the Danish artist, Mr Van Ruith, who lives at the Cumballa Hotel. His pictures are very clever, both landscape and figures, and he paints flowers also.

Mr Van Ruith has odd experiences with his models. Sometimes — often, he says — he gets a nice figure, a good looking (or picturesque looking) woman, she will come once and then never appear again. The other day he had two men of low caste. He asked his servant what caste one of them was — 'Oh, he is low caste, he will eat meat.' 'What is that man?' said Mr Van Ruith, pointing to the other. 'Oh, he is very low — lowest of all.' 'What does he eat then?' 'Oh, he eats what the sahib does,' indicating Mr Van Ruith, himself! Mr Van Ruith acted it all, in telling us, 'Fancy, the lowest caste of all, the worst of all, can eat what we do. That is what they think, and then Mr Peterson says such nonsense in his lecture the other day — he says they are made of the same stuff as we are!'

Sunday 30 March 1884

A beautiful breezy morning. The sea has little white breakers all over it. Some of the trees have a look of spring with their young green leaves, but many look wintry, for, as in Egypt, the acacias have lost almost all their leaves, and our avenue of gold mohrs (they are acacias) look very poor and bare, and give a very feeble shade in the drive. It is a bad year for the mangoes, and we have only a few on our trees. The unusual cold at Christmas spoilt the bloom they say. Some of the mangoes drop off. They are green and unripe, but we make 'mango fool' of them, which is very nice. John likes it at his *chota hazri* (little breakfast).

I am very late this morning after our party last night. We had asked Mr and Mrs Geary to come again and they did so, Mr Geary saying as they came in, 'I hope I have not made any extraordinary mistake this time!'

In this week's *Spectator* there is a paragraph on a judgement John gave a few days ago. It was a curious case in which some brothers, who had been outcasted, agreed to pay a large sum of money in order to be readmitted into their caste and be allowed to marry girls of the caste. The man who managed the whole thing brought an action for part of the money that he said had not been paid. Certain sums were to be paid to the fathers of the brides through this man, and John ruled that he could not recover such money, as it was in the nature of a purchase of a wife, or wife brokerage, which is totally against English law; and John summed up by saying that although in the low castes the custom of paying for a wife did exist, there was not anywhere, even in Hindu law, any authority for the proceeding, and that it would be wrong 'to give marriage brokers a legal status, such as would enable them to enforce their contracts by law.' 'I think it is immoral and against public policy,' he said, 'even in the present state of matrimonial relations in India. The tendency of such a decision would be to degrade still further the position of women, and to perpetuate the inequality of their relations with the other sex. In my opinion the contract is void under Section 23 of the Contract Act.'

The Indian *Spectator* approves of the decision, and thinks that it will do much good when the marriage brokers, or *dalals*, find that they have no legal claim for their money.

2 April

Last night we dined at the Governor's, at Malabar Point. It was quite a small party, the most sociable of any entertainment we have been to at Government House. John took in Miss Fergusson and made her talk and laugh. When she is interested and amused she loses her shyness and looks quite animated. The Governor took me in. He was pleasant and interesting also, and we had some nice talk. He has been urging the government in England to build another lighthouse in the Red Sea, where it is much wanted, on the end of Perim; and at last it is to be built. He goes to Aden tomorrow by the mail.

Miss Pechey and Miss Dewar went to see Lady Salar Jung last Monday. A Parsee lady, Mrs Pundiki, took them; Mr Pundiki and his brother are Sir Salar Jung's agents here. Lady Salar Jung is the grandmother of the present Salar Jung, and she is staying with the Pundiki's. The house stands in a garden. There were tents all about the garden for the many attendants of Lady Salar Jung. Miss Dewar says they went up a flight of steps onto the veranda, and on the steps and all along the veranda were the remains of little fires where the servants had been cooking, even the little pots, some half full of food, were left all about. Then there were bedsteads — the common wooden bedsteads they make here — all along the veranda, head to foot close together. The beds were only mattresses made of coconut fibre — no sheets or pillows. At last they came to a room opening onto the veranda, where they stopped and were presented to Lady Salar Jung, who was seated on a bed drawn up near to the window, smoking a long chibouk. Two chairs were placed outside on the veranda for Miss Pechey and Miss Dewar. Miss Wadia, a friend of Mrs Pundiki's, interpreted for everybody. She told them not to shake hands with Lady Salar Jung — they did not know why. It might be because the lady had just returned from a pilgrimage. Lady Salar Jung was dressed in bright lilac silk trousers that fitted closely like stockings until above the knees, when they were loose. She had a white muslin embroidered jacket on, and some soft white material like a scarf wound about her; that was all, and a cushion on her lap to lean her arms on. Mrs Pundiki, her hostess, is a big stout woman. She had seated herself on a bedstead that was just outside the window, but a little to the side so as not to impede Lady Salar Jung's view. In the midst of the conversation a loud crash was heard, and looking round they saw that stout Mrs Pundiki had descended through the bedstead and was fixed helplessly, her feet uppermost. Of course there was a rush of people to extricate her, but for some time no one could pull her out. Lady Salar Jung did not so much as turn her head towards her unfortunate hostess, but continued her conversation in a perfectly unmoved voice. Miss Dewar could not help laughing, but Miss Pechey succeeded in looking grave and attending politely to Lady Salar Jung's remarks. They would like to have seen a little girl — a granddaughter of Lady Salar Jung's — but they were told she was not dressed and it would take so very long to dress her that it would be impossible for Miss Pechey and Miss Dewar to see her that morning, but that if they would kindly come back next day at 9.00 o'clock she should be quite ready for them. They could not arrange to do so on account of Miss Pechey's engagements, so they made their excuses and bade them all 'Goodbye'.

Miss Dewar says the number of servants was something wonderful. It does not seem to matter whether attendants are clean and neat, it only matters that there should be a great number of them, that is the dignity. There can be nothing for these people to do all day. A rich Muhammadan here, Cummoo Suliman, from whom we hired our horses, and who will get you anything you want from a chair to a house, told us the other day that he 'fed 500 mouths every day.' I think that must include all his work people, and of course he pays them wages. But anyone who gets a salary, however small, 20 or 30 rupees a month from some small government appointment, is expected to maintain any number of poor relations — perhaps ten or fifteen.

Saturday 5 April 1884
It is very hot today, but there is a little breeze which helps one to bear it. Yesterday was far the worst day we have had since I came out in November. It was 88 degrees in John's study, a degree or two less in the dining room, but most oppressive everywhere. I did not know what heat was before. I have never in the hottest weather in Egypt felt anything like it. There, with the thermometer out of doors much higher, when for instance a Khamseen wind is blowing, inside the house we rarely had it hotter than 76 or 80 degrees. I cannot think houses are built on the right principle here. In Egypt our very thick walls and square built houses seemed almost to defy the weather. Here the houses are built in a long straggling way and you can have in no part such a

space between you and the sunshine as we could get in our Egyptian houses. Here we seem wholly dependent on nature, like the peasants in Millet's pictures — if she is favourable we prosper, that is we have a nice wind and are cool, if not we are hot and miserable.

I have had the white bullocks this morning for the last time. It was hot sitting out till 9.30, but I wanted to finish them. Yesterday sitting in the shade at 8.00 a.m. was almost unbearable. I have done a small hasty sketch of the bullocks to send home to the children.

Today, we are to have the examination of the ambulance class; Dr Hatch is to examine us. Some of the members are very nervous at the idea — I hope Nellie will pass. Dr Burgess (the antiquarian), who was here a few weeks ago, told us that when he was upcountry, many miles (100, I think he said) from any railway or town, he was passing near a river, when some men came running to him to tell him a boy had been drowned. They would have left the boy for dead, which he was to all appearances. 'Now it so happened,' as Miss Edgeworth would say, that Dr Burgess had been reading only a few days before the directions for saving the apparently drowned. He immediately proceeded to treat the boy according to these directions, moving the boy's arms to expand the chest, and so on. He continued for an hour before the natural breathing began again. Then he went on with the rest of the treatment until the boy was restored to life and consciousness. Dr Burgess said the surprise and gratitude of the natives were unbounded, only what was very embarrassing to him, they insisted on bringing all their sick people to him, and begging him to prescribe for them. In our ambulance class we have been practising this treatment on a little Hindu boy laid on a table. To make amends to him for being pulled and poked about, I always have a plate of cakes ready for him at the end of the lecture.

Khandalla, Wednesday 9 April

Here we are, at our little house on the hills again. It is such a change from Bombay — 'Dreamy, steamy, musty, fusty Bombay,' John calls it. The air here is so light and pure and the breeze so beautifully cool in the morning and evening, I can almost fancy, if I shut my eyes and listen just to the sounds of bird and insect life, that I am in England — in the country or at the seaside with Mamma and the dear children, or at Burghfield, with all its lovely sights and sounds — and we are counting the time till John's return from Egypt. The wind is making such a musical sound in the casuarina trees, as in *Feats on the Fiord*, when 'the wind in the stillest night in Norway makes music, from thousands of tiny harps in the fir trees.' I suppose the casuarina is a kind of fir tree — the leaf is the same only still finer.

We came up yesterday afternoon — Ellen and I, and Joseph and one of the *hammalls* (housemaids, only they are men). It was hot driving to Byculla station and the first ten hours in the train were hot, but we were fortunate in having a much better day than any day last week. When we were going through the station, to the platform, there were a number of poor rough natives — men and women — in front of us, showing their tickets and passing through the gate. I saw the ticket collector motioning them to stand back, and did not understand at first that it was to make way for us. I told the collector (a young European) 'I did not wish them stopped for us,' but they waited till I had passed. Of course one is sorry for such a thing, but it must not be put down to the English rule, a native collector would do just the same — probably much more roughly — if he saw a sahib English or native coming.

Thursday
John was to have come up Tuesday night, but he was so tired at the end of a long day's work on Monday that he decided to come by the early train on Wednesday instead. He has been today across the ravine, and he found on the hill at the side, instead of the desolation he expected, a native village, fields in cultivation and cattle grazing. Three cows strayed into our compound today; John found one of them comfortably feeding in our new little kitchen garden. We impounded them, and this evening an old man appeared — the cow-keeper — begging to have his cows. John told him he must not let them stray again, and then I told him I wanted to sketch two of his cows, and he salaamed and grinned, much relieved at no punishment and promised to bring the cows if I would ask his master.

Khandalla, Saturday 12 April 1884
I have come into my bedroom hoping to find it a little cooler, or rather a little less roasting than the sitting room, the front wall of which is only a wooden lattice. Yesterday for several hours the thermometer marked 92 degrees. Today (12.00 o'clock) it is 86 degrees. Midday here, on the Ghats, is certainly worse than at Bombay, partly I suppose,

because the house is small and the walls thinner, but I believe the actual heat at Khandalla, in the daytime, is greater than in Bombay. The mornings and evenings, however, are delicious. I was sitting on the veranda this morning, sketching from soon after 7.00 o'clock till 9.00, and it was delightful. John climbed up the hill on the other side of the road, but he came back before 8.00 o'clock, it was so hot in the sun. It is difficult to arrange one's time properly, because the cool hours, when you can walk or work, are just the hours when you can get refreshing sleep. When you first go to bed you cannot sleep comfortably, it is so oppressively hot, but towards morning it is much better; you lose the feverish feeling and can then generally sleep.

It is just what the doctor I met at Miss Manning's told me — he never let his wife get up at 5.00 or 6.00 o'clock, but insisted on her sleeping when she could sleep, and this advice he gave to everyone. Our sitting room will be better when the roof of the veranda is finished. At present there is only the iron roof; when the wooden roof, below the iron, is added, we hope there will be a great improvement. But I think while we have only lattice work for the front wall of our parlour, we cannot expect it to be a cool room in summer, or a warm room in winter. It was very cold at Christmas when we were here. However, it would cost a good deal to put up a stone wall and windows, so we must go on, as we are, for the present. J is working in his study, which is in a separate little building; it is a little better there than here, as he can use the inner room, and so get away from the latticework outer wall. But he has not done half as much work as he hoped to do. With the thermometer at 92 degrees and no *punkahs*, it is difficult to do law work. However, he feels much better today in spite of the heat, and is now attacking the 'Jain case'.

Yesterday, as we were sitting in the study, trying to think it much better than Bombay, a man came up to us carrying a dish covered with a white cloth, and salaaming to us. What could it be? Who could send us a present here? We took off the cloth and there, between two pieces of a banana leaf, was a little heap of strawberries, real English strawberries. We forgot the heat, and India, and everything. They were a present from the station master, a Hindu who is famous for his garden and his strawberries. John has often had a friendly chat with him, and so, I·suppose, he kindly sent us these strawberries. We had them at lunch, and I had some cream with mine; it was so English. Presents had not ceased, for in the afternoon up came another man, carrying a dish, a large piece of ice on it, and on the ice two fresh fish. These were sent by the man who keeps the *dak* [Travellers'] Bungalow. A friend of ours at Poona, Mrs Stokes, is famous for the number of presents she gets. One day when she was showing us some fresh acquisition, she said, 'You see how many presents I get.' 'How do you manage it?' asked John. 'By being pleasant,' she answered. 'I wish you would teach me, then,' said John. 'Ah! that is a secret,' she replied — I think it is a secret John knew already.

There are colonies of red ants in our garden, and they are now very busy making their nests. They build them in trees, at some little height from the ground. I do not know what animal they escape from thereby, but they must have a good reason. The nests are, some of them, as large as a man's head; others, much smaller. They are made of leaves, green leaves, still growing on the tree. The ants draw them together, and fasten them with a white cobweb, leaving little round entrances into the nest, walled round with thick cobweb. If there is a gap, if the twigs they have drawn together do not give leaves enough, they fetch a fallen leaf and make a neat patch. We caught an immense beetle last night, and we have preserved it; I think it is the same as one in the collection we sent home for Leslie's and Lilian's cabinet. The monkeys we have not yet seen. Perhaps, now the water course is almost dry, they do not come so often to the ravine. A month ago, when Miss Pechey and Miss Dewar were here, their maid, Ann, saw a little baby monkey just at the top of the slope, and thinking it would be a nice companion for her beloved 'Bongie' she scrambled down among the jungle after it. But a large monkey jumped out of a hole, chattering at her, and she fled. Perhaps it was the baby monkey's mother.

Easter Sunday, 13 April
It is hard to believe it is Easter Sunday, here on the mountains, no church to go to for our beautiful Easter service; the only sound the constant buzz and humming of insects, and a little way off, the tinkling of the bells of the bullocks, as they go along the high road to Poona. Some of the bells are musical, at this distance, and I am fond of listening to them, and fond of watching them, the patient bullocks pulling the heavy carts and their patient drivers passing all day along the road, going only two or, at the most, three miles an hour. Every now and then

11

we hear a quick rattling sound, and a brisk little *tonga* goes by, with English people in it, probably visitors, like ourselves, from Bombay or some big town, come here for the Easter holiday. Watching the road from the window here, in all the heat, and stillness, and dreaminess, it seems very like

> Looking through the mirror clear
> Shadows of the world appear
> There she sees the highway near
> Winding down to Camelot.

Only it goes to Poona, not to Camelot, and instead of the cool, beautiful English fields, that 'clothe the wold and meet the sky,' there are yellow, parched hills on either side, stretching away in one unbroken glare.

Bella Vista, Tuesday 15 April

Our little holiday is over, and we are back again in Bombay. I might know we are home by the tormenting mosquitoes, which are attacking me at this minute. I have just wrapped up my right wrist in my pocket handkerchief; the left (not holding the pen) is more free to move when the enemy comes.

I *did* see the monkeys at last at Khandalla, though some way off, on the opposite side of the ravine. Unfortunately John had just gone out. Nellie saw them first. There they were, some 40 or 50 of them, running and leaping on the hill opposite, very light grey, and as large, I should say, as Mr Hooper's dog 'Tiger'. They all went down into the ravine, probably to drink in the little pool that remains there, though the stream and waterfall are quite dry now.

Mrs Stevens, whom I met at Khandalla, told me she had seen great numbers of monkeys at Matheran. One day she watched some mother monkeys with their young ones. The mothers put their little ones on the low branches of a tree and then rested themselves, or played with their grown-up companions. The baby monkeys amused themselves by running up and down along the branches; but when there was any noise, or any sign of danger, the mothers caught up their children instantly, and ran off with the little ones sitting on their backs, clinging round their necks. I am beaten by the mosquitoes and must leave off writing.

12

Friday 18 April

John has had a little fever, but is much better today, after several doses of quinine.

The day John left us at Khandalla the gardener felt ill with fever. I went to see him. He came out of his little hut, wrapped up in the rough cloak the country people on the hills wear, no turban on. He crouched down on the ground looking most doleful, as the natives do, if they are at all ill. I do not think I should have recognized him. The day before he had looked so nice, sitting in the field for me to sketch him, with his white tunic and red turban. It was just like Thackeray's picture in his Paris sketchbook of Louis XIV, without his robes of state. I prescribed some medicine I ordered, only he asked that it 'should not be mixed with our water.' So we got a little can of his water and mixed his medicine. I asked him if he would like to go home for a few days, but he preferred to stay where he was. In the evening, talking to Joseph about him, I discovered that he had a little wife living with him, in the hut in our compound. We had never seen her, or known of her existence. I sent for her and found her a little girl of 11 and lame. She had been married to this man at three years of age, and after their marriage had had an accident — a bullock cart went over her and crippled her for life. Neither could get free, if they wished, from the infant marriage. It is fortunate for her that her husband is kind to her. He told Joseph, he would not leave her with his parents, who live some miles away among the hills, for fear they should make her work on the road, or in the fields, and hurt her. I asked her if she had ever learnt anything — nothing, except to grind corn, and make bread. When we are at Khandalla next, I shall see what can be done. None of these low-caste women can sew. Their clothes are only one or two long scarves wound round them; sewing is not necessary, to them, I suppose. Our *peon* here has been making a little cotton jacket, cutting it out and sewing it. Nellie asked him whom it was for? 'For his wife,' he said, 'she could not sew herself, so he was making it for her.'

23 April

Our school party yesterday went off very well. I think all the girls enjoyed themselves, although at first some were extremely shy. They arrived at 4.20, three carriages full — 17 of them with the mistress, Miss Fenemore — all of them in white. The girls' Sunday dresses used to be very ugly and Miss Fenemore got leave from the committee to let them wear white for 'best'. Five or six of the girls were pupil-teachers or head girls, waiting to go out into service, or other employment. When they arrived, I asked the girls if any of them would like to drive along the short road, before coming into the house. I knew they seldom saw the sea. Many wished to do so, so our big carriage and one of the others, went off again, and the girls had a little drive along Breach Candy. The others came into the house and we looked at sketches and photographs — rather solemnly, the girls being so shy. Miss Dewar had come to help me and later on Mrs Stead came. When the girls had returned from their drive, I suggested that some should go out in the garden to play at battledore and shuttlecock, and this was very success-ful. Others sat down to draughts and spellikens. At 5.30 we all went to tea — 21 of us altogether. The children did not seem very hungry and did not eat a quarter of what English school children would do, but Miss Fenemore told me she thought they were too much excited to eat. Coffee was more popular than tea I found, as they do not get coffee at school. We rather wanted someone — like my sister Ellen — to make a little fun at tea. Mrs Stead, though so very good and kind and bright, is not at her ease with children, and Miss Dewar is rather shy too. After tea we did much better. I proposed games and we all played at 'My ship has come into harbour'. This was very successful and we went on a long time at it as the girls liked it. Then we played 'I've been to China' and the girls were very merry over that. Then we played at 'Post', I reading out the names and kind Miss Dewar rushing about, the first to be blindfolded.

Then at 7.15 Joseph appeared with trays of ices, which we thought would be a treat to the girls, and which our cook made. John came in for the last quarter of an hour and some of the girls sang to us, a very tragic song about a soldier, and then the Canadian Boat Song. Then they all said 'Good-night' and went off to Byculla; a beautiful fresh breeze was blowing and they would have a pleasant drive home.

There were a few little fair-haired English children among the girls. It was rather curious playing 'Post', for all these Eurasian girls, not one of whom I suppose had seen England, took the names of towns in England; only one called herself 'Sydney' and no one took the name of a town in India.

Evening, Thursday

I have been out all morning, and so lost my usual Thursday morning for writing letters. I had to call on a lady, a long way from here and then went to a bazaar for Mr Squires' schools and to our workshop, where I had not been for some time. I found that Louisa, the poor girl who was so troublesome, had been doing better lately, so I asked the matron, Mrs Donaldson, if she might come over one afternoon to see me. Mrs Donaldson said she should be very glad for her to come, as there was no one to show the girl kindness — so she is here now. The daughter of the head needlewoman came with her, and they are now having tea in the garden — the little garden at the back of the house — with the fountains playing, just by them, and the tall palmyras rustling, or rather clashing, their great leaves together over their heads.

Miss Dewar kindly came in to help me, but now John has returned from a very hard day in court and wanted a drive, so Miss Dewar has gone with him. She kindly wanted to stay with the girls, and for me to go out with John. She is always so kind and ready to help me. I asked her the other day if she and Miss Pechey would come in to dinner, to meet some friends — we wanted them to help us I said, as John was tired. 'This is not a proper invitation,' I explained, 'this is to help us.' 'You had better never ask us if you want us to refuse,' said Miss Dewar, 'for we shall always accept.'

2
May

Meeting Indian ladies, caves and temples at Karli, a school concert

May Day

Such a hot steamy Indian May Day. The Lancashire saying 'Ne'er cast a clout till May be out,' would not apply to Bombay. Some days the heat seems unendurable. However, tomorrow week is the last day of this term, then comes our holiday.

Yesterday I went to Miss Pechey's to help in entertaining some Indian ladies whom Miss Pechey had invited to spend the afternoon with her and Miss Dewar. As these ladies were 'purdah ladies', Muhammadans who keep themselves shut up from the sight of a man (except their relations), we had to receive them in 'purdah' style. Nellie and Ann were below, in the hall, to open the door and show the ladies in, the butler and all the men having been told to hide themselves away. Our visitors were late, and we were afraid, they were not coming, but at last two closely shut up carriages drove into the compound, and soon afterwards three ladies and a little girl appeared at the drawing-room door, enveloped in their 'balloon-like' silk cloaks. One of the ladies was stout, but the other two were thin and interesting looking. The husband of one of them, Mr Ameeroodeen Tyabjee, came with them, and he was very pleasant, friendly and merry, evidently pleased to come and to bring his womenkind. He had on a black watered silk cloak, or rather long coat with wide sleeves, and trimmed with gold braid at the edges, long white trousers (about as loose as sailors' trousers in England), and a white and gold turban. He and all his brothers have been educated, or, at least, spent many years, in England. I asked if either of the ladies had been to England. 'no,' he replied, 'we wish

16

they would, but they will not come out of purdah, and I think the last few years it is worse than ever — our ladies keep so close.' After a time some more ladies arrived. The wife of the barrister and member of council, Mr Budrudeen Tyabjee, is rather a stout cheery-looking person, and seemed very ready to talk and be pleasant, although all our remarks to each other had to be interpreted. She brought three daughters, with her, one a girl of 13 'was just beginning purdah,' as her uncle explained to us. She wore the sari, or long scarf, which goes over the head and can at any moment be drawn over the face. The younger children wore little round caps embroidered with gold, very like the students' caps at Heidelberg, those worn by the students who belong to the 'fighting colleges'. The little girls' dresses were very much like those of children in a circus in England. One had a black silk embroidered jacket, her red and gold cap, a very full white muslin skirt, spangled with gold, white stockings and stumpy little shoes. Her hair hung down her back in four long narrow plaits, and two front plaits were taken back over a blue ribbon, leaving her ears, with large earrings to be seen. She could speak some English and so could the other girls. They go to a mission school, and the mother said they were very happy there. Then came refreshments, tea and coffee, cakes and fruit. The ladies all took something, but Mrs Budrudeen did not seem to know what to do with her dessert knife and fork — she held them both in one hand. Only one lady talked English, and she and I had a merry little chat together. I asked her to come and see me, and then she asked me if I would come first to her, but she was going away for a month to Gujerat, and would write to me when she returned. 'But,' she said, 'you will not remember my name when I write to you.' I asked her if her name was not Tyabjee. 'No, that is my uncle's name, my husband's name is Azra Achmet, and my own name is Kumranessa.' I said then names generally had meanings what did hers mean? 'Oh, I will not tell you what it means,' she declared laughing. 'Well, my name is Nora,' I said, 'then I will tell you what my name means, the 'woman's moon', 'the lady's moon'. I admired some embroidery on her sari and she told me she had done it herself, 'but,' she added, 'it is your stitches, it is tatting and crochet.' The dresses were mostly of English or French silks, made I suppose for the Indian market, but they were not beautiful in colouring like the silks the Parsees wear, and which come from China. Some of the dresses were like those I remember dear Aunt

17

Harriet wearing, long ago, a shot grey and lilac. When our friends departed they all asked us to come and see them, and Mr Tyabjee proposed tomorrow afternoon. So we are going, Miss Pechey, Ethel and I at about 5.00 o'clock, and I think I shall take my sketchbook, and make a pencil sketch of one of the children. I said yesterday I should like to draw one of them one day and the mother, Kumranessa, agreed directly.

Sunday 4 May 1884

Our dinner party last night went off all right. We were 20. Everyone talked and looked cheerful so I hope they liked it. Monsieur Follet, the French consul-general, took me in and John took in Madame Follet. They are nice people and speak and write English better than any foreigners I ever met. Monsieur Follet was consul in Australia at Sydney for many years and then in Wales, and his children are consequently more English than French by education. One of them sings nicely and the other is fond of drawing. Madame Follet told me they had just left a scene of great festivity in their compound. Their head coachman had come to them and told them he 'wanted to marry his son' and asked either for five days' holiday or leave to have the *tamasha* in the compound. They gave him leave to have the marriage celebrated in their compound; and now the friends and relations have all assembled and all day long and far into the night the revels are kept up, the tom-toms going continuously, Madame Follet fears that notes of remonstrance will flow in from aggrieved neighbours. Yesterday a black sheep was sacrificed, first decked up with garlands of flowers, poor thing, and then drugged. In the evening torches were lighted, but this Madame Follet thought dangerous as the huts are made up, so much, of bamboo, and in this weather everything is so dry and ready to catch fire, so that torches could not be allowed. The bridegroom is 14 years old, the bride 10.

While I write the birds are making such a noise — crows, sparrows, bulbuls, pigeons (or doves) and several great hawks are hovering overhead, uttering their peculiar cry. Three or four squirrels have been having such a game, chasing each other up and down the straight stem of a tall palmyra that grows close to the veranda. If only they would cock up their tails as English squirrels do they would look very pretty, for their skins are a delicate grey colour, with dark stripes.

We have caught three more snakes, all poisonous; a little cobra yesterday close to the kitchen, and the day before a huge snake seven and a half feet long. They call it a *dhamin*. It was just getting away, into a hole, when the gardener saw it, and caught it. Three days ago a poor woman was killed by a cobra in the garden of an old bungalow. She went out for some water and felt a little prick in her foot, that was all, and three hours afterwards she died. A snake charmer came and offered to charm the snake which he said would bring the poor woman to life.

Friday afternoon Miss Pechey, Miss Dewar and I went, as arranged, to the house of Mr Kumrudeen Tyabjee, a solicitor, one of five brothers, who have all done well in the world, all beginning by an education of some years in England. When we got to the house, the children of the family were standing on the veranda, with Mr Tyabjee, to receive us. We went through a room and up some stairs, and there, on the landing, was the hostess, and some other ladies, who all gave us a very kind welcome and took us into the drawing-room. It was furnished in European style, but not prettily, and there was no *punkah*. I believe the women's apartments never have *punkahs*. The ladies were elaborately dressed, in brighter colours than when they came out to Miss Pechey's. Even in their own house they always keep the sari over the head, but they were of thin gauze and scarcely hid the head or neck. One lady, the sister-in-law Mrs Hassan Tyabjee, was a very jolly lady. No other word describes her. She was rather stout, but very active and she laughed and made jokes all the time. They seem to be a happy, united, family and I should think are a specimen of the best Muhammadan families here. A daughter of Mrs Hassan sang to us in Hindustani on a funny little harmonium. She sang sweetly, but she touched the notes like a beginner, playing only single notes at one time.

I was shown an enormous portrait album, with photographs of all the relations, and portraits of English friends of the gentlemen. There were portraits of some Indian gentlemen friends, but when I asked who one rather striking-looking person was, Mrs Hassan laughed and said: 'How should I know? I never see them.' The youngest child of the house was brought in, a little girl two years old, with a sallow complexion and very black curly hair. She had a little black silk skirt on down to her ankles embroidered with gold, a white shirt and over it a scarlet gauze jacket edged with emerald-green trimming, shoes and stockings. The older children looked more suitably dressed, at least to our ideas. There

19

was nothing fresh and childlike in such a dress for a child of two years. A boy of about nine had a tunic of pale blue watered silk, simply made, and white cotton trousers.

All the children went away a few minutes after we arrived and I did not like to propose to draw one of the grown-up ladies — it would be too much like making a curiosity of them, I thought, on a first visit — but I asked them to come and see me (after we return from Khandalla) and they promised to do so. Then I shall have an opportunity, I hope. At about 6.00 o'clock ices were handed round by the *ayahs*. They handed spoons round, bowl foremost, perhaps meaning politely not to touch the bowl themselves. After ices, came coffee, very good coffee but not Arab coffee. After that came fruit and pastry, and a sweetmeat called *hallowa*, but not like our *hallowa* in Egypt. The pastry had some wonderful stuff inside, which I really could not eat when I got it on my plate, but I ate some of the outside crust, and soon, to my relief, one of the ladies came and took my plate away and brought some *hallowa*. At last, at 7.00 o'clock, we got up and said 'Goodbye'. Mr Tyabjee asked us 'just to walk into the next room for a minute before going,' and when we got there we found three garlands of white flowers and roses, which the ladies hung round our necks, and on the table was a box of scent bottles, and Mr Tyabjee put some scent on our hands. Then, at the very last, they filled our hands with little white flowers, something like daisies closed up, or very small chrysanthemums, broken off short without stalks, and gave us each some *betel* nut leaves which were doubled up and enclosed a sweet. At the point a clove was stuck through and fastened it together. This *betel* nut leaf is the one token of friendliness that must be given to visitors on parting. I intended to taste mine when I got home but unfortunately they were thrown away.

A voice from a long chair in the last state of exhaustion, John's, 'I wish England had never taken India, and then we could not have come here. Put that down, in your diary.' John is dressed all in white, no necktie. The only thing to wish is 'to take off one's skin, and sit in one's bones.'

Khandalla, Sunday 11 May 1884

We are again at Khandalla and this time we find the climate far better than it was at Easter. It is still hot for some hours in the middle of the day, but the thermometer has only gone up to 84 or 85 degrees, instead of 92 degrees. We must expect some hot days, but if we have a good deal of this weather, the change will do John a great deal of good I am sure. It was a great 'flitting', coming up here for five weeks, like a big gypsy encampment on the march. We came in three relays, or rather four, for the young horses and the victoria came separately by road, not by railway. They started Thursday morning at 4.00 o'clock and have just arrived a quarter of an hour ago. The coachman and *sais* [groom] are washing them down after the fatigue of their journey; though horses in England would not think much of what they have done, 60 miles in three days. This last part, they came very leisurely, for they left the last halting place (seven miles from here) at 1.00 a.m. this morning and got here at 8.00 — seven miles in seven hours. The landau, and my horses, as we call them, are to leave Bombay this morning, and I suppose they will arrive Tuesday night or Wednesday morning. Coolies are to pull the landau up the Ghats, as it is so heavy. As we came through Narel, on Friday, we saw numbers of coolies waiting to carry ladies and luggage up to Matheran. That is a distance of seven miles and a coolie carries a box up there for five annas, about sixpence halfpenny, or seven annas if it is a big one. It seems very little pay. I don't think I could give them five annas for seven miles. Here women carry the luggage from the station, all but the very heavy cases. Ethel and I, Nellie, Joseph, Simon and the *peon* came up Friday afternoon with boxes, packing cases, bundles of bedding, baskets, chairs, pots and pans, carpets and lamps and Tiger, the dog. Also Simon's wife and two children, and Joseph's wife and child. Altogether 19 of us have migrated from Bombay to the hills for the hot weather. The cane and mud stables are a great success, so cool and comfortable. The roofs are thatched and below, between the rafters, twigs of the mango tree with the leaves on are stuffed in, which add to the thickness. The mud plaster will be washed away in the monsoon, but the wooden supports, which are very strong, and the roof will endure. The contractor, who has done all the work at this house since John bought it, is a fine looking old Maratha. He does not do his work punctually to the agreed time, but all his work is very well done.

14 May

We have had some hot days since I last wrote in my diary. Yesterday was a curious misty day, a forerunner of the monsoon, I suppose, but it was not refreshing; there was not the slightest breeze. Even the delicate leaves of the mimosas did not stir. When I rested in the afternoon I felt as if the sun had got through the roof and was shining straight down on my head — 'those sunbeams like swords' are not pleasant when you cannot get away from them. The big carriage and horses arrived this morning having managed the journey very well. Ethel and I went round to the stables to see them, and found the horses enjoying some hay and the coachman and *sais* washing the carriage. Ameer, the coachman, is a fine looking man, a *Purboo*, by caste. He looks well even in his stable clothes. The *saises* dispense with clothes almost entirely except when they go out with the horses, which must be economical, as well as comfortable. We have fared better with our carriages than friends in Bombay did. A few weeks ago they bought a victoria at a sale on Malabar Hill. After the sale was over they sent up some coolies to fetch the carriage (there were no horses with it). Their butler was watching for the arrival of the carriage when he heard a loud crash. Foreboding something wrong he went out, and there he found the carriage at the bottom of Malabar Hill lying on its side smashed to pieces. The coolies had drawn it too fast down hill, lost command of it and it had dashed down and gone against a wall. When the butler found it every coolie had disappeared. The poor people who had just bought the carriage of course had no redress. Nothing could be got from coolies, if they could have caught them.

We are hoping, that Miss Pechey will come to us for a Saturday and Sunday, if she can leave her patients for a day or two. A little while ago she performed an operation on an Indian lady, a Hindu. Miss Dewar had been helping Miss Pechey and the operation was long and painful. At the end Ethel was surprised by the lady putting up her arms and laying a hand tenderly on each of Ethel's cheeks. Then, in a grateful voice she said, 'I respect you more than I do my sisters' — so the husband who was by translated her speech.

Friday 16 May 1884

John and Ethel have just come back from Karli. They started at 6.00 o'clock and drove along the Poona road across the plain to the foot of the hills. A Hindu boy went with them as guide. A climb of 400 feet takes you to a sort of platform three-quarters of the way up the hill — there the caves are cut into the rock. The big temple is like the nave of a church. John says, it is exactly the size of the lady chapel in Norwich cathedral. Near the big cave there are cells cut into the rock in tiers, where the guardians of the temple used to live, and where some ascetics and pilgrims still live. A spring of water comes out of the side of the hill and there are big trees that overshadow the entrance to the temple. When they had examined the temple, they spread out their breakfast on the ground under one of the big trees, and all the people, 'padres' as they call themselves, Fathers of the Church as John calls them, with their wives and children came to look on. Then John got up in all the dignity of a judge-sahib and said in his best Hindustani, 'Every one must go away — I want no one.' Whereupon they all retreated to about 20 yards off and stood there watching. After breakfast, John and Ethel strolled about and came across a poor old ascetic, who was travelling to all the holy places in India, in order to make his happiness in the next world certain. He had only some rags on for clothes and his hair was very long — nearly to his knees and matted. They never cut their hair or wash themselves while on these pilgrimages. But John says there was something striking in his face — it was very emaciated, with big eyes, wide open, looking as it were over you into the plain; his features were clear cut. John felt he would like to give him something, but was doubtful whether he would take it; Ethel suggested that John should try, and so he beckoned to him, but he did not move. John then climbed up to the little platform of rock outside the cell, where the old man was and offered him a small piece of silver. The old fellow stood still but said '*Sahib kya munkta?*' (What do you want?) John held out the money, the man put out his hand and John dropped the coin into it. The old man did not say a word but stood looking out in his abstracted way and John retreated feeling, he says, as if he had been making an offering to a god — not giving alms to a man. All the people down below were watching the scene, and directly John got down pressed round him — men, women and children clamouring for baksheesh. Coming back across the plain, John says, they saw a wonderful bird, as big as a pelican but with much longer legs and a very long neck. It was a greyish blue colour with a long narrow red beak. The boys who were carrying the basket and wraps stopped rather frightened at the great bird and ran back to John. Perhaps we can learn in Bombay what the bird was. They brought me back a lovely branch of a flowering tree — orange and yellow, with leaves something like Spanish chestnut leaves.

John says I must add that he found it a very good plan to tell the guide to tell the people that he was a *burra sahib* (a great man) and must not be troubled; and until they saw the transaction with the holy man, when, I suppose, the temptation to beg became too strong for them, they did leave him and Ethel alone.

The barber has been here today and brings the news that some gentlemen at the hotel here went out shooting yesterday, and brought home a tiger, ... also an animal that the barber described as 'like a tiger but not a tiger.' We think it must be a cheetah.

This is the great season for weddings, and we see many marriage processions pass along the high road. One has just gone by. On a piebald pony was seated the bridegroom, and, in front, went some men with musical instruments — a drum, a sort of horn and I don't know what the others are. A number of friends go with the bridegroom, and they stop at their friends' houses — just as the Bedouins do in the wedding processions in Egypt — and play and sing. We passed a procession yesterday and the person on the pony was so covered with wreaths and ornaments that we could not see if it was the bride or bridegroom — I suppose it was the bride.

We have a great deal of music going on now. Besides the tom-tomming in the native village, a band plays constantly two fields off. There is a large Roman Catholic school here and the boys have a band among themselves. Two of the Fathers called here on Friday to ask us if we would come to a school concert, and if John would preside on the occasion. They want to collect a little money for the new instruments. The priests were German — evidently — Father Fischer and Brother Waldmann. They were very genial and merry — as Roman Catholic priests often are — however poor they may be. This school does a great deal of good; English, Eurasians and natives all go to it. We shall go and see the school when the boys are at their lessons. The concert is to take place next Wednesday at 5.00 o'clock on some flat ground, above the station.

Thursday 22 May

Yesterday the concert at the Roman Catholic school here took place. It was given in order to get some money to buy new instruments for the boys' band — and the result was very satisfactory; they got more money than they at all expected. The concert began at 6.00 o'clock. It was out of doors on a pretty little hill just outside the village, which is covered with mango trees and bamboos. There is just space enough without trees to accommodate the school and an audience of 80 or 100 persons. The boys played very nicely, being conducted by the bandmaster, Brother Waldmann. The Fathers sang two German part songs together beautifully, without any accompaniment. The first glee they sang was called 'The Huntsmen' and the other 'The Swiss Boy'. I thought there was something very pathetic in these men — all devoted to a self-denying life, all here, in voluntary exile, standing there in their plain black cassocks surrounded by their pupils, some fair English boys, but most of them dark Eurasians or Indians, and all singing together, 'I am a Swiss boy and love my home' and 'I love pleasure and fun.' John, being patron, he and I were given a sofa in front, and I was very glad of a comfortable seat, for the concert was long and I was tired. It grew dark before the second part began, and lamps that had been hung in the trees were lighted. The effect was very romantic — with the yellow sunset sky and the tall and feathery bamboos, across the light, and below, the village tank, giving a pleasant feeling of coolness. Later on, as the twilight vanished and the sky darkened, out shone the noiseless fireflies said to be red or reddish in their light, but they are not. Their light is cold, just like the light of a glow-worm, and as they appeared, hundreds together, I thought of *Locksley Hall* and the Pleiades rising 'like a cloud of fireflies tangled in a silver braid.'

At 8.00 o'clock the concert came to an end and, before the final 'God save the Queen', the rector of St Mary's stood up and made a little speech, thanking us for our help, and others too, and speaking enthusiastically of the good that music does to us all. He spoke with a foreign accent — they are all Germans — but very fluently. He hoped, he said, that the boys would be able to do something in return for the kindness that had been shown to them, and give nice music to the inhabitants of Khandalla. 'And den,' he said, 'we must expect dat we shall have nicer *concairts* in Eternity.' He spoke entirely from his heart; he did not know that the transition was rather abrupt from the boys' band to music in heaven. After he spoke and John had said a word or two, up got a Portuguese gentleman, Monsieur d'Aguiar, who had taken a great interest in getting up the concert. He had sung too — 'The Boatswain's Story' — a long ballad about a ship pursuing a whale up to the North Pole; but all that people could hear was at the end of every verse, 'And that is the truth, said he.' Monsieur d'Aguiar, however, looked so smiling and radiant, so very happy in his own performance, that you felt good-humoured in looking at him, and you could not help at the end clapping loudly the 'Boatswain's Story'.

Well, Monsieur d'Aguiar got up, and said that he must propose three cheers for the 'Honourable Mr and Mrs Scott,' and when the three cheers had been given 'one cheer more for Mrs Scott.' It was very kind of them, but very unexpected. Then there was a cheer for Monsieur d'Aguiar and one for Sir Jamsetjee Jeejeebhoy (who was present) and then we came away. Sir Jamsetjee Jeejeebhoy came home with us to dinner, and so did Mr Griffiths (head of the Bombay School of Art) who is in Khandalla, also, for the hot weather.

Sir Jamsetjee is a nice kindly man and does a great deal of good work in Bombay. He has schools of his own for Parsee boys and girls, and he takes a great interest in politics. John has been helping him in some notes that Sir Jamsetjee was asked to prepare for government. I should like to call on Lady Jeejeebhoy, but I do not know if she would like it. Sir Jamsetjee has never been to England. His father went to London, and took with him, as one of his servants, his barber, a Hindu. But on their return the poor barber suffered for his boldness in going to England, for he was immediately outcasted, and being outcasted is a terrible punishment, even if the outcast is befriended by so powerful a person as Sir Jamsetjee. Being outcasted means that no one of the caste will speak to you or eat with you or come to your wedding — or buy from you or sell to you — and when you die no one will come and perform the rites necessary for you to gain paradise. But, in fact, on paying certain sums to the temple in charity, the outcasted person is readmitted and in this case the barber did so gain his readmission into the caste.

Miss Pechey and Ethel left us last Tuesday. I think the few days' change has done Miss Pechey good, but it is a hard trial for her to go through the hot weather with no assistant to help her in her work.

Sunday 25th

Yesterday was a much better day. Instead of 93 it was 88 degrees at the hottest time, and those few degrees made a great difference. I am so glad, for John's holiday would do him no good if the weather continued as it was on Thursday and Friday.

We went over to Lanowli yesterday, and I got a little pencil sketch of a tent and the woods behind. But it was not the most beautiful part. Miss Sheppard drew with me and, as she is quite a beginner, it was best to take something simple. She has a good idea of drawing, and of colour too, and if she will only work I have no doubt she will get on. In the wandering life of a commissioner (her father is chief commissioner of the northern part of the province) there are such grand opportunities for sketching. The Lanowli woods are very small in extent, but very beautiful. The trees are, many of them, fine and gigantic creepers coil themselves round the trunks and hang like huge snakes from branch to branch and from tree to tree. It would be difficult to give an idea of these woods in a sketch, but I must try.

Mrs Sheppard sees a great deal of the natives, in their wanderings; she speaks Hindustani, Marathi and some Gujerati. She has queer experiences. The people of the villages, through which they pass, come out to see the 'burra sahib and the ma'am sahib' and often bring offerings of milk. Knowing that it gives great offence to refuse to eat or drink, Mrs Sheppard sometimes is in a trying position. At one village, the headman, the *patel* as he is called, brought her some coffee in a pot. Mrs Sheppard hesitated for a moment seeing there was something in the coffee — it might be only coffee beans. The *patel* said directly, 'Oh ma'am sahib likes the coffee strained.' He looked round for something wherewith to strain it, but nothing being at hand, he whipped the scarf off a man's back, who stood near, strained the coffee through it and handed the coffee back to Mrs Sheppard! At another village a man brought out a basin of milk and offered it to Mrs Sheppard who was on horseback. Some sweetmeats were floating in it, which did not look tempting. The man asked if the ma'am sahib would have the milk alone, and immediately plunged his very dirty hand into the basin of milk and subtracted the sweets. Mrs Sheppard took the basin, and holding it in her hand as if she were about to drink, touched her horse with the spur. The horse plunged and over went all the milk. Then with many expressions of thanks and explaining that she had not time to wait for another supply of milk, Mrs Sheppard bid the man 'Good evening' and galloped off.

At one place, where they pitched their tents, Mrs Sheppard put a notice in the local paper to say that she was 'at home' every morning from 10.00 till 12.00, and would be glad to see anyone who wished to consult her or who was in trouble. She told me she often did this. Well, a letter came to her from a Eurasian woman, telling her she was in great trouble, in dire poverty and that she was very sorry she could not come to see Mrs Sheppard but if Mrs Sheppard was passing near her house, she should be very grateful if Mrs Sheppard would call. Mrs Sheppard went to her at once. The house was larger than Mrs Sheppard expected, and the rent, as she learnt, was 30 rupees a month. The mistress received Mrs Sheppard and told her that they were in dreadful distress, that some days she had no bread for herself or her children. 'And you keep a cook?' asked Mrs Sheppard (who I suppose had seen signs of servants about the place). 'Oh! yes, ma'am I must have a cook.' 'And you keep a *dhobi* [washerman]?' 'Oh! dear yes ma'am how could I do without a *dhobi*.' 'And you have an *ayah*, to look after the children?' 'Oh certainly ma'am I must have an *ayah* for my children.' 'Well my good woman, if I were in your place I should dismiss the cook and cook my own dinner. I should dismiss the *dhobi*, and wash the clothes and I should look after the children myself and make the eldest one help me. You're not at all a case for me,' and so Mrs Sheppard wished her 'good morning'.

It reminded me of some of our cases of distress in Alexandria. I remember one instance when the father was out of work and at home (not ill). The daughter did plain needlework, but the amount she could earn was not sufficient to keep the family. I asked the mother why she did not take in needlework herself also. 'Oh,' she replied, 'it was quite impossible, she had the house to attend to.' So the family lived on the work of this one girl, eked out with help from some ladies who paid their rent. Several times, a young woman who begged for needlework, as charity, objected to carry the parcel of work to the railway station herself; 'her brother' or someone, would call for it. It was evidently too undignified to be seen carrying a parcel; it was not undignified to accept any amount of charity.

The thermometer is at 87 degrees and it is 5.00 o'clock, but the breeze is very pleasant and in another hour it will be much cooler. There is a service, though no sermon, in the schoolroom at Lanowli at 6.30. It is a contrast in the way of comfort to the Bombay churches, where comfortable armchairs and *punkahs* going overhead make the heat as little trying as possible. In Bombay the churches may be hot, but they are *never* close, as in England, where one is often in a church that is very cold and yet is close and stuffy. Here the large windows all wide open and the waving *punkahs* prevent anything like closeness.

John had a pleasant walk over the hills early this morning with Mr Griffiths. They went up the other side of the 'Duke's Nose' and had a wide view over the Ghats. They heard a great many birds — a bulbul, the Indian thrush, a green parrot, the 'seven sisters' and the 'whistling schoolboy'. The seven sisters are birds that fly six or seven together and chatter constantly, as if they were quarrelling. Coming down Mr Griffiths and John met a man, who was carrying two bundles of wild banana or plaintain leaves. These leaves are very large, growing six or seven feet long and a foot wide. They are used by Brahmins as tables for their meals, and must be picked and carried by one of their own caste. They are cut into pieces about two feet long. One leaf tray cannot serve for two meals and it must not be touched by anyone but a Brahmin.

29 May

John went down to Bombay this morning by the 7.00 o'clock train and he will return tomorrow. He was obliged to go, to look up a great many reports that he needed for the Jain case — he could not bring all his law library up here.

This evening, as soon as it was cool enough, I went down to the village, to go on with a sketch I began a few days ago. I thought, at first, I would draw the little native 'smithy' and I asked if the blacksmith was there. 'Yes, but he was sick,' and he was not working. I did not know the poor man was really ill while I was sketching, but today I sent Joseph to ask how he was and he brought back word that the man had a very bad leg, and was very ill. I sent Joseph back to learn more about them and he found that they were very poor, that they had had a 'jungle doctor' who 'had done him good' but, as they could not pay him any more, he had given up coming. I went to see the poor man and found him sitting with his wife (or mother) at the door of his little hut. His leg was all wrapped up and when I asked what he had under the bandages, he said 'leaves that the jungle doctor had ordered.' I told him if he would see the doctor belonging to the railway company here, I would pay for the visit. At first they refused saying they were afraid of an English doctor — he would cut his leg, and all he wanted was the 'jungle doctor' and good food, as the doctor had told him he needed. A respectable man, belonging to the 'Travellers' Bungalow' came up, and stood by, interested in what was going on. He told us that the man was, as he had said, very poor. There was no one to work the little forge, and no money coming in, now the man was ill. I knew the only thing to help the man really was to get him to see the railway doctor — a Portuguese, said to be really clever. So I told him if he would see the doctor, I would send him to them tomorrow, and would allow them a little money for a few weeks, to get food. On this, they consented to see the doctor.

Joseph will fetch him, tomorrow morning, and go with him to see the poor man and then bring him in here, on his way back to Lanowli, to tell me his opinion. Most of the people here are very poor, but even when they are almost starving it is very difficult to persuade them to leave their village and go only the 70 miles to Bombay, when they can get work in the factories directly. This lame man is a Muhammadan; Sheik Kassam is his name. He has a nice face and so has the old woman. His forge is such a primitive affair, a huge pair of bellows outside his hut and a little iron stand and a few tools and some old pots and pans. I must draw it, though I cannot see the man at work.

Friday 30th, Evening

I am sitting on the veranda watching a grand sight — a fire on the hill opposite. It is 8.30 and a dark evening, only now and then between me and the glare of the fire, flits the tiny spark of the firefly, looking cold and blue, by contrast. The fire has been burning since 5.00 o'clock, and before it was too dark to see the country we saw plainly the great blackened space left by the fire — now there is a long line of fire, broken by patches of darkness. It looks like a row of gigantic footlights, lights just ready lighted for the play to begin, and the spirits of the Ghats, like the giants that lived in the Kiesengebirge, may be coming out to play in the night. Dear Aguste, our dear, beloved governess, used to tell us those wonderful German legends until we lived in a world of imagination, not in Hampstead, but in 'an unsubstantial fairy place'. The fire has spread a long way, but it could not reach us. There is all the ravine between us. It will be out, I think, before John gets near. These fires are very common in the spring. The country people burn the grass, thinking it improves the ground, and that they will get a little crop to grow well on the burnt patch. But it really injures the ground, destroying all roots and seedlings, and the government tries to prevent it. I fancy this big fire today is burning unmolested because the officer of the forest laws, Colonel McRae, has left Khandalla. The chief commissioner too, Mr Sheppard, struck his tents this morning and went off to Poona. He was afraid the monsoon might burst and then his tents would be spoiled.

I went to see my 'village blacksmith' this afternoon. He and his wife shook their heads over the 'English doctor' for he had only bandaged the leg up and not put on any leaves or even ointment. I assured them it was all right, that I had seen the doctor after his visit to them, and that the man wanted medicine, and good food, and the leg would heal in time. I asked him if he would eat our food if I sent him some, for though these people are Muhammadans, they are so affected by the caste customs of the Hindus, that they might not have been allowed to take it. However, the man said *'Hai,'* [Yes] directly, and so when I got home I had some soup made for him and sent it down.

3

June–July

Snakes, the rains, the Jain case,
Indian baby given opium

Khandalla, Thursday 5 June 1884

Mrs Stokes and her sister have been two days with us, and have just left us to return to Poona. They are thoroughly Irish, warm-hearted and friendly, very merry and perfectly natural. This morning John took them to the Karli caves, and Mr Griffiths and a friend of his went also. They started at 6.30 and took their breakfast with them. The day was hotter than was pleasant, but nevertheless they had a nice expedition and all enjoyed it. Coming back again walking over the hot plains before they reached the road and the carriage, was the most fatiguing part, and Mrs Stokes looked very tired when they returned at 11.00 o'clock. She said she quite agreed with a lady here, Mrs Cox, who told John the other day that 'she had now seen all the cave temples in India that she need see, and she was not going to see one more.' And, she added, 'she could not wish her worst enemy to go to Karli.'

Last Tuesday, John and Mr Griffiths went a long way over the hills, taking their breakfast with them. They drove in a *tonga* over a rough country road as far as they could, and then they walked through the jungle. John says he was amused at the way in which Mr Griffiths got a man to come with them and carry their basket. The *tonga* driver had to stay with the *tonga*. Mr Griffiths spied a group of natives some distance off. They were in a mango tope (little grove of mango trees). John and Mr Griffiths set off to fetch one of the men, but when they got near and called out what they wanted, the men shook their heads and one observed that they were busy picking mangoes and could not come. 'Come,' said Mr Griffiths, 'someone *must* come and carry our basket;

we will give you some pice' [small coin]. It ended in two of the men coming very willingly, and some women following (from curiosity, I suppose) too. They climbed up through the jungle till they came out onto an open plateau of rock, with a splendid view of the Ghats, all round, range beyond range, in all their weird, fantastic shapes. Mr Griffiths went to the edge of the rock and looked over. There was a clear fall of about 800 feet. While they were admiring the prospect, they heard a sudden rush through the jungle not far off. John says, it was much more than the noise any cow would make bursting through bushes. Where he stood, he could not see anything, but the two hill-men shouted out, '*Bagh!*' [tiger]. They heard the creature, plunging away, down the hill. The men were positive as to its being a tiger.

Miss Leahy, (Mrs Stokes's sister) has been staying at a little hill station, 25 miles beyond Poona. In the compound of one bungalow a panther was shot one night whilst she was there, and another was seen. Colonel Stokes came to India as colonel four years ago. He had been here before, but it was all new to Mrs Stokes. The Bermudas, where they were stationed before, did not in any way prepare her for India, not for the people at least, if it did for the climate. She told us of some of her experiences when they first arrived in Bombay. They had not been there a month, when one day, while Colonel Stokes was out, a man called and asked if he could see 'ma'am sahib'. As she did not understand Hindustani, she asked her butler, who spoke English, to interpret. The man from his dress was either a Hindu or Muhammadan, probably a Hindu. He began with many salaams to ask if ma'am sahib would get him the contract for the regiment, and that ma'am sahib should never be without fodder, for their horses, as long as she lived in Bombay. Mrs Stokes, thinking he wanted to supply them with hay, replied that they had already given their custom to a corn dealer. 'Oh, no' said the man:

The ma'am sahib did not understand him, at all. He did not mean that. Would ma'am sahib get the sahib [Colonel Stokes] to give him the contract for the regiment, and if she would, their own horses should be supplied for nothing, all the time they were in Bombay. Ma'am sahib could show the sahib the bills and get the money from him, but he [the merchant] would always send the bills back receipted, and ma'am sahib could keep the money.

When the meaning of the man's proposal dawned on Mrs Stokes, she says she was so taken aback that she had no good reply ready, but she told the butler to tell him that the ma'am sahib had nothing to do with it and he must go away at once, and that Colonel Stokes would be home directly and would be so angry he would kick him off the compound. The man departed, grumbling out 'that if ma'am sahib would not, plenty of other ma'am sahibs would.' Colonel Stokes, when he came home and heard about it, was sorry Mrs Stokes had not found out the man's name. Mrs Stokes was even not sure what the contract was he wanted. It must have been a large affair, as Colonel Stokes said, to make it worth his while to offer such a bribe, as the feeding of four or five horses for several years. Bribery goes on, we know, in England as well as in India or Egypt, but I suppose a tradesman, of the most reckless morality, would hardly come openly and propose to a wife that she should cheat her husband.

Yesterday afternoon we went to the Lanowli woods, and I began a sketch, while John and Mrs Stokes walked about, and Miss Leahy searched for ferns. The *sais* stayed with me — the men are getting quite knowing about my artistic wants and get out my paints and brushes and wait contentedly for any length of time watching my drawing. I heard the birds making a great noise, in a tree about 10 or 12 yards off, but I thought it was only some bird discussion going on, when suddenly the *sais* called out, '*sap!*' [snake] and pointed up to a branch in the tree. There I saw a snake, five or six feet long, curling and twisting itself about and the birds chattering and fluttering just over it. Whether they were charmed by it, or whether they had nests in the tree and were afraid of the snake finding their young ones, we could not tell; we did not see any nests. After a time the snake apparently went to sleep; it lay quite still and the birds left it and were silent too. The *sais* said it was a cobra. After this, I certainly will not sit in a wood, sketching, without someone by me. Intent on my painting, I should not see a snake if there were one near.

Colonel McRae told us he came upon a huge anaconda (a big snake) one day (somewhere in these districts, I think). All they saw at first was a great tail sticking out of a hole in an old wall. He took hold of it and pulled, his men by him were ready with sticks to kill it. But while they were watching this hole and the tail, suddenly a huge head appeared out of another hole, and made a dart at Colonel McRae, getting within a few inches of his face. Colonel McRae says he let go the tail and 'bolted'. The creature retired within its hole. But the men managed to kill it at last. The *peon* who had a sword stood ready, by the hole where its head had emerged, and the others poked a long stick, into the other hole where its tail had disappeared. Presently the poor creature, being irritated, out came its head again, and the *peon* chopped it off, with a blow from his sword. They measured it, and found it was 16 feet long, and at its thickest part, Colonel McRae said, it was as thick as his thigh.

Khandalla, 12 June 1884

We are all sitting on the veranda listening to a wonderful sound — rain falling. It sounds lovely, and you cannot help believing that the trees and plants are enjoying it, much more at least than they 'enjoy the air they breathe' up here in the hot dry dusty weather we have had. There has been a thunderstorm too, not coming very near to us, but travelling round, over the hills, and our ravine has been full of mist. The rain began to come through the roof into the parlour, so we had to send for the contractor's men, and they came and mounted on the roof and soon put the tiles right. It is so strange, and so nice, to see all the ground wet. I have not seen any wet earth (excepting what the gardener waters) since last October. We are thinking of our black horses and the two men who started yesterday morning at 5.00 o'clock on their homeward journey to Bombay. They would be resting when this storm came on at 2.00 o'clock, but whether in a village or only under trees we cannot tell. The men have not got their monsoon coats yet.

The day before yesterday John and Ethel, when they were out for their early walk, found a poor dead deer half eaten. It must have been done by a cheetah or a panther, no jackal or hyena would attack a deer. It was about the size of a fallow deer. It was only 100 yards from our compound. We did not think that they came so near, but our house is lonely. Yesterday afternoon I was at home, as I was too tired to go out for a drive. So I thought I would draw one of these wild-looking hill-men, if one would stand for me. I asked Joseph to go to the end of our compound and stop the first picturesque looking man he saw. Joseph went off, rather mystified but amused too. Ellen went with him to see that it was the right sort of person to sketch, and almost directly they returned with a hill-man. He was just crossing our compound when they stopped him and brought him here. He was quite ready to 'stand',

and I made a little rough sketch of him. Joseph cannot always understand these people, their language is so different to his, but the man
who is in charge of this house when we are away comes in when there
is a difficulty and interprets between them. While I drew the man, I
noticed he coughed a great deal, so when I had finished and Joseph
came up, I asked him if he had caught cold, and offered him some
lozenges and a mustard leaf. He accepted my medicines readily, but it is
rather difficult to put poultices on a man who wears no clothes to speak
of. Before he left, happy with his payment of half a rupee, a man and a
boy came to fetch him, to some work. They all went off together, after
looking with great interest at the portrait. John and Ethel were away by
this time, driving. Half an hour afterwards the man and boy returned,
and came up to me, the man touching his left eye and telling me something in Marathi. I guessed he had hurt his eye and thought probably he
had got something in it. I was just wondering if I could perform the
'pencil operation' on him, which the doctor had taught us to do at our
ambulance classes, when Joseph came up and interpreted. The man had
been chopping wood and a piece had flown up and struck his eye. I told
him to bathe his eye well and then keep a wet rag over it all night, and
every night till it was better, and gave him oil silk and rag, but of course
he had no sponge so I had to cut him off a piece of mine which was not
very generous, as it was an old one. There are no civilized shops in
Khandalla. Next time we come I will have a better supply of things.

Friday

We have pouring rain, again, and thunder and lightning. The parlour
looks forlorn, for the rain is coming through the roof again in one place,
and dripping down into a vegetable dish I have set to catch it. John is
going down by the new train at 7.00 this evening. Then he will get a
good day tomorrow for work. Ethel and I are going tomorrow morning.
Three detachments have already gone: the men and young horses on
Wednesday, the landau, my coachman Ameer, and the bay horses this
morning; and now by the afternoon train, Simon (our cook) with his
wife and children, and Joseph's wife and children. All the men are
delighted to go home to Bombay. Now the rains have come it is not
comfortable for them as the kitchen is some little way off, and they
have to run through the rain with the dishes. The *chobdar* is very careful of his clothes, and Nellie sees him take off his turban and his white

36

tunic and leave them in the little pantry here, while he runs through the rain to the kitchen and back.

Yesterday morning as I was sitting by the road sketching, up came the man with the bad eye. He was very cheerful and came to tell me he was much better for the bathing. He had brought another hill-man with him, who asked me if I would treat him. I heard by the poor fellow's breathing that he had asthma. I told him that I would give him a note to the railway doctor at Lanowli, and that he could go this morning to see him. So he has been this morning and the doctor has prescribed for him. It is rather perplexing when these people apply to you and expect you to cure them of everything.

The *massall* (the servant here) came the other evening, at 9.00 o'clock, to tell us his baby was very ill. They live in a queer place, difficult to get at, though not far off. I asked Nellie to go to them, and she took Joseph with her, and some remedies. It was a curious scene, as Nellie reported. The baby was in a wretched room half open to the air and half below ground. It had a bad cold on its chest. They said it would not take any food, and so the poor mite had been put to bed (or to sleep rather, for there is nothing you can call a bed), having had nothing to eat since 8.00 in the morning. Nellie took it up, fed it with a few spoonfuls of food we had sent and told them to put a poultice on it, explaining to the father through Joseph how to do it. We had no linseed, but they got some from the village and crushed it. It was so late, 9.00 o'clock, that all the inhabitants of the huts were at home and consequently eight or ten people crowded in after Joseph to see what was going on. This same baby had been ill before. Then, when Nellie went, the mother, instead of coming forward as an English woman would do, to speak about her own child, laid it down on the ground and retired behind the door, leaving the father to tell everything, and take all directions. It was the same when our cook's child was ill. The mother did not stay by her little girl when I looked at her and enquired about her health, she retreated into the next room, peeping round the door occasionally. Certainly Joseph was with me, but she does not mind being seen by him or any of the men. One wonders when the poor women will rise into a better position, how many years it will take to make any impression on them. Seeing how things are here, it seems almost strange that we grumble at anything about women's position in

England; yet, no doubt, there are some things that can be altered for the better.

Bombay, Thursday 19 June 1884

A great storm of rain is going on. I cannot see the sea, only a white wall of mist and rain, and the poor palm trees turning their great leaves helplessly away from the storm, all their dignity gone, as John says like a lady with her dress blown about in a high wind, no gracefulness left. The crows are quite silent, in despair. I saw two of them sitting together disconsolately, on a tree by the veranda, their poor black feathers dripping wet. Directly the rain stops and we have a break of sunshine they cheer up and caw again. For ourselves we prefer them when their spirits are not good enough to caw and croak.

The great Jain case is finished, at last, and tomorrow John delivers his judgment. It seems strange to English minds that an 'idol' can possess property, and how 'an idol cannot alienate a gift.' Some of the native papers will probably attack John, as he is making a rich and powerful Hindu pay up his share of a large sum that has been lost, through his and the other trustees' negligence. There will be a report of the case, however, and I will copy it, or insert it, in my diary.

Saturday 21 June

The great day has come and gone. The Jain case is over. The newspapers are reporting the judgment in full, half is given today and the rest will follow on Monday. John says there was a large number of the caste present. The majority, evidently, sided with the managers and trustees, who were popular and whose mismanagement they would have condoned. But though the custom has been, in most temples, to allow very careless management and misappropriation of the money offerings, Hindu law is clear on the subject, and so are the rules laid down in their sacred books. Manu, a great authority, says: 'Whoever seizes the property belonging to the idol or to the priests shall be born a reptile for a million of million of years.' Though these trustees are not, actually, convicted of fraud, money belonging to the temple was certainly misappropriated when it was lent to mills, in which the trustees were all interested; and when a large sum was lent to the son of one trustee and never returned.

Sunday 22 June

Yesterday we had wild storms, a rough sea rolling in, breaking over the sea road, angry and muddy. The sea here is never the beautiful clear, glassy sea we had in Egypt. When it was rough there it would still come tumbling in, lovely green and blue water and snow-white foam. But we had a break in the rain and I went out to see two invalid friends. I went first to Mrs Slight, the French lady with a Scottish husband. I found her better and able to be up in a dressing gown. She had been suffering very much from neuralgia and fever. I did not wonder when I heard what had happened to her. I forget whether I have mentioned before that she is a great rider, rather an unusual thing for a Frenchwoman. She was out riding a fortnight ago on the Mahim sands, five or six miles from here, quite alone, without even the *sais*. It was about 6.00 o'clock in the evening. She had not been well, indeed she is never strong and, she told me, as she was riding along the sands she felt she was going to faint. So she took her foot out of the stirrup, intending to dismount, but does not remember anything else until she woke up with the sensation of cold. The waves were washing over her, the tide having come in, her faithful horse was standing close by her. Two natives were coming along the shore and they ran to her assistance. She could not make them understand where her home was, but they took her to the nearest house and went off for assistance. She sent for a friend who lived at Warlee, the fishing village on this side of the woods, and fortunately this gentleman was at home and came to her. He sent off for a carriage, sending at the same time a messenger to let Mr Slight know that his wife was safe. He had been very anxious naturally. By midnight Mrs Slight was safe at home.

I went next to see the artist, Mr Van Ruith. He looks very delicate, poor fellow. The doctors tell him he ought to go away to a more bracing climate, but how can he? He has friends here and a sale for his pictures; and he cannot stand cold. His picture for the Governor is nearly finished. It represents a scene on the shore that happens here once a year: the *Balena* or 'Coconut Day' as the English call it.

On a certain day in August, the Hindus throw coconuts into the sea as offerings to the god of commerce, Gunputti, as they believe the violence of the monsoon is then over and coasting vessels can begin to sail again. The picture gives a good idea of the scene, the crowds of natives with all the variety of Hindu and Muhammadan and Parsee costumes, but the preponderance of white in the Indian dress makes it difficult for the artist to get such a rich effect of colour as one sees in any Egyptian crowd.

In the afternoon I went to Miss Pechey's to meet Miss Sakharam, a Hindu lady belonging to the Brahma Somaj, the reforming section of the Hindus. Her stepfather, Dr Sakharam, is professor of botany at the university, besides being a doctor with a large practice among the natives, so large that he has *five* dispensaries in various parts of the town for his own work. He is a great botanist and keeps two clerks employed in nothing else all the year round but finding, drying and preparing specimens of plants. Miss Sakharam had arrived just before me. I was struck by the first sight of her as she sat in her graceful sari talking to Miss Pechey; her whole air was so modest and dignified. She is 19 years old but looks older, dark brown with a sweet thoughtful face. At first we looked at photographs, and books on Indian birds, beautifully illustrated, that Miss Pechey had borrowed from the Asiatic Library, but after a time, when John had come in and was talking to Miss Pechey, Miss Sakharam and I were sitting together and she told me she was in trouble, and explained to me what it was. It began by my asking her if she had ever seen the High Court. 'No,' she said, 'I have never been in the court. Must a woman go herself into the court if she has a suit?' I explained that a woman must appear if it was a criminal suit, and then she went on: 'I have a suit of my own, coming on, in the High Court. I want to see the barristers but my family do not like me to.' I asked her who were her counsel and was glad to hear they were Mr Inverarity and Mr Talang. After a minute, she asked, 'Is there another judge named Mr Scott in the High Court?' Of course I told her there was not, and then she added: 'The first proceedings come before Mr Scott.' This made it awkward for me. I knew I must not offer any advice. Miss Pechey, not having heard this, came up and suggested that Miss Sakharam might meet Mr Inverarity at *our house*. I had to say, that could not possibly be, but there was no reason why she should not do so at Miss Pechey's, if her stepfather agreed.

Her case is a sad one and I am very much afraid she will lose. Her own father left her a good fortune. When she was 11 years old she was married to a young man; they went through the ceremony and each returned to their respective homes. 'In our caste,' she explained:

We do not join our husbands till we are 15 or 16 or 17. I have never seen him since that day. I have never spoken to him. I do not feel he is my husband at all. Three years ago he became consumptive; he cannot go out, he cannot work. He has not a pice [an eighth of a farthing], nor his uncle either. They want me, because they want my money.

She said sadly: 'I have always been fond of learning and fond of reform, and so my people (her caste) go against me and try to say I am not respectable, and now I am summoned to go into court.'

John went away at 7.00 o'clock as he was going to a gentlemen's dinner party at Mr West's. Just before he went off a party of Muhammadan ladies came to call. They did not seem to be very strictly 'purda' ladies as they had no objection evidently to the butler coming up to us with fruit and cakes. John, however, retreated as they came in, thinking it probable they would object to a gentleman. One of the ladies was a patient of Miss Pechey's. She had a baby of two months old, and Miss Pechey had attended her. She was stout with rather a heavy face, which lighted up pleasantly when she laughed. I should have guessed her age to be anything between 18 and 24; she is 14. She wore a light blue sari, deep yellow short tunic, and greenish gold coloured trousers. She had no stockings on, but slippers (without any backs to them), which she kicked off when she had seated herself, as did the other ladies also.

Monday
There is a leader in the *Bombay Gazette* on the Jain case and there are several extracts from native papers in the *Times of India*, all, I am glad to say, approving of the judgment. We heard yesterday of several influential Indians speaking with great satisfaction of the judgment. The solicitor for the defendants told a friend, a day or two ago, that no one in court had been able to guess which side the judge thought was in the right, even at the very end of the hearing of the case, which had occupied 34 days.

Wednesday 25 June 1884
There was a break in the monsoon yesterday, and it was bright and sunny. Today, again, it is fine. Since the monsoon began, ten or eleven days ago, we have had a rainfall of 13 inches. A gentleman was telling

John the other day that he remembers one monsoon in Bombay when during one shower (or rain storm rather) of four hours duration, nine inches of rain fell. Some friends of ours have braved the monsoon and been at Khandalla for the last week — Mr and Mrs Peile. We lent them our little house. The daughter is delicate and the doctor advised their remaining on the hills until Poona was cooler. However, after a week of it, they could not stand it any longer, and they were going on to Poona last Monday. The rain had come through the roof into the sitting room, in spite of all the contractor had done to make it secure, and at last it poured through the roof into the dressing room. Mrs Peile says the walls are spoilt. The rainfall is far heavier at Khandalla than it is here. We have about 80 inches in the three months (or three and a half) but at Khandalla they have 200.

Yesterday, the Hindu lady I had met at Miss Pechey's came to spend the afternoon with me. She brought her two little brothers and little sister. I had said I hoped she would come and see me before I knew of the complications caused by her having a case in the High Court. They arrived at about a quarter to five. Ethel was here and afterwards Miss Pechey came in to see her. I was glad they came in for I had some callers and so was obliged to neglect Miss Sakharam for a little time. I asked the children if they would like to go out and play in the garden, and Nellie brought out the battledores and shuttlecocks for them. They gazed in astonishment when we showed them how to play, but had no notion of playing themselves. Miss Sakharam said 'they would like very much to go out in the garden but,' she added, 'our children never play, you know.' If the old saying is true 'All work and no play makes Jack a dull boy,' I think 'no work and no play' either, must make him still duller and that is what the children's lives here seem to me often to be. They have no good games, and they seem to be turned into little men and women so soon. Miss Sakharam told me that the early marriage stops the girls' education altogether at 10 or 11 years of age. For though in their caste they do not join their husbands till 16 or even 17, the girls are not allowed to continue their education at school. She said the little girl, after marriage, was expected to be frequently at the house of her mother-in-law; whenever there was company, for instance, she must be there to offer flowers to the guests. 'And all such nonsense,' added Miss Sakharam, bitterly. Her own marriage had interfered sadly with her love of study. When the young man fell ill, though she was not expected to go and see him even, her family said it would not do for her to be going out to school. More than once Miss Sakharam repeated, 'Oh I should like to have matriculated. I do not want to marry (only it is our custom), I only want to study — that is my wish — I want to learn and then help the native ladies of all races.' She asked me to come and see her, and pressed me to come 'this week'. She leads a busy life, not only because she studies, but she does a great deal in the house. She takes entire charge of the little girl and younger boy, washing and dressing them and having them with her almost constantly. Her grandmother cooks for the family, and her mother is not strong, but if the grandmother is away, or ill, then Miss Sakharam does the cooking.

Thursday 3 July 1884

John had a long day in court yesterday, sitting from 10.00 till nearly 8.00. At 7.00, and just as I was wondering when he would come, Mr Peterson came in, kindly, to tell me that the case was not over, the counsel for the defence was still speaking, and then there was the summing up to come, and the jury to deliberate. So I had my dinner (for I was very tired) and just at the end John came. It had been a brutal murder case, and therefore, doubly, trying. A man had murdered a little child of five years old for the sake of its ornaments. It is a most common form of murder here. The people are so fond of decking their children with silver chains, bracelets, anklets and earrings, as they can afford it, and then the children play about unprotected and offer constant temptations to theft if to nothing worse.

In this case, the prisoner had confessed his guilt to the policeman, but no confession to the police is allowed here to be given in evidence, for torture was so constantly employed by the native police to extort confessions (as it is now in the native states) that government, to put a stop to the dreadful practice, decided that evidence given by the prisoner to the police should not count against him. If this man had not, himself, shown people where the silver waist-chain was hidden, there could, scarcely, have been evidence enough to enable the police to trace out the rest of the events. It will, probably, end in the death sentence being commuted, to transportation for life.

We have had several of our servants ill. Some I have treated myself, but for the *chobdar* who is delicate and also Joseph's wife I have had good advice, and I am glad to say both the *chobdar* and Joseph's wife are better.

Yesterday was a busy day for me, quite unexpectedly. I had invited three young women from our workshops to spend the afternoon and have tea here, thinking that John would be late at sessions, and so not want me to go for a drive, and that Nellie, as usual, would take a good deal of the tiring part of the entertainment off my hands, going down to the sea, or about the compound with them, but just after they arrived a poor woman came to me, sister of the *amah* who is with Marian. She had been down in the morning to tell me her little niece (the *amah's* baby) was very ill and I arranged for her to bring it to me and then for Nellie to go with her to Miss Pechey between 3.00 and 5.00 — the hours when Miss Pechey sees patients at home. But these people have no notion of time and so with no reason at all to give why she was late, she brings the baby at 5.30. It was very ill, poor little thing, and I could not send it back without seeing Miss Pechey, so kept them here. Ellen went with them to Miss Pechey but there were people with her and by mistake she was not told our poor woman was there. I entertained my friends from the workshop in rather a distracted frame of mind — what my mother calls 'having one's brains pulled two ways at once.' At last they all sat down to tea and they seemed to enjoy the cakes, so I hope something was satisfactory. Miss Dewar came over, kindly, and told me she thought Miss Pechey would soon be here. She came in at 7.00 o'clock, and pronounced the baby to be very ill indeed, and said, that it required the most careful nursing, medicine and poultices, and food every quarter hour, a teaspoonful at a time. Of course poor ignorant people (however loving to the child as these are) could give no such care, so the only thing was to keep them here. *Chobdar* being away ill, I gave them his room and the woman, though alarmed at the idea of staying without any relation, agreed to do so. Nellie sat up all night and when I went in at 2.00 this morning we thought it seemed a little better. Miss Pechey has been this morning and says she thinks 'now it will live.' It is the baby I sketched for Johnnie and it was then a merry healthy child. I ought to have sent up for it, to come down before, but not knowing it was at all ill, and being rather pressed with other things, I forgot it. I think we were just in time to save its life.

While I write the grandmother, uncle and little cousin are all paying it a visit. Nellie has been resting a bit and I have been attending to the baby. We have put it into clean clothes and when it is a little stronger and can bear a warm bath, Nellie will give it a good washing. By questioning the uncle, closely, I learned, that they have been giving this baby a small quantity of opium, twice a day, ever since it was two months old — it is almost a year. That is a universal custom among the poor here. I suppose, as long as the baby was nourished, properly, it stood the opium, but on being weaned just as we went away to Khandalla it got into bad health, and grew gradually worse.

Saturday 5 July

Yesterday was a Muhammadan holiday, and consequently the courts were closed. I was very glad John had a day's rest at home, though he had plenty of work to do here. Today he sentenced the dreadful men who cut off their wives' noses. Dr Peterson was telling us that this form of revenge on wives is very ancient in India. There is a very old fable in Sanskrit in which the wife, knowing that her husband is going to cut off her nose, dressed up her maidservant in her clothes and leaves her to be mutilated instead of herself. The husband (who had gone out) comes back and cuts off the poor servant's nose. No mention is made of the after fate of the poor creature, but the wife appears before the astonished husband with her face uninjured and tells him how she had prayed to the gods to restore her nose, and the fable ends, 'and the man was an obedient husband ever after.'

The *amah's* baby is better and would have been almost well by today, if its relations had not made it ill again. Yesterday morning Miss Pechey found it so much better that it was to have more food, milk and sago, carefully boiled, and a little fever medicine, as it was uncomfortable and fretful with its teeth. Well, we gave it everything as ordered, but in the afternoon Nellie observed that the child was unaccountably sleepy, and towards evening if was difficult to rouse it enough to take its food. We felt suspicious, but I thought surely the aunt would never give it opium when we were doing everything for the child. However, when Miss Pechey came for her evening visit, she said directly the child had had laudanum. Was it not dreadful? Miss Pechey said the woman must be searched and the family forbidden to come near it. Our cook's wife came and searched the woman — nothing was found on her, but hidden under the bedclothes was a leaf with opium on it. It was a shock to find that the family, while so smiling and grateful to us, apparently were cheating on us like this.

Miss Pechey said the baby now, instead of being allowed to sleep two or three hours at a time (as she had said it might do as it got better), must be roused constantly and given food, and must have more medicine to counteract the opium. We had had a woman to sit up the night before, a friend of Kamalabai (the woman doctor), and expected her again, but she did not appear or send word why she could not come. I knew Ellen had been up a great part of the night, and I was loth to let her sit up again, though she was ready to do so. Joseph went off to bring an old woman he knew.

By this time John had gone to bed, but I was sitting in my dressing room on the back veranda, the broad-leaved plants looking so beautiful at night lighted up by the hanging lamp in the porch and the palmyras rustling their great leaves together overhead. At last Joseph appeared, followed by a very low, rough-looking old woman. It seemed to me impossible such a poor old creature could be trusted to carry out medical directions, or that the baby's aunt would attend to her if she did. While I was showing her the food, however, and speaking to her through Joseph, she ended the matter herself by telling us that she was a 'high caste woman' and could not possibly touch the food, or the low caste baby, and off she walked. Nellie urged me to go to bed. I had had several disturbed nights and was not very well myself, so I retired, but could not for some time 'draw the quiet night into my blood' and go to sleep.

Now we have secured a more hopeful nurse, another friend of Joseph's, who nurses a great deal among the Parsees. I think I can depend on her. Of course we cannot undertake to prevent the relations poisoning the child with opium when once it goes home. Marian wrote and asked me to see the child, as it was ill and her *amah* very anxious. We have just telegraphed to Marian, telling her the baby is better, but that the opium giving must be stopped if the child is to recover. As little Gerald (Marian's baby) is nine months old, I hope she will wean him gradually and send the mother back to take charge of her own child. The father is away at Poona and we have, of course, no legal authority over the child. The aunt here is very angry evidently and threatens now to go home. If she does and gives it opium, I do not see how we can save it. Miss Pechey, when she was here just now, wondered if they wanted to do away with the child, as it is a girl, but I do not think so. I think they are fond of the child, but they have no patience to walk about with a fretful child and the regular way is to give them opium to keep them 'good and quiet.'

Miss Pechey has been in this evening and together we saw the uncle of the baby and spoke to him about the opium. Miss Pechey warned him that they would kill the child if they went on giving it opium. Then Miss Pechey left, but I waited and spoke to the man (through Joseph) and tried to make him understand how wrong it was to cheat me when I was doing everything for the child. The man, who has at least more intelligence in his face than the woman, appeared sorry and said it was very wrong but that it was their custom, always, to give their children opium and they did not mean to harm the baby. Tomorrow the child is to go home and I told the man I would give him milk for the child for some time if he would fetch it or send for it. I can only hope they will leave off the opium.

Saturday 26 July

Mrs Jardine came this morning to paint the Arab horse dealer. It was so stormy that I hardly thought she would come, but she is so enthusiastic about her painting, that no little obstacle would keep her away. Our Arab came first on Wednesday and when we asked him when he could come again he answered gravely, that he could not say, that it depended on whether he saw the moon or not. If he saw the new moon on Thursday he could not come that day, but then he could come Friday and as many days afterwards as we liked, but that if he did not see the moon Thursday, he would come to us. Then he should probably see it *Friday* and not be able to come to us that day. The explanation is that the fast month of Ramadan was just coming to an end and that directly he saw the new moon, Bairam (the feasting month) would begin and then he would, I suppose, devote the first day to mosque-going and eating.

4

September–November

Nasik, Bench and Bar at Bombay,
Mohurram, Indian hospitals

Nasik, Monday 8 September

WE saw a little bit of the town of Nasik the day we came here, but it is only a corner of the town that you drive through in coming from the station to this house. That little bit looked so Indian and picturesque that I want to see the rest, and make some hasty sketches, if I cannot do more.

Today, in the pouring rain, the poor pilgrims look most melancholy as they pass along the road to Trimbak. This year is the holy year. One year in twelve, the Ganges is supposed to flow through into the river here, the Godavari; and then the faithful come and worship, to expiate, not their own sins, but the sins of their ancestors. Trimbak is 18 miles from Nasik; it is there that the sacred water of the Ganges is supposed to flow into the Godavari. It is curious to watch the pilgrims, a long line passing across the common at the end of the compound, ambling along on old ponies, one after another, reminding one rather of the picture of the 'Canterbury Pilgrims'. But *they* look happy and merry, and these poor people look tired and worn. One man — a very holy person — has come to worship at Trimbak. He holds one arm up over his head, and is said to have held it so for 12 years. I suppose he could not put it down, now, if he would. The nails are four or five inches long.

There are many ancient temples here, and at Trimbak some cave temples, which I hope to see when I am stronger. We can get an old carriage from Deolali, and Baby and Nurse can come too if it is a nice day. Mr Baker goes in a *tonga* to court, the street where the court is, like many others, being too narrow for a carriage. Yesterday a man

48

presented a petition to Mr Baker asking for employment. The petition is in Marathi in the printed character. The letters have been cut out — first drawn evidently — and the whole thing looks like a piece of beautiful lace-work. I am going to send it home to the children.

Nasik, 12 September 1884

Today has been a beautiful balmy day with bright sunshine but clouds enough to throw great shadows on the range of mountains to the north, the Ramsej range, they are called after the god Rama, who is supposed to have had many adventures in this part of the country. To us, one of the hills has a more recent interest, for there two months ago a friend of Mr Baker's, Mr Muloch, was torn by a panther. Besides biting him, the beast threw him against a tree and, his head getting a severe blow, the doctors feared at first that the brain might be injured. He was brought here, and nursed in the room which is now Baby's nursery. Mr Muloch is a great sportsman and no doubt would have killed the panther, but his gun did not go off when he aimed at the panther, which was within ten yards of him. His being stunned seems to have saved him as the panther thought he was dead and went off. The beaters then came up, and brought him here.

Yesterday afternoon, being fine and warm, I went out to the end of the compound and when I got there I saw so many wild and picturesque pilgrims that I felt I must, then and there, draw one, so I asked *chobdar*, who was with me, to stop a dark gentleman with a queer musical instrument, beads round his neck and wild black hair and request him to 'stand' for me. I rather expected a refusal, but though he looked surprised, he stood still and his companion, a holy man, stayed also. So I sat down in the middle of the road and made a hurried pencil sketch of him and then of the holy man. But I wanted to make a better drawing of the holy man so we asked him if he would come the next morning to the bungalow. At first he said 'No,' he was on his way to Bombay, but when I told him I would pay him, he changed and said 'Yes,' he would come.

13 September

It is such a lovely day, I wish John were here.

My holy man came yesterday, and stood for one and a half or two hours. He has a stern worn face, as if he did more fasting than was good

49

for him. He walked lame and said he was very tired and hungry. Nurse Alice (my nurse who is still with me) asked him how he was going to Bombay. On foot, he said. She asked him how long it would take him. Ten days, he said. It is about 100 miles from here. He added if he got anything here then he would go by train. So I could not help giving him more than I had meant to give, for with his lame leg it was so hard to have to walk to Bombay. The third class is very cheap all over India, always crowded with natives, and I knew a rupee and a half would take him to Bombay. We asked him what his name was and he said 'Lukshanan' and he came from Khandish.

Sunday 14 September

We got our funny old carriage from Deolali yesterday, and in the evening Mr Baker and I went out. He came home rather early from court and we started at 5.30. I had seen nothing of Nasik beyond this compound and the very short drive to pay my calls on Friday, so all was new to me.

We drove through part of the old town, rough narrow streets, with queer little native shops, and people sitting about at the doorways or lounging in the street. Everyone seemed to know Mr Baker and saluted us and stared at the unusual sight of a four-wheeled carriage — *tongas* are the only vehicles here besides bullock carts. We went up a steep road at last, where we had to get out and walk. At the top of the street we came out suddenly onto the edge of a hill, a little green bit of table-land and then the ground going down in rough banks and slopes to the river below, the Godavari.

The view was so wonderful and came upon me so unexpectedly that I could hardly realize it was not a picture we were looking at, one of Turner's it seemed to me come to life. The great shallow winding river was below, with houses and trees on either side, and the temples on the banks, and people crossing by the ford, and, further on, the bright green fields and groves of trees and, above and beyond all, the grand range of the mountains, some of them half lost in clouds, and at their feet a white mist clinging to the valley, making me think of the view from the citadel at Cairo, somehow when the Nile is flooded and you see the Pyramids beyond.

We had only stood a minute there, when from a house behind us issued an old gentleman in white garments and a red turban, who came up 'salaaming' and smiling, and invited us to come into his house. Mr Baker knows the old fellow well. He has a small pension from government and he lives very contentedly in a queer old house and is said to be the greatest gossip in Nasik. After a friendly greeting between him and Mr Baker, and Mr Baker having introduced me, we all went into the house and upstairs, to the principal sitting room. Going upstairs I thought I must feel like a sweep in old times climbing up a chimney. It was pitch dark and no balusters, but so narrow that you could feel some support by putting your hand on the wall on either side. The sitting room we came into was a big bare room with common chairs and tables, English not Indian at all. We sat down by the windows and I made a little pencil sketch. Hopelessly beautiful as the view was, still I meant to try, so as to give them a little idea at home. Mr Raghuji Trimbak kindly asked me to go whenever I liked and I shall try to go again. When we rose to say 'Goodbye' he begged us to sit down 'one minute' and then in came a young man — his son I suppose — who gave him a scent bottle, a little tiny bottle that had something like oil in it. He poured a little of the liquid onto our hands. It was scent made from sandalwood and has a very strong smell. Then he took up a tall graceful silver vase, the top instead of being open being made like the 'rose' of a watering pot. This contained rose-water and he poured this onto our pocket handkerchiefs and generally watered us with it. Then the son put into the old man's hands a number of pink roses picked short off without any stalks, and some other flowers, and Mr Raghuji put some roses into our hands, and then the ceremony of parting was over, and we shook hands and came away — the polite old fellow coming downstairs with us and to the top of the street.

24 September

Our journey down from Nasik was very beautiful. My eyes were tired of looking at the moving landscape. The colouring was really gorgeous, for the mountains were a deep blue and the plains below were covered with the rich verdure of the monsoon. The grass was a vivid yellow green, then there were fields of crops in bloom, then there were marshy tracts covered with flowering grasses — pale pink mostly and a little golden yellow flower in great patches. The wild flowers all along the line were beautiful. The wild *bendee* with a flower almost exactly like a yellow hollyhock, large, and pale yellow with a black centre. The *bendee* is a vegetable; you eat the pod with the seeds in it, and when cultivated the pod grows to a great length, often a yard long. On the banks by the railway, almost within reach of our hands, was a bright yellow broom looking so English and nice, only the leaves were rather different. I noticed a beautiful creeper with yellow flowers and wondered at first if it was a yellow convolvulus, but it was the wild cucumber. In one field we saw a huge bird, I don't know what it was, but we saw it very distinctly. It was dark greyish blue about the body with a red neck and a white head and a very large bill like a pelican's. It was walking sedately along, not far from the station. It stood quite three feet high, I should say.

Bombay, Saturday 11 October 1884

A lovely morning again, but so still and hot and enervating. I understand a little how the 'lotus eaters' felt. Tennyson might have been here in Bombay to write his poem on such a day as this. John got home at 11.40 last night. He had had a long hard day; he was up before 6.00 a.m., worked three hours, went to town and sat from 11.00 till 6.20, came home, dressed and went off to a big dinner given to the Bar by Sir Charles Sargent.

All the judges were there excepting the Hindu judge, Nanabhai Harridas, and he came afterwards, as did the Hindu barristers. Hindus, of course, cannot eat with Europeans without breaking their caste. The Muhammadan barristers were at dinner, as they can eat with us. It was a *burra khana* (great dinner) of 40 people. John had Mr Farran one side of him (the acting attorney general) and on the other Mr Perishaw Mehta, a Parsee barrister, and the best speaker in western India, a better politician than lawyer John says. The leading Muhammadan barrister, Mr Budrudeen Tyabjee, was there. When, after dinner, the Hindu barristers arrived, it was very nice, John says, to see the perfect equality and *esprit de corps* among all the members of the Bar, English, Parsees, Hindus and Muhammadans. Such a union of the Bench and Bar had never been attempted before, excepting on the occasion of a chief justice leaving the country.

After dinner they formed into knots, smoking and talking, and two leaders, Mr Inverarity and Mr Branson, told strange stories of their experiences. John has forgotten most of the stories, for he was very tired, but one he remembers was of a man who confessed with circumstantial detail to the murder of his father. But when the case came on for trial, Mr Inverarity defending him, it was proved beyond the shadow of a doubt that other people had killed the man and that the son had had nothing to do with it. Then Mr Branson told a tale, even more strange, of a man who wished to take revenge on a caste fellow whom he hated. He got two men to come and wound him and then to swear that it was his enemy who did it. They stabbed him, but not very badly, whereupon he called out: 'That's not enough, that will only give him a year.' So they stabbed him again, this time so severely that eventually he died. They ran off to the nearest police station and gave evidence against the enemy, who was, accordingly, arrested. The result was, however, that the plot was discovered and the two men transported for life. The party broke up at half-past eleven. John says, although he was tired, he enjoyed it. All the Bar were so friendly and nice to him. It showed his two years' work here had been fairly successful, John said; more than 'fairly', I think.

Khandalla, 20 October 1884

A real blustering English day. The poor plants look forlorn, 'caught and cuffed by the wind.' We have been down to look at our new path. John feared the heavy rain might wash away some of his earthworks, but it is all right, and the waterfall is fuller and looks beautiful. We saw an army of ants marching along, everyone carrying something under him, but we could not make out what. Then we came upon a mass of little red creatures, something between caterpillars and worms. In the evening there are hundreds of long red worms, crawling and twirling about — we think they may be these red creatures grown big, only, if they are, they have lost their hairy look. Mr Griffiths says there are worms here that only live one day — perhaps they are these. We saw some lovely butterflies yesterday. John and I pursued them, with a finger-glass in one hand and a sheet of paper in the other — but as soon as we got near one and thought we had it, away it flew. However, at last I caught one, which I must send home to the children. One can't help feeling it rather cruel to catch them and shorten their little lives, and yet how else can we learn about them? John has had such irritation from stings that he has lost two nights' sleep, and so today he sent over to Lanowli for the doctor, Dr Pires. He came and pronounced the rash to be caused by these hairy caterpillars. Every hair has a poisoned tip, and he says it is quite sufficient for the caterpillar to have walked over John's clothes to have left its poison behind. He has sent John some ointment.

Today I have been drawing a fine old man and a bull. Last week one morning John called to me to come out quickly and see some 'Vishnu bulls'. I ran out, and just by the stables were three bulls, but so covered with trappings that it was almost impossible to say what they were. The men were dressed in a different way to the ordinary hill-men we see here. Their turbans were enormous, so wide that they were like our children's sailor hats, for giving shade. One old fellow seemed to be the leader. He was very tall and had long loose red trousers with a vivid yellow turban. They came marching towards us with great dignity, when all of a sudden one man started out from the rest and began waving his arms, and shouting at the bull he had been leading, while one of the other men struck up a queer sort of music with a drum he carried. The man ran round and round the bull, calling to it, and then suddenly the bull made a rush at the man, lowering his horns, as if to toss him. I fled backwards, not feeling at all brave or inclined to try 'looking the bull in the face,' as one is told to do. But the bull stopped, and the man shouted again and the bull charged again, but this time he thrust his nose onto the man's shoulder — quite into his neck, and so they ran about. For a moment I thought the bull's mouth was open and that he was biting the man, but of course it was all show. After this the bull was made to perform some tricks. The man asked him questions and it lifted up one forefoot and then the other, making a queer noise by way of answer — something between bellowing and grunting. The man told him to 'salaam' us all and it went round lowering its head for a bow to each of us. Then the man asked it how many rupees it wanted, and when he came to 'four rupees' and the bull grunted for 'yes', there were shouts of approval and laughter from the men. These bulls are sacred to Vishnu. They travel long distances, going as far as Calcutta or Madras. The men take their wives and children with them. They live on what is given them. As the bulls are sacred to Vishnu no native — no Hindu, that is — will refuse a small offering, even if it is only a handful of rice.

Khandalla, Sunday 2 November
There has been a service in the little church here this morning, and Mrs Turner and I have just returned from it. It is seldom that there is a serv-

ice here, but a clergyman has come from Bombay as acting chaplain and will be here for a month. He came out from England only two or three months ago, and fell ill with typhoid fever, and was so ill that the doctors did not think he could recover. However, with Dr Blanc's skill and Nurse Pridgeon's care he did get well. His wife and child had started from England to join him just as he fell ill. What a joyous meeting they will now have.

One thing in the little service today was very nice. There were three Indian ladies and several dark gentlemen. The ladies looked graceful in their saris; their dress seems suitable for the gravest or gayest occasion. A lady, who knows many Indians well, told me that what constantly attracts native women first to our religion is the freedom that it offers to women. I thought of that today, looking at those kneeling, draped figures, and the words 'the liberty wherewith Christ has made us free.'

Last Thursday and Friday were Muhammadan holidays, the festival of the *Mohurram*. It is the anniversary of the death of the brothers, kept by carrying about models of their tomb, and performing religious rites before them for two days, at the end of which time the *taboots*, as these tombs are called, are dipped in water and the ceremony is over. I had forgotten the day was anything unusual, and was sitting writing, when I heard someone on the veranda, and there was the *shikarri*, with his little boy, got up in their best clothes, the little boy holding a plate in his hand on which was some money, a rupee and small coins. I got up, and we smiled and 'salaamed'. I could just make out that he had come to 'call' on me. On the plate was some brown stuff, like powder, sweet smelling. The *shikarri* took up a pinch of it and put it into my hand, whereupon I guessed that some return on my part was expected, and I presented the little boy with a rupee.

A little later I heard a sound of native music, and looking out I saw a number of men and boys coming up our drive; a tall pole with white cotton scarves round the top was carried by one man, another beating a drum, and others singing. The *chobdar* was sending them off, but I stopped him, and the men came on. The *shikarri* was among them. As they got nearer, I saw most extraordinary looking creatures — a man and two boys painted like tigers — the boys were naked and the man also, excepting for his loincloth. They were painted with yellow and red stripes and wore caps on their heads with something like ears; their mouths and chins were scarlet, and they all had round discs on the backs of their hands. The man in addition had a long tail which ended in a fine yellow tassel, and which was supported by a boy who ran behind him, holding the tail in one hand and a chain that was fastened to the man in the other. I suppose they meant to imitate the movements of a tiger, but it was ludicrously unlike any animal I ever saw. Whatever the man did, the boys did. First they all walked about with a regular stage stride; then they faced each other, brandishing their arms; then the man appeared to be irritated, and jumped about till the boy who held his tail suddenly took off both tail and chain; and then the man lay down and twirled about his legs and arms; and the boys lay down and did the same. This was all. We gave them a little present, and they went away smiling and salaaming, tigers included. It seems that these men make a vow, at the beginning of the *Mohurram*, to personate some animal for the four or five days that the festival lasts. As soon as the *taboot* is dipped in the water, they are released from their vow. One evening when we were driving home after sunset, we met the *taboots* being carried through the village. It was a very picturesque sight. Some men carried the *taboot* on poles on their shoulders, while others danced or played music before it, and others carried great torches. The *taboot* is made of some white material, mostly of paper I believe, in the shape of a mosque and with bright green columns — the Prophet's colour. In Bombay the *Mohurram* causes a great sensation, and large numbers of police are posted about the town to prevent quarrels between the Shiahs and the Sunnis. An effigy of Hassan is carried about; it is on the anniversary of *his* death that the festival takes place, I am told, and crowds of Muhammadans follow, working themselves up into a state of great excitement, as one man narrates the events of the murder.

Khandalla, 16 November

We have had a strong east wind blowing for three or four days, so cold in the evening that we had to get into the warmest part of the sitting room, where the carpets are hung up. Even then, we could not stand it yesterday evening and retreated into the nursery. We shut the door onto the veranda, but as it is, like the rest of the front wall, trellis work, it was rather like the old circus joke of 'shutting the gate of the field to prevent your catching cold.' Last night I shut everything in my room, but even then it was very cold. We put a bottle, filled with hot water, in Baby's cradle and hung a shawl all over the mosquito net above the back of the cot. The thermometer went down to 65 degrees and we shivered. Dr Field, the new doctor at Lanowli, has just been to see Baby, and he says he never felt such a disagreeable wind. He comes from Bhusowal, a place in the plains, where he has been for two years, since he first came from England. I am glad to say, he is having some bedrooms got ready attached to his dispensary at Lanowli, and he said he would take anyone I sent to him. There is no nurse, only the compounder, the man who makes up the medicines. I asked Dr Field how he would manage. 'As he had done at Bhusowal', he said, where he had a great many native patients. He made one of the family come with the patient, and look after him and cook the food. In many cases, and with all those of high caste, they could only eat food prepared by one of their caste. Although it seems a strange arrangement to anyone fresh from England, it is infinitely better than the patient being nursed at home. In this way there is control by the doctor, and a good roof and solid walls at least round the patient. If the *shikarri's* poor little child had been sent with its mother to such a place at the beginning of its illness, it could probably have been saved. Sister Jacobina, who is matron of a hospital at Karnal, tells us she has to arrange often for the relatives to come and cook for the patients, although she has a staff of nurses. The high caste Indians would not come to the hospital otherwise. She says in a letter I had from her a few weeks ago:

> I have a nice hospital now with the dispensary, the largest house in town, belonging to a Nawab and called *Shish Mahal*. It had been lying waste, for three years, and was said to be haunted, but I took no notice of that and I hope a spirit of peace and love is possessing it now, and that it will help many poor and sick.
>
> The arrangements are so different from any European hospital. The Hindus won't eat hospital food, so I let them cook their own, as long as they do what I order. I have a little fireplace, for them, and I have quite good caste of Hindus and Muhammadans.
>
> The English people are particularly kind to me [Sister Jacobina is German] and help me in so many ways. We are four workers here. In the morning we go together to our work. In the afternoon I usually see my private patients .... I collected money for a new carriage which has lanterns. I was often called out in the night and the streets are very dark and bad, and I nearly

drove once in a big hole. Last winter I met with an accident [she was upset in a bullock cart] and sprained my ankle, severely.

This year I have hard work, the sickness is so great. Karnal has many standing tanks, and two canals, and the sanitary arrangements are very bad, hence the great amount of fever. All Europeans have gone and we mission ladies are alone in the station. Even the English doctor, now, has gone on a tour in the country.

Three of our mission ladies have been laid up with fever, but I am thankful to say, I have kept well, through it all, till now, though I feel very over-worked indeed. God knows I have no time, and the sick people always tell me, 'only you must not get ill now.' On the whole they are very grateful.

Tuesday 18 November
I have just been to the end of the compound, by the high road, to see how I could finish a sketch, of a bullock cart, which I began when I was last here. The light is right about 8.00 o'clock but this east wind is so strong that I am afraid I must not try to sit out, then. It is very tiresome, for the mornings are lovely and, but for the wind, I could paint so well then. I have done a sketch of the watercourse, but then I am sitting some way down the bank and am sheltered. I saw a long line of bullock carts passing along towards the village when I was by the road. They looked very picturesque winding down the hill and up again as the road dips there. Then a number of cattle passed — one was a splendid fellow, with a great hump, and a lovely grey skin, shading off from a deep grey to almost white. I must get a bullock cart here in the shelter of the house, I think, to finish my sketch.

Last week dear Baby was poorly and I was anxious about her. Now, though she is really almost as well as usual, she is better here in Khandalla for a few days longer.

Ethel left us yesterday, and went back to Bombay. Miss Pechey is always lost without her friend, and wrote threatening 'to go into an hotel, if Ethel did not soon return.' Miss Pechey is the gentleman, and Ethel the lady of that establishment. Ethel is fond of collecting insects, and has had the *shikarri* hunting for scorpions for her for some days. He brought some handsome reddish coloured beetles the other day, and we shared them. He brought us also some enormous pods — he says they come from a large tree, the size of a mango tree. I tried to make him understand that I wanted some leaves as well.

Last Saturday (as Baby was much better) we went over to Lanowli, for Ethel to see Mr Shipp's collection of insects. Mr Shipp is railway manager at Lanowli, where a great many of the officers of the Great Indian Peninsular Railway Company live. He has good opportunities of getting insects, as the Railway men bring them or send them to him. He has a beautiful collection, well arranged. Some of the best were caught in our ravine. The locusts were quite different to those we see in Egypt, which are thick-bodied and heavy and of a greenish colour. These are more like a mantis in shape; slight and elegant, and in colour, a pinkish brown — about the wings, very pink, so I understood how it was John called them a 'pink cloud of locusts in the air.' There were a number of black beetles, like our scarabs in Egypt. Mrs Shipp pointed out three, that were about an inch and a quarter long. They had strong, thick scales over their wings, and their legs must be very strong, for Mrs Shipp told us she and Mr Shipp poised a dinner plate on the back of one of these three, and it walked away with it quite easily. Then they put another plate on the first one, and kept on adding plate after plate till the little creature carried seven plates on its back. It seems most wonderful, surpassing the stories of tortoises and turtles.

Yesterday morning Ethel and I went over again to Lanowli to see the school maintained by the GIP Railway Company for the children of their servants. Mrs Shipp, who takes a great interest in the school, met us there. We were very much interested in all we saw. The first sight of the rows of scholars, from the tiny children in the infant school to the elder ones in the fifth standard, was very striking, so different it is to our school in England, though this is called 'the English school'. There were the little English boys and girls side by side with the Hindus and the Eurasians — little flaxen-haired fair things next to the dark brown skin, black hair and black eyes of the Indian or the half-caste. All were dressed in English fashion, though some boys we saw could hardly speak English. All were neat and clean and almost all looked very healthy. They seem to be very fortunate in their schoolmaster, Mr Andre. When I asked him if the children came readily, he said, 'They won't stay at home,' and then he told me he always came into the schoolroom every evening from 7.00 to 8.00 (though school is over at

4.00) and was there, helping his own children in their studies, and also any others who chose to come and get his help. He says they can work at subjects then outside the school curriculum.

Bombay, Sunday 30 November

Friday night, after we had gone to bed and John was sound asleep, I heard a knocking at one of our windows, and a voice saying something in Hindustani. John got up and found the watchman with a letter in his hand from Sir Charles Sargent, asking John to go up to his house at 7.00 a.m. the next morning. So yesterday before 7.00 John went off. At a quarter to eight, as I was sitting writing on the veranda, a carriage drove up and Sir Jamsetjee Jeejeebhoy got out. He had come to consult John about a great meeting the Indians are getting up to present an address to Lord Ripon. We sat and talked for half an hour, and I introduced Baby to Sir Jamsetjee, and at last John returned. After half an hour's discussion about the meeting, Sir Jamsetjee departed, and then John got to his own work, which he had to get done for the court by 10.30, and only just had time to eat his breakfast.

5

December

*Prize giving at Roman Catholic schools,
arrival of new Viceroy, Volunteer ball,
remarkable tributes and farewell to
departing Viceroy, Lord Ripon*

Wednesday 3 December

YESTERDAY I went to a meeting, which was very interesting to me — a large gathering of Christian natives in the schoolroom of the Free Church. Lord Radstock addressed the people. It was an impressive sight, the crowd of dark Indians, men and women, all, or almost all, in their native costume — even the native missionaries — all listening attentively and joining heartily in the hymns; the tunes were native. A young Indian woman played the harmonium; she sat perfectly still while she played — like a statue excepting for the movement of her hands — but she played nicely. Lord Radstock spoke, in a very simple way, addressing himself, principally, to the Indians. He spoke entirely of the love of God and the happiness that religion brings; there was not one word of threats and denunciations, as one hears too often. He spoke of the power of forgiveness to win love, and told the story of Joseph, but without mentioning any names, and of how he kissed his brothers 'before even they had said they were sorry.' Then he turned towards a number of Indian school children and asked, 'Who was this grand man — like a king?' and they answered at once 'Joseph — Joseph.'

After he had spoken for some time, a native missionary interpreted the speech. Then, there were a few prayers, some given by Indians in Marathi.

61

Sunday 7 December 1884

It is such a pretty morning, the sea looks bluer than usual, and there is a dreamy, misty stillness, that seems like Sunday in an English country village. Perhaps today seems all the quieter because of the bustle that will begin tomorrow. Lord and Lady Dufferin are to land in the afternoon. All the officials, judges included, will be waiting at the Apollo Bunder for the new viceroy, but there is no provision for ladies, so I shall not have the honour of waiting, in the heat for an hour, to see the earl and countess step ashore.

Last week was what Mamma would call a 'full week'. Monday evening we had Mr West and the learned German from Vienna, Dr Hultzsch, dine with us, Miss Ellaby and Mr Wordsworth. We had a pleasant evening. Dr Hultzsch is here on a literary mission; he is searching for old Sanskrit manuscripts. Last Sunday evening, he and Mr West and Mr Wordsworth called, just as we were ready to go out for a drive. John walked off with Mr West and Mr Wordsworth, and Dr Hultzsch drove with me. We went along Breach Candy, our usual drive. The moon was nearly full, and it rose behind the palm trees as we came home. We looked, and admired, and Dr Hultzsch told me an old Hindu legend about the moon.

He says the story goes that in old times men were looking for the elixir of life. Round the sea lay the great serpent; and one day there was a fight between men and the serpent; and in the struggle the sea was agitated; and out of its depths rose up the holy mountain; and out of the shining waves came the moon; and there came also the wonderful drink, the elixir of life. But before the men had caught it, a dreadful demon seized the elixir and drank some. Then the mortals fell upon the demon, killed him, and cut off his head and his tail. But as he had tasted the elixir of life, they could not destroy his immortality and the head and the tail fly for ever in the heavens. The head is called Rahu and it follows the sun. The tail is called Koota and it follows the moon. When they get too near, and touch the sun and the moon, there is what mortals call an eclipse.

I suppose the old Scandinavian myth of the snake encircling the world with his tail in his mouth — emblem of eternity — has its origin far, far away, in some old Eastern faith.

Wednesday came the picnic to Elephanta that I could not go to, but John did and enjoyed it exceedingly. The sun set first, and then the moonlight over the harbour and all the islands and the great city make such a fairy-like scene, it is worth a tiring expedition to see it all. John thought they should be back here quite by 10.00 o'clock, but it was past midnight when he got home, and I was imagining accidents to the little steam-launch when he walked in. In spite of the lateness, however, it had done him good; the fresh blow on the sea had driven court and suitors, barristers and solicitors out of his head. I think he must get more sails in the harbour.

Lord Radstock and his son have gone on now to Poona and Allahabad and other places, continuing their 'mission'. I forgot to say last week — or rather I had not time — when speaking of the meeting for Indians, that my Hindu friend Rukmabai (Miss Sakharam) was there. I took her home afterwards; Nellie brought Baby in the carriage to fetch me. Rukmabai asked me if I would come in and see her mother, and show her Baby. I hesitated on account of her lawsuit, which is still unheard, and also because I knew Baby was very tired and hungry, but Rukmabai looked so disappointed that I could not hold out, and so we went into the house with her. There was a large hall paved with stone and, on one side, a table with writing materials for Dr Sakharam, and opening out of the hall, his dispensary.

We went through the hall into a room — or rather another hall — and there sitting on the floor, with three children playing round her, was Mrs Sakharam. She got up as we came in, and her daughter introduced us to each other. She has a nice kindly face and simple manners, as all the Hindu women I have seen have. She does not talk English, so her daughter interpreted for us. Mrs Sakharam took Baby in her arms, and was very loving in the way she held her, perhaps because her own little baby, two months ago, did not live — it was born dead. Baby, though she generally cries if a stranger takes her, was quite happy all the time. I was so glad.

Wednesday 10 December

I have so much to tell of this week. I meant to write up my diary, day by day, properly, but new viceroys arriving turn everything upside down. The next thing last week was the annual prize-giving at St Mary's College, Mazagon, the large Roman Catholic school in which we had been interested at Khandalla, for some of the Fathers and many of the boarders were there in May, when we were at Khandalla and there was the concert in aid of the 'band' at which John presided.

Ethel went with me and Baby and Nellie came for the drive. John arrived there soon after we did, coming from the court. As we drove up to the college, we saw quite a crowd of people and carriages and a police officer commanding the entrance. We presented our card of invitation and were walking on towards the seats and platform which were all in the open air, when I recognized Father Fischer, whom we knew at Khandalla. He took charge of us, and found us very good seats, just in front. The centre seat, however, was destined evidently for some grand personage, for it was elegantly draped with a bright green table-cloth, and an embroidered cushion softened the wooden chair. Ethel and I looked and wondered. Was it for the Catholic Bishop of Bombay, Bishop Meurin? A Portuguese gentleman near us carried a huge bouquet, but no one sufficiently exalted had apparently arrived for him to present it to.

Soon John arrived, and we saw Father Fischer meet John and nearly embrace him as he took him by the arm and brought him up to us. Still the grand chair was vacant. Now Bishop Meurin arrived, and the rector of the college met him and our Portuguese friend rushed forward and knelt before the bishop; so did many others, ladies too, and the kind old man looked pleased and friendly as they kissed his hand. But he too passed by the tablecloth and took his seat on the next chair. Then the proceedings began.

We had a concert given by the boys, and excellent it was, excellent in choice of music and in the execution. I wished many times Papa had been with us; it was just what he would have liked. One boy, a German lad of 14, played a beautiful solo on the violin. His father is band master to the Nizam (at Hyderabad) and, no doubt, he inherits his father's talent. One song, called 'The Three Kittens', was sung by a number of quite little fellows from the lower school. They acted as well as sang, imitating the scratching and fighting of the kittens and, at last, the reconciliation. It was done with great spirit. At intervals during the concert, fireworks went off. The first, which was a rocket, went off with such a noise that Ethel and I thought some accident had happened. When the concert was nearly over there was a stir and commotion, and we saw several of the Fathers go towards the entrance.

And then in came the great man of the evening, the papal legate, Monsignor Agliardi. He has come, from the Pope, to arrange an episcopal dispute, at Goa. The great man walked up towards the throng of people, and we all rose. The bishop knelt, and after him the rector, and many others, to receive his blessing; and then Monsignor sat down with great dignity on the tablecloth and the concert continued.

Then came the prize giving and a nice little speech from Father Fischer. Monsignor, however, got tired of handing books to the boys, or else thought others should share the honour, for he turned to the bishop and the rector and the prizes were handed to them, and some to John and to Ethel and me, to give also to the boys, and then others in the front row also. Then the rector introduced John, and he and the legate talked Italian. Monsignor has a clever, striking face, kindly, but a man of the world. His robes were rich — a cloak of reddish purple silk and a cardinal's hat, and a large cross hanging in front. At last the big bouquet was presented, and Monsignor Agliardi looked smilingly happy.

Everything ended with 'God Save the Queen' played by the school band. The priest who teaches music, Brother Waldmann, is German, as are most of the Fathers; you can see how his whole heart is in the music. He stood there in his simple black cassock, waving his rod, and as earnest and excited as Mr Foster, the conductor of our musical society at Hampstead, who rules his ladies and gentlemen as despotically as ever Brother Waldmann can his little boys. The scene was pretty. The college is a fine building, and the chapel by it, with tall palm trees separating the two, and the college all hung with flags and Chinese lanterns. As the evening grew dark, it all looked very unreal and you could almost fancy the great palmyras were stage properties, paint and cardboard, only they would never have been in such 'good drawing'.

The next day we were at another Roman Catholic ceremony, the prize giving at St Xavier's College. St Xavier's, founded by the Jesuits, is the head of all education among the Roman Catholics in this presidency. There is another St Xavier's College at Calcutta, as important and powerful as the one here. The governor gave away the prizes, although the papal legate was there. There was a dramatic performance — Sheridan's *Critic* was acted by the elder scholars and was done, on the whole, capitally. Mr Puff was acted with great spirit; Mr Sneer was good, though perhaps not quite sneering enough. Don Whiskerando, acted by a dark Indian lad, was capital, and so was Tilburino. It looked odd, in the programme and in the prize list, to see such names together as Andrades, Waite, Rosare, Jijibhoi Pestonji, Mistri Akbar, Nazarrali, Haidari and so on.

Wednesday 10 December (9.30 a.m.)

John has just come back from a ceremony at Parel, the opening of a hospital for animals in connection with the Society for the Prevention of Cruelty to Animals. The hospital is the gift of a Parsee millionaire, Mr Dinshaw Manachjee Pettit. The house is an old two-storied building in a large compound and surrounded by trees. The Earl of Dufferin declared the hospital open. He made a nice little speech, John says. He said 'Bombay was celebrated, even in England, as caring especially for the welfare of the lower animals and notably for those that minister to the wants of man.' There was an immense crowd of Indians. Mr Bayley (of the High Court) is chairman of the society, and he made a good speech. He told of a bullock cart that was arrested on account of the miserable condition of the bullocks and it was found that it was conveying the luggage of General Grant (the American president) to Government House. Then he went on to say that the committee proved by the action they took that, like the law, they were no respecters of persons. The bullock-driver was taken before a magistrate and fined.

Thursday 11 December

Yesterday was a hard day for John, not hard work in court, but hard work at entertainments. First, there was the ceremony at Parel; then he got a few hours' work at his judgments, for today; then at 1.30 he went off to a luncheon given to Lord and Lady Dufferin by the commander in chief, General Hardinge; then down to the dispensary to be present (as one of the committee) when the earl and countess paid it a visit; then back here at 6.00 o'clock; and then the ball in the evening at Parel.

But I must go back, and try and tell, properly, how things happened. Last Monday morning, at about 8.00 o'clock, we heard two guns fire — 'the mail; then Lord Dufferin has arrived.' A pause, then three guns. What does that mean? The orders from Government House were that all the officials should be at the landing stage at 4.30 p.m. Would poor Lord and Lady Dufferin be kept waiting in harbour all that time?

Arrangements to welcome a viceroy cannot be altered easily, so there they did wait, and only at 4.30 they landed. They had an enthusiastic welcome from Indians and English alike. The streets were very pretty decorated with flags, and the troops were out, and the ever picturesque crowds of Indians. I did not go down, as we were going to Government House to dinner in the evening, and there being no seats for ladies it would have been very tiring. So our invitations had come, at last; that great question was settled.

When the Duke and Duchess of Connaught were here, we had been at Parel in good time and had had a long time to wait, so this time we thought we would not be too early, and we were a little too late. We were the last comers. I was hoping Lord Dufferin would remember that John was the man he had wanted to have in Egypt, but John, of course, threw cold water on my hopes. However, when we got into the drawing-room and the governor introduced me to Lord Dufferin, he said directly: 'Is your husband here, Mrs Scott?' and added: 'I want very much to see him. You know, I wished to have him in Egypt. I wish it could have been arranged. I think he would have saved us a great deal of trouble there.' And then John came near and the governor presented him and he and the viceroy had a talk, but it was interrupted soon by the announcement of dinner. I could not see whom John took down to dinner but I was well off, as the bishop took me in. He is so pleasant and so well read that it is always a pleasure to get a talk with him. Opposite to us was Monsignor Agliardi in his silk robes, but instead of a hat, a small red silk skullcap. Next to him was Mr West. They talked French. Mr West is working hard at French now, daily, in view of Egypt and his duties there. I tell him he is getting on, though of course at an immeasurable distance from John! He reminds us of Mr Lapenna, in his power of work, and of concentrating all his energies on the important study of the moment. I had plenty of time to watch him and the great man, for the bishop had a long talk with the lady on the other side of him. At the end of a good dinner Monsignor helped himself to a glass of liqueur, which he drank, with his usual calm dignity.

After dinner came the 'reception'. It was a grand sight, the throng of people of all the various races, religions and castes of India pouring in through the great open doors, coming to meet the new ruler of this mighty empire. Lord Dufferin comes in a happy moment, for him.

Everyone is prepared to like him, and all parties are vying with each other in declaring that he is the 'right man in the right place.'

The first people presented after Lord and Lady Dufferin had taken their stand with Sir James Fergusson and his daughter by them, were some stray gentlemen. They looked anything but happy as they advanced and bowed and shook hands and passed on. Then came an English lady, looking really as if she were going to cry. We felt very sorry for this vanguard of guests, but it was irresistibly funny too. Then the people came pouring in and you lost your individual friends in the crowd. At last came up the first Indian lady. It was so pretty to see Lord Dufferin's reception of her. He took her hand, bending down to the little slim figure with a fatherly tenderness. It seemed as if he were saying: 'Now I am welcomed by the daughters of India.' She passed on, and was followed by a great many more Indian ladies; I think they must have waited till the English people had come in, for I only saw a few English ladies presented among the Indian ladies. There were two Indian princes in beautiful uniforms, one of them wore the 'Star for the Mutiny'. But there were not nearly so many Indian grandees as when the Duke and Duchess of Connaught were here last winter.

Wednesday evening there was a ball at Parel. We went, though we do not dance, as John thought we must, but we did not enjoy it much and only stayed about an hour. My principal pleasure was sitting by Madame Follet (wife of the French consul general). She is very nice — the whole family are — and we looked on and admired and criticized, and laughed at the extraordinary dresses some ladies wore. The governor is very fond of dancing, and he was 'whirling and twisting' most of the evening to the 'mazy'. We were rather surprised, however, at seeing the new viceroy do the same. He went round the big room with much energy. I thought, myself, he had better been talking to John.

Yesterday morning it all ended, however, and the guns going off at 8.00 o'clock announced the departure of the viceregal party from Bombay. We had our dear home letters, some of them still that John had not read, and as he rested a little while before going to court I read him the children's diary.

'How well they are,' John exclaimed, 'well — morally, physically and intellectually. The same can't be said of me — morally, physically and intellectually I feel in a state of dilapidation.'

December

Saturday 13 December 1884

We are later this morning than usual. John was not up till 6.30, and I only came here (onto the veranda for my *chota hazri* — little breakfast) at 7.30. Here comes Baby from her morning drive, looking very rosy and comfortable and solemn. I often think of what Annie used to say struck her when her children were young — the silence of a little baby. Now she will have her bath and be dressed again in the Indian fashion. But she does not go out in her nightgown as some babies do.

Well, we went to the ball last night. It was a volunteer ball given by Mr Bayley, who is the lieutenant colonel, but we only stayed about an hour and were home again soon after 11.00. The drive back was so pleasant, the fresh night air and the stars overhead. There were a great many people there, and as the uniform is scarlet the scene was a gay one. The town hall is a fine building, and the chief room was capital for a ball. The large-leaved plants and palm branches decorate a room so easily here. The crotons, with their parti-coloured leaves, made ready-made nosegays in themselves. The evening was far more interesting to me than the Government House ball the other night. There was such real thorough enjoyment. It was, of course, a different sight to any dance in England, three fourths of the volunteers (excepting the officers) were Eurasians and their wives and daughters as dark as they were.

At a scene like this you realize what a large half-caste population there is. Physically they are said not to be very strong, and they are certainly rarely tall or broad in stature. Last week, when we were at St Xavier's College, a gentleman who has been here for 30 years told me that when he came there was not a tenth part of the Eurasian population that we have now. He said it was one of the difficult problems of the day — what was to become of all these people. Another question that grows more difficult, rapidly, is what to do with the educated natives. There are thousands of young fellows now well educated enough to take clerks' places, but there are not openings for a quarter of them. I hear that many educated Indians are obliged to be content with sepoys' wages or going on messages, when they could be writing in a merchant's office, or making up complicated accounts in a bank. What is needed in India are technical schools, and then works could be undertaken in the country that now are impossible.

However, to come back to the ball. It was nice to see the pleasure it gave. Of course it had its amusing side too, and we watched the funniest couples careering round. 'There goes a runaway couple,' said Mr Anderson, who was standing by me as a little man in a red coat and a dark brown lady in a white muslin dashed wildly past, pursuing their course regardless of all such obstacles as other peoples backs; then slowly, struggling after, came another little couple, bumping and being bumped back, by everybody. Mr Bayley looked quite in his element, receiving everyone with kind hospitality, from the governor and commander in chief, down to the shyest little Eurasian girl. He is very tall and looked well in his colonel's dress uniform.

Sunday 14 December

I am sitting on the veranda. It is my birthday and my sweet Baby is just by me in Nellie's arms — a precious, beautiful present since the last birthday. She is getting much older in her ways. I think she is rather forward in noticing things, and she laughs so prettily now and stretches out her little hand to take hold of us, or of anything we are showing her. She has been much admired lately, which of course is only natural in my opinion. Last week an Indian lady came to see us and was delighted with Baby; it was really touching to see her tender ways to little Baby, who quite approved and graciously allowed her little hands to be smothered with kisses from the sweet, loving face. This lady and her husband, Mr and Mrs Aranachalam, were on the *Cathay* with John coming from Ceylon.

Mr Aranachalam is a judge in Ceylon. He is an MA of Cambridge (he took a high degree, John says) and is a very intelligent, well educated man. His family is the leading Tamil family of Ceylon. They are very rich, but you only guess that fact from the magnificent jewels on the neck, arms, ears and nose of the lady. She speaks English well, but slowly, and is rather shy of speaking before gentlemen; he talks just like an Englishman, absolutely as if it were his native language. He is a fine looking man, broader built than most Hindus and with a highly intellectual face. One or two of the Muhammadan barristers approach somewhat to Mr Aranachalam's type. Other people noticed Mr Aranachalam's striking appearance too. John had asked them on the ship to come and see us, but we heard nothing of them till last week. They had been to Hyderabad and Poona. It was not pleasant, however, for Mrs Aranachalam at Hyderabad. The purdah system is closely maintained there, and she found herself stared at wherever she went. At the races she was the only Indian lady on the grandstand; she was glad to come away. Mr Aranachalam is here for his holiday, and he brought his wife with him to accustom her a little to travel and foreign ways, as he hopes to persuade her to go next time to England with him.

We found that they would like to go to Government House to one of the receptions for Lord and Lady Dufferin, so John said he would see what could be done. John dislikes asking for anything, but it was not asking for any relation or friend of ours — in Mr Aranachalam's position he would naturally be asked, if they knew of his being here; so John wrote to the governor's private secretary, but this was on Monday and in the afternoon Lord Dufferin was to arrive. The reception was to be on Tuesday. All day Monday, no answer — Mr Aranachalam wrote to say that if they had no invitation they should leave Bombay next day. However, Tuesday afternoon a note came to John saying that an invitation would be sent to Mr Aranachalam. So I wrote to him, telling him it was all settled. It was fortunate I did so, for the invitation card did not come in time, and they would not have gone but for my letter. They went, therefore, without any card to show. They wanted me to take Mrs Aranachalam, but of course I could not as we were going earlier to the dinner. However, when they came, they soon found us, or John found them, and they were much interested in the sight. They were invited for the next night, to the ball, and then, I am glad to say, Lord Dufferin had a talk with Mr Aranachalam and introduced Mrs Aranachalam to Lady Dufferin. They had had no difficulty in getting in. Of all the crowd of people I don't think one was asked to show the invitation card — any one well dressed could have got in, I think.

We persuaded Mr and Mrs Aranachalam to come and dine with us the next day, Thursday. Mrs Aranachalam would not eat food cooked by us, but she agreed to come, and sit at table, and have some tea. The lady doctors and Ethel came to meet them. After dinner, when we had left the gentlemen to smoke, the little lady talked a great deal to us. She said 'she should not mind herself eating our food, but her family and friends would object, but that when she went to England she should eat anything.' They have their cook and their own cooking utensils wherever they go in India.

I forget whether I have mentioned that we are getting up a little 'art club'. It was Dr Cook's idea. He called to ask me if I would help him. I think it is certainly the first time I have been asked to join in anything since I came here that was not a charity, and only a scheme for pleasure. It was rather a nice change. We had a preliminary meeting last Friday afternoon, and we made the rules and elected the members. There are 16 of us. Among the gentlemen artists the army is well represented, there being four officers out of the seven men. We are to meet once a month from 5.00 to 7.00 p.m., and show our drawings, criticize and be criticized. I proposed the name 'Portfolio' — the name of the club Louisa belonged to years ago, and that she used to take Ellen to. It is a better name, than 'Sketching Club', which has too confined a meaning. We made Mr Peile president, and Dr Cook and I are secretaries.

Monday 15 December

The programme for Lord Ripon's reception is now published. He will arrive Wednesday evening, but he will get out at Parel station, just near Government House and be received privately. The next day he is to make a public entry into Bombay. It will be a grand sight. Then the addresses from Bombay, and a great number of towns in the presidency will be presented. All the judges are to be on the dais with Lord Ripon, so John will see well. Then comes the laying of the foundation stone of the new municipal buildings. John wants me to go to that, as he thinks it will be very interesting. I wish I had strength to rush about and see all the ceremonies, but it is very tiring even in England, and far more here. We are invited to dine at Parel Thursday evening, and there will be a reception afterwards. The feeling here towards Lord Ripon is so different to what it is in Calcutta that I hope everything will go off well and give him some comfort, after all he has had to hear from the Bengal planters and their confrères.

Tuesday

We dined last night at the commander in chief's. It was polite of him to ask us, for John had not called on him, but he met John the other day. General Hardinge is only here for a short time, just for the cold weather. He is staying at Malabar Point, one of the governor's houses. It was nice driving there. Malabar Point is a little narrow promontory, stretching out into the sea. We had a pleasant evening. John enjoyed it thoroughly. He got interesting people to talk to. When the ladies left the dinner table John was next to General Hardinge and they had a great deal of talk. The general has been much in France, and he had many anecdotes of old days, and present days, to tell. He was talking of the change of manners, even in the last 20 years, and he said he often found that the people who knew him least used the least formality in addressing him. 'That's your modern manners,' said he, and then he told a story of a grand French lady — a marquise — who was condemned in the Reign of Terror to be guillotined. The president of the tribunal said to her, *'Citoyenne Cécile, avez-vous bien entendu le sentence?'* *'Monsieur, le Président,'* she answered, *'si je suis Citoyenne Cécile, donnez-moi ma liberté, si je suis Madame la Marquise donnez-moi mon titre.'*

The governor took me in to dinner and I liked my talk with him. After dinner I was sitting next to deaf Mrs Jefferson, the Dumbells' friend; she is a dear old lady, everyone likes her, I think, but it is rather embarrassing to have to shout to her down her trumpet. She speaks loudly too herself, and so your conversation is heard all over the room. She is great at people's relationships and genealogies and I had strings of names given me. It is not with her mere society talk; she is most kind hearted and takes a real interest in a wide circle of friends and acquaintances, but still it is difficult to get up the proper sympathy at the moment, especially as all your 'ohs' and 'indeeds', your 'how very sad!' and your 'how very nice' are heard all over the room.

Wednesday 17 December

Yesterday afternoon I went over to Miss Pechey's to meet a lady and gentleman who had arrived that morning by the mail. The lady is English, the gentleman Indian — a Muhammadan from Bengal. He has been called to the Bar in London and has now a good practice in Calcutta, and is an honorary member of Council. The lady is young and very nice looking, bright and natural. The gentleman, though dressed as an Englishman, is completely Indian in face and appearance. They have a friend, a German lady, travelling with them, who has come to spend the winter with them. I am glad Mrs A has this friend with her, but with every help, and the happiness of her husband's strong attachment, I fear she will have a great many trials to go through. No one meeting an educated Indian gentleman in England can possibly conceive the enormous difference between the home life of the best educated Indian and that of a cultivated Englishman. I could not help feeling anxious about her — bright, smiling and happy, going to a life all new to her. If she can battle through, and outlive slights and coldness and find enjoyment at home, and interest in helping the Indian ladies of her husband's family and others, of course she can do a great work. Here, even, it would be easier for her, but in Calcutta it must be very difficult.

This afternoon I am going to meet some Indian ladies at Miss Pechey's. Baby is invited also (I fear not so much for her intrinsic value as for her forming a subject of conversation for the Indian ladies). I hope Miss Manning will approve when she hears that Baby has begun, at four months, to attend our meetings of Indian and English ladies.

Evening

Baby's debut in Indian society was not quite a success. She gave one look at the glittering dresses and strange faces round her and then, down went her little lip, and she burst into a piteous cry. But I think it was a good deal the darkness of the room that Baby did not like, and she had not had her usual afternoon sleep. After our Indian friends had left, or rather just as they were descending the stairs, John drove up to the house to fetch me. Three of the ladies were standing by the hall door (every manservant having been sent out of sight long before); when they saw John they started back. Then Miss Pechey asked John if he would drive round to the stables and stay away there while the ladies got into their carriage, which of course John did.

Then John and I went off to Malabar Point, for John to call on the commander in chief. He was out, but General Annesley was at home and he asked me to get out too. We went and sat on the rocks overlooking the sea. It is so beautiful there. As General Annesley said, it is just like being on a ship only without any motion. The sun had set but there was a rich glow in the sky and then, as we sat on talking, the lights of the town began to show brighter and brighter, and the necklace of lights that encircle Back Bay brought Palermo to my mind, as it often does. Then a haze of light over the centre of the Indian town showed where the illumination had already begun for Lord Ripon. We had not heard the guns at 5.00 o'clock. Baby was crying, so of course even Lord Ripon was unimportant, but they had gone off, 31, to announce his arrival at Parel. General Annesley told us that they had been travelling about a great deal since they were here last. Some months ago they were at Kolapore and paid a visit to the Dowager Ranee and her granddaughter, the wife of the poor lunatic Rajah. They were admitted into the *zenana*, but were in an outer room. There was a wide open doorway, just covered with a slight gauze curtain, through which they could see everything quite plainly. The Ranee put her hand round the edge of the curtain and shook hands with the commander in chief saying, 'I have a great friendship for you and I have made you a cushion,' and she handed him a velvet cushion beautifully embroidered.

Friday 19 December

Yesterday was a great day in Bombay. We shall never forget it. The welcome to Lord Ripon was so enthusiastic, it must have been overpowering, almost, to him. There is so much to tell; I do not know how to tell it all before the mail goes. The first ceremony yesterday was the Presentation of Addresses to Lord Ripon at the town hall. The viceroy and the governor left Parel at 1.00 o'clock and made a public entry into Bombay — the route having been arranged beforehand. The streets were thronged with Indians. The town hall was densely crowded, and the sight was most interesting, as delegate after delegate came forward and presented an address. Mr Kemball, who was there, says that the crowd was so dense it was impossible to get any place where you could hear. One address alone was signed by 150,000 persons.

At 5.00 o'clock the convocation was to take place at the university. Ethel went with me and we drove down at 4.00 o'clock. We were in good time, and were glad to have the opportunity of watching all the people before the viceroy arrived and the speeches began. John went from court to the university. The University Hall is a separate building, and the fellows, officers and High Court judges, members of Council, and commander in chief were all to assemble at the university and, with the chancellor, the vice-chancellor and Lord Ripon, form a procession and march to the hall. The scene was very animated and gay before the great people arrived. The crowd of undergraduates in their gowns, which marked them as belonging to one body, but with every possible shape and colour of headdress, from the Parsee's tall shiny hat to the wide-stretching scarlet turban of the Maratha. Then the rows and rows of seats in the body of the hall crammed, the majority Indians, but a good show of English too. In the front row sat conspicuous an Indian native prince — a boy of about 14 in a gorgeous costume and glittering with silver and gold and jewels. He was the fattest boy I ever saw, and when he stood up he looked more like a gigantic baby of two or three years, than a lad with muscles and sinews.

After waiting some time, there was a stir and excitement and we all rose, while the loud cheering of the crowds, outside, told us Lord Ripon was coming. Nearer and nearer came the wave of sound, and then up the steps and along the great hall came the long procession, headed by the usher carrying the mace (if that is the right word). Then the rich lilac gowns of the fellows, then all the syndics, then the deans of all the faculties, Dr Blanc in his soldier's uniform, dean of the Faculty of Medicine, the judges of the High Court in their scarlet robes, the members of Council in diplomatic uniform, the Bishop of Bombay, the Roman Catholic bishop, the chief justice, the commander in chief and, last of all, came the vice-chancellor and chancellor, resplendent in black and silver gowns, and with them the viceroy, Lord Ripon, a little man in a heavy black gown, brightened only by his light blue ribbon. The cheering was taken up, inside the hall, as the procession moved up, until the chancellor had taken his seat on the dais, the vice-chancellor beside him, and Lord Ripon had seated himself, quietly, in the front row by the fat prince.

Then the vice-chancellor (Mr West) rose and spoke: 'Mr chancellor and fellows, this university has the right, conferred on it by an act in 1874, of conferring degrees on persons, deemed by the university, worthy to receive them,' and then he went on and, in a noble speech, he told us what Lord Ripon had done for India, how all his life he had laboured for the cause of education and the cause of peace. He went through Lord Ripon's long political career, speaking in the highest terms of the consistent uprightness and benevolence of his character — it seemed to me as if I heard my dear father's voice speaking when he said, 'And Lord Ripon has found here, as in England, and in all the world, that the highest ability is united with the highest benevolence.' He spoke of Lord Ripon's forbearance when attacked, of his never once stooping to retaliate, of the Christian charity that characterized all his actions, 'And I say that his Christianity has been a boon to India, not in spite of it has he won the hearts of the millions in this great country, but because of it, because of the love and kindness its spirit teaches him to show to every one.' I wish I could remember all he said. I mean the exact words of a great deal, for I think I shall never forget the meaning of the speech.

Then the vice-chancellor came down from the dais, and walked to where Lord Ripon sat, and took him by the hand, and led him up to the chancellor, and Lord Ripon knelt and received the Degree of LL D. But I must finish my account tomorrow, for now I must send off the letters and get ready for the great ceremony of the laying of the foundation stone for the new municipal building.

Khandalla, Saturday 27 December 1884
For six days I have written nothing in my diary. I had to leave off writing, just when there was most to write about. My finger (which had been painful) got worse and my doctor, Miss Pechey, ordered me a sling, so I had to give up writing and painting.

I wanted very much to tell of the doings last week as they went on, but it was no use, I had to give in. I wrote to the children with my left hand, it would amuse them, the funny writing, but it would not be legible enough for a diary.

I will go on from the dinner at Government House. Lord Ripon was very pleasant and talked a great deal. He spoke of the warm reception he had had in Bombay and said half laughing, 'You know I've had a good deal of abuse, and so I find this a pleasant change.' And then, alluding to Mr West's speech, he said 'I was not prepared for all the things he said of me, I did not know I was such a good fellow.'

After dinner there was a reception and a great many Indians were presented. I think there were more Indian magnates present than at Lord Dufferin's reception. Several princes had come on purpose to see Lord Ripon. The Rajah of Indore, Holkar, as he is called, had written to Lord Ripon, telling him he was coming to say goodbye to him. We were standing a little way off, watching the last comers being presented, when we saw a big stout man in a plain white Hindu gown come forward, and suddenly put his arms right round Lord Ripon, and give him a hearty kiss on both cheeks. As soon as he had released Lord Ripon, he turned to the governor, and embraced him. It was funny to see the operation, and it seemed funnier still when we heard that the last relations between him and the viceroy were on the occasion of a severe reprimand being given to the Holkar on account of his government being so bad.

One Indian gentleman looked odd in English dress clothes — tail coat etc. — and a turban. At dinner Lord Ripon had said, when I mentioned Miss Pechey, that Lady Ripon would like very much to see her, and so when the lady doctors and Ethel were presented Lord Ripon introduced her specially to Lady Ripon.

The next day — Friday — was a busy one, for the departing viceroy, deputations and ceremonies, winding up with an entertainment at Sir Jamsetjee Jeejeebhoy's.

The courts had to rise early, again, for all the judges were to be at the laying of the foundation stone of the new municipal buildings. I drove down and called for John at 4.00 o'clock. We expected to have some difficulty in getting through the crowd, but there was none of any kind. The roads were lined with spectators of every caste and race, but there was perfect order, everywhere. There was a wide space, where the ceremony was to take place, with a good many trees on it. A wooden paling enclosed the spot where the stone was to be laid, and there were tiers of seats like an amphitheatre for spectators. The ground was covered with gay carpets. There were banks of flowers — roses, heliotropes, geraniums — against the dais where Lord Ripon was to sit. There were arches of palm leaves and flags of all sorts waved above us. On a little table near the dais stood the beautiful casket, containing the address from the municipality, ivory and silver, worked in high relief. The corporation had voted 4000 rupees for the casket alone; they certainly gave the departing viceroy a hearty farewell.

We were very early, and had to wait half an hour in the sun. Everyone had expected there would be an awning and, consequently, few people had brought umbrellas or parasols. Mr Bayley and some other old Indians had come in sun-helmets, but John had not. As we were waiting, the Rao Sahib Mundlik came up to us.

John: Well, Rao Sahib, you see, we are all taking to Indian ways, now, — here we are sitting in the broiling sun — England's day is over.

Nora: I shall keep my English umbrella, I cannot give that up.

John: (waving his umbrella in the air). Yes, we'll cling to my umbrella, the last sign of English power — the last rag (waving it in Mr Mundlik's face).

Exit the Rao Sahib laughing.

At last our hot half hour was over; near us we saw poor Miss Pechey, Ethel and Miss Ellaby, and they had no parasols, but I had given mine already to a lady behind me so could not help them.

Now the band struck up and we heard the cheering — first distant and faint, and then louder and louder, until the viceroy and the governor entered, and we all rose. The Englishmen uncovered, but Lord Ripon quickly signed to them to put their hats on again — he knows what the sun is at half-past four o'clock. Then the chairman of the corporation — a Parsee, Mr Perishaw Mehta — came forward and read the address. It was well written and well read — in a slightly foreign accent (as most of the Parsees speak). I thought it must be a happy moment for Lord Ripon. As each of the liberal measures of his government was mentioned — especially those affecting municipalities — the clapping was great, and the enthusiasm passed beyond the barriers and deafening cheering sounded from the crowds outside — some happy few, who had climbed into trees or on to the top of palings, being able to see as well as to hear and shout.

Then came the laying of the foundation stone. I had never seen the ceremony before and it was impressive to me: the burying of the newspapers of the day in the glass chest — the *Times of India* and *Bombay Gazette* plainly visible as they descended into their tomb — to be unearthed, when, and by whom, perhaps hundreds of years hence? And these newspapers praising the justice and liberal policy of the English viceroy; when they are next read our government may be as much a thing of the past as the Roman rule in England. The band too played such a sad mournful strain while the chest went slowly down, you felt quite sorry for the poor newspapers.

Then an Indian workman standing by took up the silver trowel, and all the members of the corporation stood round, and he spread the mortar over it — the great block of stone came swinging slowly down, down, till it touched the stone below, hollowed for the glass casket, and then Lord Ripon took a little ivory mallet, and tapped the great stone, and said it was 'well and truly laid.' Then there was a great cheer, taken up outside, and the viceroy made another speech, and the governor spoke — short and to the purpose, as he always does — and the grand ceremony was over. But Lord Ripon was not to rest then; he went off to St Xavier's College, to the prize giving, when all old collegians were invited to attend to do honour to Lord Ripon. John had intended to go, but he was so tired with hard work in court, and another festivity in store, that we drove straight home — rather 'headachy' from the sun.

At 9.00 o'clock we went off — Ethel with us — to Mazagon, to Sir Jamsetjee Jeejeebhoy's. When we were within a quarter of a mile we saw there was something going on, unusual in the dark narrow lane, the fashionable quarter of former days — policemen stationed along the road, illuminations, the universal *butti* much in request (a common tumbler that is filled with oil and a cotton wick). The wider streets and richer houses were adorned with flags. Across one wide thoroughfare was a long banner with large letters, 'ADIEU, BELOVED VICEROY OF INDIA.' A blaze of light presently showed us we were at the house, Mazagon Castle. We drove up and as we alighted Sir Jamsetjee met us — grand, in black cloth, embroidered with gold and silver — the Baronet of India; his kindly, honest face welcoming us each and all. The ladies of the family did not appear, though he is an advanced liberal, but we heard afterwards that they were in mourning and that they had remained in the lower rooms. They did, however, see Lady Ripon and Miss Fergusson when they arrived.

The sight was very interesting — such a number of Indian gentlemen, the host himself an Indian — giving their approval, and welcome to the viceroy and his liberal policy in India.

The Holkar was sitting outside on a veranda. He was said to be sulky, and he certainly looked so, though detachments of gentlemen from time to time went to him and tried to pacify him. I noticed a little boy in scarlet going about, led by the Parsee high priest, and I was told he was the son of the Holkar, and he wanted, very much, to be introduced to the *burra sahib*, Lord Ripon, and so he was.

Then there was the Rajah of Kolapore, such a jovial, honest, friendly fellow. Mr Kemball brought him to me and introduced us. He knows him well, and likes him very much. Then I had a talk with a magnificent prince in green velvet, gold brocade and jewels ad libitum. He is called the Prince of Lamri, but I think he must be the identical prince who kissed the Sleeping Beauty or danced with Cinderella. He twirled a jaunty moustache as he bowed, and smiled, and talked English, as well as possible, only once he made a mistake, when he said, 'I went to Oxford and to Cambridge too, with my master.' He meant his tutor.

We left early, as we always do, but we were very glad to have been there. The next day was the end of the most wonderful demonstration that India has seen — a hearty loving welcome and a tearful farewell to her English ruler. Where was the 'patient, deep disdain'? — loud huzzahs and praises almost extravagant in their warmth. I wish Matthew Arnold had seen it, and Mr Townsend too, who quoted those words to me.

The final scene of all was at the harbour. John was there with the judges, and all the Indian and English officials. They would have been there, anyway, whoever was the departing viceroy; but the great crowd — the vast throng of the natives — the people of India — had come of their own free will.

Before I go on to the next week, and Khandalla, and our usual life, varied unpleasantly to me by my sore finger, I must put down a few of the mottoes that were displayed everywhere in the streets for Lord Ripon.

- 'Tell Ma we are happy' [Mother — Queen Victoria]
- 'Goodbye, Pa Ripon!'
- 'Goodbye, Ripon dear,
   All your friends are just here!'
- 'Ripon the Just'
- 'When far away and over the sea,
   Ripon, dear, think of we!'

By Saturday evening, everything was over and Bombay returned to its usual ways. It had been hard work for many people, for the police, most of all. Sir Frank Souter (head of the police) said 'they had never had such work, for 20 years, as they had had in these three days. Yet there had not been the slightest accident — no report of a single row had been made to him.' It speaks well for the Indian police and for the English officers.

6

30 December–March 1885

Elephants at Khandalla, Mr Scott meets a Hindu priest, the Towers of Silence, Hindu and Muhammadan friends

Bombay, 30 December

THE following Tuesday we went up to Khandalla, that is Baby, Nellie and I went, and also Ethel — with Joseph and the *massall*. John came up, the next morning, when his holidays began, and Miss Pechey followed by the next train. It was such a change from the hurry and excitement of the week before to the quiet free country life up there among the hills. We never enjoyed it more. It was quite cold in the morning, and evening, and not very hot in the middle of the day. But we had none of that dry searching east wind that made Baby poorly in November; indeed we had a good deal of damp the first few days and some heavy rain. The water course was replenished, and a tinge of green came over the burnt-up grass — it was so pretty.

One morning, just when I was talking to the old contractor who was listening to my harangue with folded hands and an air of the greatest innocence (though he must have known that not a single door he had been putting up would shut or open properly), Ethel came running in — 'Be quick, come out — there are some elephants coming along the road. Mr Scott is stopping them.' Away we ran, leaving the contractor bewildered, and at the end of the compound found John and two great elephants with men on their necks. John was asking the men to stop and let us sketch and photograph them, but no, they said, they must go on to the village; they belonged to a regiment and had come to fetch some cannons. One elephant was a huge creature with handsome tusks, cut and ornamented — it seemed to be the leader. After these first two came ten others along the road — they did look so picturesque, towering over the grey wall of the compound, and standing out against the blue shadows and morning sunshine of the hills behind.

They were all tethered, eventually, in the village by the public stables, and a great commotion they caused. Horses are very much frightened at the first sight of elephants. It was fortunate that none of us were driving out, for our black horses are very frisky when anything alarms them.

In the afternoon John went down with Miss Pechey and Ethel to the village, and saw the elephants and men, and found that leave must be got from the colonel before they could come to us. John wrote a card to the colonel, who agreed directly, and the next morning two elephants arrived — the big one with the tusks and another smaller one. Ethel took several photographs and I made one or two sketches, but it was difficult, as the elephants were scarcely ever still. Ameer asked if he might bring out the horses, and lead them past the elephants, and so he did. At first they were very much startled and jumped about, pricking up their ears and tossing their heads, but after half an hour he was able to get them to pass pretty near to them and, by the end of three or four hours, they were quite friendly together and let the elephants almost touch them with their trunks. Ethel got one photograph of them all together. I hope it will turn out well. The bay horses we had left in Bombay. The elephants were generally very obedient to the mahout, but when the big one was made to lie down and I wanted him to remain in that position for a few minutes, he refused to do so, in spite of raps on the head and expostulations from his rider. I asked the men why he would not lie down, and they said the stony road hurt him. So I sent for some hay for him to lie on and then he condescended to stay a few minutes for me. The elephants had no trappings or saddles on them and John wondered how the men got up and down. When I came to pay the men, however, I saw how they did it. The man took hold of the great ear and began sliding down the side of the neck, whereupon the elephant lifted up his foreleg, bending the knee, which made a step for the man, and then lowering it gently the man slid down to the ground.

Khandalla, 4 January 1885
Mrs Baker left us yesterday. She was here last September year, just before I came out, and was staying at the inn at the other side of the

village. It is in rather a lonely part, and the inn was generally empty, so wild animals came nearer to it than they do to the village. I suppose at least that is the explanation of an adventure that Mrs Baker had. She was out rather late, in the dark, and was driving up a hill in a little *tonga* with only the driver and her old dog, a Scotch terrier, Fanny. There were no lights in the *tonga*, and I suppose, going up hill slowly, they did not make much noise. Suddenly, the pony stopped and began to back down the hill, and Fanny jumped out barking madly. Mrs Baker thought the pony could not manage the hill, and was just going to get out when the driver called out 'Sit still, a tiger, *bagh*'. Mrs Baker could not see what it was, but they shouted as loud as they could and some natives, from below, came running up with sticks and pitchforks. They found a poor bullock, half eaten, which the villagers said had been killed the night before. The animal, whatever it was, had evidently returned to finish it. They went on to the inn, and most thankful poor Mrs Baker was to feel herself within its walls. But the people watched, and saw a panther come right up to the garden of the inn, and then disappear.

I think I mentioned in my last diary, that a panther or cheetah was supposed to have been in our compound a fortnight ago, just before we came up. There was a commotion and people watched for it, but nothing was found. Mrs Baker has lived in very out-of-the-way places in India. Wherever she has been, she has taken an interest in the children of the place, native or English, and generally had a class of children at her own house to teach. But the life of a junior civilian is somewhat a wandering one, and sometimes, when they had only been settled a few months in a place, Mr Baker was ordered off to some other station. Once she was very ill, and they had to come down to Bombay from a remote town in the interior. She was carried in a *palki* (a sort of sedan chair) and Mr Baker was in the bullock cart with the luggage. The men carrying the *palki* outstripped the bullock cart and were some way ahead. Mr Baker saw them, in the distance, turn off the road into the jungle. Wondering what this could be for, Mr Baker jumped out of the cart and ran after the *palki*. He had noticed the place where they had disappeared, and found them a little way from the road. The *palki*, with his sick wife in it, was set down among the bushes, and the men were just walking off when he came up to them. He asked them what they meant by this; they calmly answered that that was as far as they meant to carry the memsahib, and they were going home. At last, with expostulations and threats, and I fancy with some use of his stick too, Mr Baker got them to take up the *palki* and carry it to the next town, 17 miles off. But he would not leave Mrs Baker again and walked all the 17 miles by the side of the *palki*. They were in the country of the Bheels, the wild people, descended from the original settlers of India, people who lived here before even the Aryans appeared.

John was at Poona for three days last week. One day while there he went to see the famous temple of Parbutti. It is really dedicated to Siva, one of the great Hindu Trinity, Brahma (the Creator), Vishnu (the Preserver) and Siva (the Destroyer). It stands on the top of a great rock overlooking the plain of Poona, and no devout Hindu goes to Poona without doing *puja* (worship) at the shrine of Parbutti, the wife of Siva.

John had a very interesting conversation with the priest at the temple. John asked him who he was and he said,

Priest: I am the high priest.
John: Where did you learn your good English?
Priest: I was a government clerk.
John: Why did you leave that post?
Priest: Because the hereditary high priesthood is in my family, and it is very valuable. All the gifts to the god, all the food that is offered and all the flowers come to me for distribution.
John: Who takes part in the division?
Priest: There are seven priests, a lot of musicians, who play for the god, twice a day, dancing girls, who dance for him, and a lot of servants for the temple. We are 75 people altogether.
John: Of the 75 shares how many do you take? 35?
Priest: No, rather more than that. I give what is right and take all the rest to myself.
John: What, money offerings as well as the rest?
Priest: Yes. Everything.
John: We fancy that the food is really given to the god.
Priest: It is by the worshippers, but the god only smells it. We eat it.
John: Tell me, if you do not mind, how you do *puja*.
Priest: Well, first, we offer flowers, which we lay before the god, and then we offer food, rice and ghee [clarified butter], or cakes, and then we wash the god.

John: What do you mean by washing the god?
Priest: Oh, we only pour a very little water on him.
John: Do you do anything to prepare yourself for *puja*?
Priest: Yes, We have to wash ourselves before we do our *puja*.
John: And have you many worshippers?
Priest: Yes. Thousands and thousands; I cannot tell you how many, but they come from all parts of India.

By the temple there is a great stone slab where the sacrifice of *suttee* was performed — widows being burnt to death. The priest, when asked, defended *suttee*, for he said widows, according to their religion, could never marry again, and ought to follow the souls of their husbands.

John: I defy you to point out any passage in your Veda or shastra [sacred writings] which says that widows may not remarry. The old priest looked up, with a twinkle in his eye, and said, 'Perhaps you are right, but it is against all caste custom and she is excommunicated if she does remarry.'
John: Well, you ought, all, to be ashamed of yourselves, for doing such a barbarous thing, when it is not in your religion.

The old man smiled again. He took all that John said, very good humouredly. At this point the rest of the party came up, and one of them began teasing the priest, about his god, and the old man retired into his shell, and would not say anything more.

Bombay, Tuesday 27 January
Yesterday, our Indian friends came, ten altogether, three of them being children. I had arranged for all our men to keep carefully out of the way. Some English friends came too and we got on very well, the only disappointment being that the wife of the Oriental translator did not appear. She wrote to say she was not well. By 4.30 we were all ready, the men all banished and Ellen on the veranda ready to receive our guests and show them in, Sister Jacobina kindly taking Baby, that I might be free to welcome our friends.

The first arrival was a carriage with two draped figures within who looked young, even bundled up, as they were. Ellen brought them in, and they threw off their cloaks and two girls, of about 12 and 14, appeared — daughters of the barrister and member of Council, the Honourable Budrudeen Tyabjee. These girls speak English, so there was no difficulty in entertaining them. Then Mrs Turner with her baby and *ayah* arrived, and soon after Mrs Ameeroodeen Tyabjee and her two nieces. Then Rukmabai came with her two little brothers and sisters; her father continuing a little better she had been able to come. It must have been a long work for her to get all these children into such gala attire — for I know she has scarcely any help now in her care of the children, when her mother is engaged entirely in nursing Dr Sakharam. The little girl, Narrabhai, whom I had last seen in a little white nightgown, now appeared in a flowered silk jacket and long skirt reaching to her feet. The youngest boy, of two, who was in a simpler costume at my last interview — as then he had nothing on whatsoever — was resplendent in a peach-coloured silk suit, and a jacket pointed at the back and edged with gold braid, trousers to match, and a jaunty cap embroidered in gold and silver. The boy of four, whose bare legs had before attracted the attention of Bracken [the dog], appeared in a rich brown satin costume, and very handsome the little fellow looked, with his splendid black eyes. I could not do much to amuse the children, having the ladies to attend to, but they seemed quite happy. Miss Spencer, from the Mission House, came, and she kindly interpreted for me, and we had a long talk with Mrs Ameeroodeen, taking her round the drawing-room and showing her the pictures. She has such a gentle, sweet face; I wish that my sister Ellen were here to draw her. There are no end of subjects for a figure painter — a much greater variety among the women — rich or poor — than in Egypt. Mrs Ameeroodeen had a rich, deep orange satin skirt edged with embroidery, a silk jacket with flowers worked on it, but the sleeves were thin gauze and edged with gold embroidery that she told us she had worked herself. Her hair is black and braided, falling in front of her ears (as our dear Aunt Mary's did), long loops of beautiful pearls, fastened at one end, like earrings to the ear, and the other end tied up under the hair. She had a thin gauze sari over her head and she wore white stockings and shoes without heels. The girls had a curious combination of colours in their dress — one had a blue silk skirt with a brilliant pattern on it, a bright red sari, white gauze jacket, white stockings and pink satin boots.

Wednesday 28 January

Sister Jacobina and I have just been strolling about the garden and, coming back along the drive, we saw a white figure, wrapped in a sheet (exactly as we used to personate a ghost in our games, and acting, long ago). When we came up to it, I saw it was Chouty — our *garawallah* (groom) — Joseph then appeared and told us Chouty was very ill. The poor fellow really did feel very ill evidently. Sister Jacobina felt his pulse and questioned him in Hindustani; she thought he ought to have advice at once and probably needed to be a few days in the hospital, though we told him he would be comfortable, and I promised to come and see him there. Now he has gone off with Joseph in a buggy and I have written to the house surgeon about him. The *chobdar* has gone off also today, as he says he is not at all well and wanted a change. So I have given him five days' holiday, though it is awkward, just now, to lose him as so many visitors come.

I had a letter from Mrs Baker yesterday asking me if we could take in her invalid friend, who wants to consult Miss Pechey, so I have asked her to come on Monday.

Sister Jacobina and I went to call on Mrs Budrudeen Tyabjee yesterday afternoon. We took Baby and Ellen. Baby is a great help with native ladies — they are so fond of children — and Baby's appearance, so different to that of their little babies, amuses them. There was a sister of Mrs Tyabjee's staying with her and she had four children with her and one, a tiny baby of five months, the same age as ours, but about half the size. This mite was dressed in a pink flowered silk jacket and trousers to match and an embroidered cap on.

It did look so uncomfortable to our notions — a baby of five months attired in such a costume, its little back too weak to sit up. I don't know what our nurse would say to it. Some neighbours came to call, but they fled on the arrival of the brothers of Mrs Tyabjee. The gentlemen's appearance was a relief, as they both talked English and they are educated men, with plenty of subjects to talk about, which the ladies (with rare exceptions) have not. I found that the girls had been told to ask me, yesterday, to go next week — not this — and that 'a little entertainment was to be got up, when I could go,' so we are to go next Tuesday and I shall ask Mrs Dumbell to go, as it is amusing and interesting to a newcomer to see an Indian party, and they asked me to bring any friends I could.

Monday 23 February 1885

Yesterday afternoon we went over the Towers of Silence; Sir Jamsetjee Jeejeebhoy and Mr Nusserwanjee, the secretary of the Parsee Punchayet, met us in the grounds below the great stone stairway that leads up onto the hill, where the sacred towers are. Miss Pechey, Miss Ellaby and Ethel all came with us. When we got to the top of the great steps, we found ourselves before the gateway into the gardens. On the wall was a notice 'ONLY PARSEES ALLOWED TO ENTER.' However, we all passed through, and inside was a little kind of courtyard with a low wall, over which we looked down at the road up Malabar Hill, which we had just left, and the beautiful view of Bombay, the harbour and islands beyond.

A number of Parsees, all in white, were standing about, some of them guardians of the place, and others probably belonging to a funeral party that had just been there — white is the sign of mourning with the Parsees. All the people saluted Sir Jamsetjee — he is much respected among the Parsees. Then we walked round the gardens. They are beautifully kept, with wide paths, and avenues of trees, and beds of flowers. In the centre is the tower where the sacred fire is burning. We went into the building, but could not enter the inner room, where the fire was. Sir Jamsetjee told us it was a small fire of sandalwood, in a brazier, on a little pedestal, in the middle of the room. They brought this fire from Persia 200 years ago. They settled, at first, in Gujerat, and some years later came to Bombay, bringing of course the sacred fire with them. There are keepers of the fire who take turns in feeding it with sandalwood, day and night. The door was unlocked, I noticed, and Sir Jamsetjee said some worshipper was probably within, praying.

Then we went on, quite near to one of the funeral towers. A row of vultures were sitting on the top of the wall; one huge bird was on the ground, near to where we stood. These vultures live in the gardens, there are about 400 of them, but they do not build and breed there. No one knows where the birds do breed, and yet there is a constant supply; and once a vulture comes it never goes away again. There are no vultures at the Tower of Silence in Poona, or at Surat, or at any other town where the Parsees are. There was a notice up, about 20 or 30 yards from the tower, 'PLEASE TO STOP HERE' (in English, all the notices were in English), but Sir Jamsetjee took us still nearer the tower. Mr Nusserwanjee explained to us that there were five openings in the walls of the Fire Tower, which were so placed that the light of the fire could be seen from each of the five burial towers. These openings were narrow slits, like those one sees in old castles for the bowmen to shoot through. Mr Nusserwanjee then showed us a model of one of the burial towers, and explained the ceremonies.

John asked him what they believed happened to the soul after death.

We believe, [he said,] that we are happy or miserable according to our deeds in this world. If we are good here then we are admitted into heaven, and are with the all-wise Creator, who is the source of all light, but not immediately; we must go through some preparations. Those who have done evil, but who have good in their hearts too, have a chance given them. They live again, other lives. We know that the Creator must be impartial, and yet we see one man is born the son of a rich man, and another man is born a cripple, or blind or very poor. That must be because in some other existence here he did bad things.

He evidently thought that was the only reasonable explanation.

After this we came away; at the gate we were stopped, however, by a man coming up with a basket of nosegays. Sir Jamsetjee took them one by one and presented us each with a nosegay, very pretty though made in the stiff native fashion. They were made of flowers from his garden, roses, mignonette, and that little waxy flower whose name I forget. We came away feeling that much of the horror that we had felt before in looking up at the Towers of Silence was gone, and that there was a solemn, religious and wise respect for the living, and for the dead, in the custom that had endured 6000 years.

Thursday 5 March 1885

Last night was the great *tamasha* at the large house on Breach Candy belonging to Mr Madowdass. It really was a beautiful sight, the house, the garden, even the wall by the sea road, were a blaze of light, and as we drove up, and got a view of the front of the house, we saw VR in blue and red lights. All up the drive there were arches of bamboos hung with little *butties*; no wonder they had to get 5000 *butties*, as Mr Hurkissondass said.

The wide steps up to the veranda were carpeted, and the veranda also, which was unusually large, was covered with a gay coloured carpet, and the wooden supports of the roof were festooned with white muslin curtains, and there was a scarlet valance (as we should call it) all along the edge of the roof. There must have been some hundreds of guests — the gentlemen for the most part in 'clear white'. One of the hosts — the son who had called here — met us on the steps and conducted us along the veranda and to seats at one end — and then some other gentlemen came up, and hung wreaths of the white Indian jessamine round our necks — long wreaths that reached to our waists. They had a powerful sweet smell and when we got into the crowded rooms, where it was hot, they were rather overpowering. Presently we went into a large drawing-room, where, in the centre, we saw a group of dancing girls — two girls and two musicians, men. The girls were short and not at all pretty; they were gaily dressed; one wore a bright green bodice, a skirt edged with gold embroidery, and a scarlet and gold gauze sari — she sang a song in a low voice, and one of the men accompanied her on a queer sort of tambourine or drum.

Mr Hurkissondass asked me if I would go to the ladies' rooms and be introduced to his wife. Mrs Wordsworth came with me, and we went off through the big rooms and out again to the veranda, but to the opposite end to that where we had been sitting before. A screen divided this end from the rest of the veranda and a little crowd of ladies was at the other side of the screen. But the doors of the screen, which were very large, were wide open, so the ladies could see a great deal of what was going on.

Mrs Hurkissondass was a pretty little woman, not more than 18 or 20 I should think. She had a pale peach-coloured silk sari on and magnificent jewels. She could not speak English, but Mr Hurkissondass interpreted for us. Presently a little girl came up in a pink brocade jacket, pink satin trousers, black and gold cap, and pink satin boots. Mr Hurkissondass told me this was his youngest daughter, a girl of nine; then came a taller girl dressed just in the same way; she was about twelve — both daughters of a former wife, her father said, but he did not seem very certain! She, like her younger sister, had a beautiful necklace of pearls round her neck. I asked if the girls went to school, but their father said, 'No. They had a tutor at home. They had not yet begun English, but they would soon do so now. They had been studying their own language first.' Then Mr Hurkissondass told me he had another daughter. 'My eldest daughter is a widow, poor girl, and from our dreadful customs, you know, her fate is sealed; everything for her is finished; she is only 15, and she is very intelligent.' Of course I expressed sympathy with her and he sent for her and introduced her to me. She had a nice face and looked intelligent, as her father said.

The degradation of the Hindu widow's lot came home to me there in that brilliant gorgeous scene, for there was this girl alone, among her splendidly dressed companions, in a brown cotton sari, a plain print skirt, bare feet and not a jewel on her. She talked a little to me, telling me about her baby girl (her great comfort as her father said), a little thing of 18 months, and I told her about my baby and so we made friends. But soon she got up and said she would go, and she went back into the bedroom that opened onto this part of the veranda, and where many Indian ladies and *ayahs* were. We went in there also, afterwards, and were introduced to more members of the family. One lady took off her bracelets and necklace and we looked at them and handled them. How a London jeweller would stare at such ornaments, such a mass of magnificent pearls in one bracelet that would make at least 12 handsome bracelets in his hands. It seems as someone says (Disraeli I think in one of his novels) 'ropes of pearls'. The necklace was also of pearls, but with large emeralds interspersed. The emeralds were very large, but not cut, so they were rather a dull green.

Mr Hurkissondass apologized for not offering us any refreshment. I suppose it is against their caste for any who are not Hindus to eat in the house. Some of the guests, our neighbour Mr Punthaky for instance, complained of there being no supper, not even a glass of water, as he said. From the way in which Mr Hurkissondass spoke of his widowed daughter's sad life, I should think that he is enlightened in his views, but even the most advanced of the Indians are terribly afraid of what their countrymen will say. The Hindu Mrs Grundy is as bad as the English one I suppose.

18 March
Yesterday I went to a party at Mrs Budrudeen Tyabjee's. Miss Fergusson was there; I suppose it was a farewell party for her. There were a good many Muhammadan ladies, but very few Hindus or Parsees. I took some friends with me, Mrs Mackay and her sister, who have come

lately from Calcutta. They had never been into an Indian house and were very much interested in the scene. The veranda was furnished with sofas and a gaudy carpet and a good many of the people sat there while the rest were dispersed among two or three large rooms. I think we should have done better if we had not been so divided. However, Mrs Budrudeen and her sisters and her daughters were very kind and hospitable, and did their best to make the afternoon pleasant.

There was a pretty meal set out in the dining room, all kinds of sweets and cakes and ices and coffee. The ladies of the family helped us to everything themselves with just the assistance of one or two *ayahs*. The elder children, girls of about 14 or 15, who speak English very well, interpreted for their mother and looked after their guests most readily. One of them carried round a slender silver vase full of rose water, which she poured over our hands. Then, when we said goodbye, the hostess herself came and hung garlands of Indian jessamine and pink roses round our necks and, with a little silver spoon, took some strong scented liquid out of a tiny silver vase and put it on our handkerchiefs; it was rather like attar of roses.

Mrs Budrudeen was dressed handsomely, as she always is; she had a thick white silk skirt with gold embroidery, and a lilac gauze sari, and wonderful jewels. Her skirt was short and you saw her ankles and anklets of silver. Mrs Hassan Aly, the niece of Mr Budrudeen Tyabjee, was there with her daughter and little grandchild, whom we met before. She had asked me to go and see her last week, but I was not able to go. She is so merry and good tempered looking that I think she must be a great gain in the family. Shut up and with so little to interest them, a woman who makes fun out of everything and is at the same time good-humoured must be a godsend.

We were at an evening party last week at Mr Geary's (editor of the *Bombay Gazette*). There were a great many Indian gentlemen, and also many Parsee ladies. Some of the ladies were very nice looking, especially one Mrs Mehta, wife of Mr Perishaw Mehta, chairman of the Municipal Corporation. They live very near to us, and I am going to call on them. There was a daughter also at the party, and I had a talk with her. She had a pretty light blue sari on and I was thinking how nice it looked when she said, 'How do you like our dress?' 'Very much, I think your dresses are much more graceful than ours.' 'But it is so difficult to manage them,' she said, 'they are very awkward. I never wear this at home or in school [she goes to school still]; I wear always the English dress at home.'

Our neighbours, the Bomanjee Punthakys, were there; they had sent me the day before some little glass bangles. I accepted them, as they were of so small a value that John said we could not return them or insist on paying. Now they have sent me *six dozen* and tell me the first few were only specimens to see if I liked them. However, even six dozen are not worth more than a couple of rupees, and John says we can keep them. The Tyabjees and other Muhammadans were in great force at Mrs Geary's. Mr Budrudeen remarked to John that there was a large gathering of Indians and he added, 'We never meet together in this way except at these kind of parties [alluding to the different races — Parsees, Hindus, Muhammadans]. Among ourselves the line of demarcation is very strongly marked.'

19 March

I have had a great deal of writing to do for John. I have three thick books of evidence taken in Kattyawar to go through and analyse. I have just done half. While I do this Ethel has been writing to John's dictation. As, however, he has the books with him in court, I can go on with my diary.

Monday afternoon we had our school tea party; 23 children, Miss Fenemore and the pupil teachers came. I sent our carriage and Ethel sent hers, and with three hired ones, all the party were brought over here at 4.40. I asked Miss Fenemore if any of the children would like to drive along Breach Candy by the sea before we began our games, whereupon every hand was held up. We sent off three carriages full, Miss Fenemore staying with us. Ethel and Mrs Yorke Smith, Mrs Fulton and Mrs Le Breton and her little boy had come to help. But the great success of the evening was a game, brought up by Mr Phipson, honorary secretary of the Natural History Society, and a friend of ours. He had called in the morning and when I told him what was impending, he offered to come and help.

The game he brought was a huge sheet of canvas painted in black and white like a chessboard. This we put down on the sandy, flat ground (where the tent is usually). We had a little table, and draught board and draughts, and Mr Phipson and Ethel played draughts, while the children stood on the squares of the sheet and moved as Mr Phipson and Ethel played. Each child had a number and a number was gummed on each draught. It was very amusing; the girls were about 11 and 12 years of age, old enough to understand the game, but not so old as to be shy, as the bigger ones would have been. When a piece was *crowned*, two girls stood together on one square. But before this game, we had tea, and that was a success too. Remembering that last time the girls were too shy to eat a good tea, I arranged differently this time and, after seeing the children sit down, left Nellie and one of the pupil teachers to make tea, and Miss Fenemore and the other ladies returned to the drawing-room.

They certainly did make a good tea, everything on the table was cleared. Simon had made the gayest looking cakes to please the children ornamented with pink and white sugar, stewed fruit (as they do not get that at school), blancmanges and oranges. Before they left, I had ices for all the children, which always pleases them. Simon makes them. They came back into the drawing-room afterwards to sing us one song before they left, the 'Cavalier', Walter Scott's words, and very nicely they sang it. But there was a little surprise for them. So in a moment the children had rolled up the rugs on the floor and stood round in an impatient circle, watching Mr Phipson as he held the basket. Then he made great fun, telling the children he should not throw till they were all still and then counting 'one, two, three' and waving his arm till they made sure the sweets were coming and started from their places, only to be told they had moved and must go back again. Of course the joke had to be repeated several times. Mr Phipson had asked me if he might give the baskets (which were pretty) to the children who got most in the scramble, but I suggested he should reverse it, and give them to those who got least, and so he did, and a little girl and one of the pupil teachers, who had very few sweets, were consoled with the little baskets.

7

April–June

*Party for 115 Indian ladies, the power
of moneylenders, author sees
the cave temple at Karli*

Bella Vista, 7 April

Miss Pechey has come back from Rajkote. She has had a curious experience. The poor lady, her patient, died. The case was hopeless when Miss Pechey arrived. She had been ill for a month with inflammation of the lungs and it had been left too long. All Miss Pechey could do was to alleviate her suffering and give her comfort, by herself nursing her all day. The husband of the poor lady, the Thakore of Rajkote, was very anxious to do everything that was possible for his wife, partly from real affection, and partly because of his fear of what people might say if the poor lady died. He had married a wife before from the same family and she had died, and he seemed to think people would say there was something wrong if this one died too. He had lost five wives altogether and had six then living.

The poor lady was very willing to be nursed by Miss Pechey, and took her medicine and food readily from her hand — the liquid food that is; rice and one or two solid things she would take, and preferred taking, from the native women. They seem to think solid food is contaminated by the touch of anyone not of their caste, but she liked Miss Pechey to give her the liquids, from a belief, so Miss Pechey thought, that nothing wrong would be in it, no poison put in, if the English lady gave it her.

There were three children, in the *zenana* (the women's part of the house), two little girls and a little boy of two, the heir of Rajkote. The little girls had a happy life, for they were allowed to run about the house, and even into the great hall of the Thakore's house, and the servants used to take them out for a walk in the morning or evening, but the little boy — the heir — never left the *zenana*. No change could come into his little life to cheer and amuse him. He was too precious to be allowed to go out of the sight of his mother; the thick walls of the palace were prison walls for him. He never went into the fresh air even, for there was no garden. The Palace of Rajkote is, really, a fortress, built at the bend of the river, which flows round two sides of the building. There was scarcely any water when Miss Pechey was there; it was the hot weather and the river bed was almost dry. Miss Pechey did not live in the palace. She was there every day, but slept at the house of a Parsee family, who kindly took her in. She had gone off from Bombay very hurriedly on receiving the rajah's telegram, taking only her medical appliances and accompanied by her butler, but she has been told since 'that it was a mad thing to do, to set off to Kattyawar without ascertaining where she was to live. If there was no European family to whom she could go, she should have taken bed and bedding, butler and cook.' Miss Pechey says herself, if the Parsee family, the Wadias, had not taken her in, she could not possibly have stayed at Rajkote. The life in the *zenana* is so utterly unlike an English lady's life, that no one could live there.

One morning very early, 3.00 or 4.00 o'clock, the poor lady was very ill, and the Thakore came to fetch Miss Pechey. They got to the *zenana*, unexpectedly, before any windows or doors had been opened, and Miss Pechey said the atmosphere was so dreadful that, strong as she is, she felt she should faint unless she got some air, and she ran to a window and opened it. The windows were covered with gratings, and the room where the patient lay was an inner room, only ventilated from the larger bedroom, with its grated window, and where six or eight ladies slept with their *ayahs* lying about on the floor. They don't know what cleanliness means, so I do not wonder, Miss Pechey says, she could not have lived in the palace.

As to anything like nursing, or attendance on a sick room, there was none. Miss Pechey had the greatest difficulty in getting the things she wanted. If she asked for the simplest thing — an egg beaten up, or a cup of gruel, she says, it took half an hour, at least, to collect the utensils. Then the cook would bring the egg, or whatever it was, into the great hall, and sit down on the floor surrounded by lookers-on, and proceed to make the food, the Thakore himself often standing by to watch the cooking. If such an unheard of thing as a poultice was to be made, Miss Pechey says, it always took her an hour to get the things together to make it.

Bella Vista, Saturday 11 April 1885

This week has been a very 'full week' (as Mamma and Conny would say) and I have had no time for my diary, painting, or letter writing. *Letters* I did not write certainly, but notes by the dozen each day, in preparation for my Indian ladies' party.

All Tuesday morning Ethel and I were hard at work, writing new invitations, and making out a list of those who had accepted. A great many of the Muhammadan ladies did not answer at all, but came to the party just the same. I had had to change the day (after sending out a great many of the invitations) as the volunteer fete was suddenly fixed for the 8th. Lady Reay was bound to go to that, to give away the prizes, and could only have stayed a very short time with me, so I changed my day, for I knew how many of the Indian ladies would wish to be presented to Lady Reay, and John thought it would have a very damping effect on the party if Lady Reay drove off directly it had begun. But we were very much afraid some guests might be left unwarned of the change, and that Indian ladies, speaking nothing but Marathi or Hindustani, might appear on Wednesday. However, only one solitary guest did arrive, and that an Englishwoman who is studying at the medical college, Miss Cook.

Some of the answers I had were very funny; one I will copy here. 'Mrs and Miss Mincherji Readymoney, beg to acknowledge thankfully, the receipt of the kind invitation, of the 4th inst., by Mrs Scott, and beg courteously, to decline to attend to Ladies Party owing to some inexplicable inconveniences. — Tank Villa, April 8th.' It is written in a childish hand.

Mrs Sayani writes that she is 'delighted, to learn, that Lady Reay will grace the party, by her presence, and that she will thus have the coveted opportunity of being presented to her Ladyship.' Fatima Begum (one of the Nizam's people from Hyderabad) refused on account of illness in her family, and then came after all on Thursday. A good many, at least several, I think, must have done the same.

Wednesday was a busy day of preparation, as I had to get everything ready by the evening. Miss Birdwood's wedding was fixed for Thursday, so there was no time on Thursday to be counted on. Ethel came in, of course, and helped me, and I had a young woman from our work-shops to help Nellie, but Baby declined to be neglected, and so Nellie had to do a good deal with the heavy young lady in her arms. I found, too, that there were several Indian families who had not had invitations and who ought to have had them, and I had to write notes and send off special messengers. That evening there was a party at Government House, and all the Bombay world was there. Mrs Stokes, John and I went for an hour. The drive was lovely, and the party a pretty sight, as usual, with all the variety of costumes.

Thursday, the great day, arrived. We were all up early, and Ethel came in to help in the last arrangements. At 10.30 we went off to the wedding. It was a pretty sight. Miss Birdwood made a very pretty little bride in her long simple white satin, and the bridegroom was a boyish-looking fair young fellow in his artillery man's uniform and clanking sword. The church was beautifully decorated, and four tiny bridesmaids, from four to six years old, followed the bride. When the service was over, they walked before the bride and bridegroom, strewing flowers as they went, Indian jessamine, stephanotis, and other pure white flowers.

Well, by 4.30 we were all ready for our guests; 5.00 o'clock was the hour, but Indians come very punctually; indeed they often appear before the time fixed, so we had to be ready. However, the first arrival was an Englishwoman, Mrs Bruce; she was very kind in attending to the Indian ladies. Then came a Hindu lady, who took the wise precaution of send-ing in her card — Mrs Vevandradas Purshotendas (what would my dear mother do with all the names). She only spoke a few words of English, and Mrs Bruce and I were trying to entertain her when Miss Pechey came to the rescue. Then the guests began to arrive in numbers.

I had stationed a young woman (who speaks Hindustani) on the top of the steps, to receive the guests and usher them in, with strict injunctions to announce clearly the name of each. I welcomed them as they came in, wondering, sometimes, who this person was, or how that person had come, when I thought she had positively refused. Very soon Lady Reay arrived and I took her into the drawing-room, introducing the principal guests to her as they arrived, but I could not stay with her. I left some-one to interpret and went back to receive more guests. By 5.30, I suppose, all the Indian ladies had arrived. Some had brought children, and many had brought a friend with them. The Indian ladies were delighted to be introduced to Lady Reay, who talked to all she could and was as pleasant and nice as she could be. I brought up my sweet little friend, Mrs Ameeroodeen Tyabjee, and Lady Reay fell in love at once with her sweet face. Mrs Budrudeen Tyabjee and the other sisters were not forgotten. Then, I must present an equal number at least of Hindu and Parsee ladies. I hope none have been left out who ought to have been presented. I tried to think of everyone, but as I did not know many of them before; it was difficult.

The Ranee of Jhutt appeared in a beautiful costume and splendid jewels, but she was a little behind the times; she threw off her shoes at the bottom of the steps and walked up in her stockings, as the custom used to be.

The drawing-room was now crowded; there were not seats for more than half the people, for we could not get the Indian ladies to disperse and go into the anterooms. The pleasure was to see and be seen — after the first half hour few of them even looked at sketches or photographs. We had some songs, sung by English ladies, and a Parsee girl played on the piano, but talking went on all the same. Even when Mrs Morland, a great musician, sang, and her splendid voice rang through the rooms, the buzz of talking never ceased. What would Papa have said! One Parsee lady, standing by me, thanked her very warmly for her beautiful song, but Mrs Morland observed: 'All your ladies do not think like you, or they would not talk so much.' Mrs Morland is accustomed to profound silence when she sings. How I wished Conny were here with me, and Lily and the little ones to help me; and the pretty faces for Ellen to draw if she were only here, for some are very pretty, and refined looking too, though I do not quite agree with Dr Hultzsch in thinking the nose ring 'very coquettish'. A few of the ladies went into the back porch, which is really only a continuation of the drawing-room, and sat there with Lady Reay. The fountain was playing in the little garden beyond, and the great leaves of the arums, and the palmyras above, made a pretty background to the gay ladies.

At 6.00 o'clock tea was ready, set out on a long table in the dining room. The men had brought in the eatables, and then vanished, and Ellen with the help of Florentine (the French dressmaker) only was there, to make the tea and coffee. We brought the ladies in — all who would come — there were just a few high-caste Hindus who could not eat or drink in our house; they stayed in the drawing-room. The English ladies worked hard, waiting upon the Indian ladies. (I wish Miss

Manning could have seen the friendly readiness of everyone to entertain our Indian guests.) Simon had cooked everything, with the help of two men for two days — there was a good deal to do. Ices are always popular with Indians, so are sweets, of all kinds. Ellen's arm ached, serving out ices. I think, another time, we might have Joseph close by, just within the pantry to do that work. Many of the Indian ladies say they do not object to servants, they do not count them; it is only gentlemen they object to seeing! As it grew dark, the *massall* (the lamp man) came in and lighted the chandeliers, and no one seemed to mind at all. I did not see anyone cover up her face, or attempt to retreat from his presence. Louisa (the young woman from our workshops) counted the guests as they went away, opened the carriage doors for them, and saw them off. We had 115 Indian ladies, about ten children, and about 50 English ladies.

There was a paragraph, in the *Times of India* about the party, and a longer notice in the *Indian Spectator*, and there is also a letter in a Gujerati paper from an Indian lady who was at the party, with a leader on it by the editor. We should not have heard of that, but our friendly neighbour, Mr Punthaky, sent us the newspaper, and has kindly translated the articles for us. I am so very glad people were pleased. Several Indian ladies came on Thursday who had never been to any European house before, some who are very strict conservatives. I hope now they will come again. Dr Cook had told me of two sisters who were coming (after a great deal of hesitation); they are cousins of Sir Jamsetjee Jeejeebhoy's, granddaughters of the first baronet. Lady Reay has asked me to give her a list of the ladies I introduced to her, with a memorandum as to who they are. 'Your party interested me immensely,' she says in her letter.

Wednesday 22 April

Our *mali* has gone off to the police office, having had a summons served upon him 'for causing hurt to the body' of a man in the bazaar. John and I were on the veranda, when up came the *mali*, with his little boy, carrying a torn garment belonging to the boy and the summons in his hand. His story is that he sent his little boy for some ink, and gave him some pice (small coins) to pay for it. The child came back with no ink and his clothes torn, and his pice gone. The boy says the *marwaree* took his money and, instead of giving him any ink, beat him and sent him away. Thereupon, the *mali* went off to the market and accused the shopman of hurting his child, and a quarrel ensued in which, he says, he was beaten. But the *marwarees* (moneylenders) have been too quick for the *mali*, and have served the summons upon him.

Thursday

I went yesterday to see Mrs Hassan Aly, and I took a friend with me who was very anxious to see a native house — Mrs Gurney Fox. Her husband is a nephew of Miss Caroline Fox of Penjerrick, whose *Memories of Old Friends* my mother has been enjoying so much lately. There are two other nephews here, Mr Charles Fox and Mr Newcome Fox, barristers, very pleasant well-read men. Mrs Fox told me that her aunt had asked her in her letters, several times, if she saw anything of Indian ladies and had added: 'Why do not you invite them to your house, instead of giving dinner parties to English people?' So Mrs Fox was glad to come to my ladies' party, and be introduced to some Indian ladies, and very glad to go with me yesterday.

Mrs Hassan Aly lives close to the Nujmoodeen Tyabjees, where Ethel and I went last Saturday. The house looks over the same tank — the Baboola tank — but it is a large house, at least the drawing-room was much larger than Mr Nujmoodeen's, though not so grandly decorated. The room, however, is so enormous that it struck one as very unusual, and I asked Mrs Hassan Aly if they had ever measured it. 'Yes,' she said, 'it is quite 100 feet.' There were only three Indian ladies, Mrs Hassan Aly, Mrs Budrudeen and her daughters, and Mrs Nujmoodeen. There were several children, and after we had been there a little while, I asked one little girl, Nazali, who spoke English, if she would let me draw her, that I might show my children how little Muhammadan girls dressed. She was very willing, and ran down to the entrance, where our carriage was waiting, to fetch my pencils and paper. She sat down on a chair, and her little brother, Azhar, stood by her, and I made a hurried pencil sketch.

It always seems such a pity that Ellen (my sister) is not here when I see so much to paint; there are endless subjects for drawing, even if she did nothing but portraits and single figures. There were some other English ladies there, but only one whom I knew well, Mrs Birdwood. As there were people enough to talk, I thought I might use my time in drawing. The Indian ladies and children were very much interested in my sketch and, of course, I had to draw being watched all the time. The grandmother of the children seemed much pleased at my wishing to draw them. She was a sweet looking woman, with a thoughtful careworn face and large brown eyes. She wore the plain dress of a widow, white muslin sari, untrimmed, and a plain black silk shirt. Her husband was the eldest brother of the Tyabjees. Before we came away, we had the usual refreshments, cakes and fruits and coffee. One thing, which I had not seen anywhere before, was a nosegay on the table, and in the middle of the flowers a stick of incense (or scent, as Mrs Aly called it), burning and throwing up a little scented smoke over the table and the guests.

The view from the windows to the west, over the tank, was very pretty; the dark red roofs of the town, of every shape and angle, stood out against the sunset sky, and away in the distance, just showing over the house tops, the grey outline of Cumballa Hill, with its fringe of palms. I should like to paint the view, and Mrs Hassan Aly was very kind in pressing me to come whenever I liked. It will be very nice if I can use some of the time spent with the Indian ladies in drawing. They do not understand a ten minutes' call, a good hour, or hour and a half, at least, you must stay if you wish to please them. Mrs Fox was much interested in her visit, and now having seen a Muhammadan family, she must see also a Hindu and a Parsee household.

Our *mali* has come back from the police court; the case was discharged; nothing was proved against him. When the summons first came, John wrote to the magistrate (a Parsee), Mr Dosabhoy Framji, telling him that he knew nothing of the rights of the case, but that the man had always been steady and well behaved with us, and had a good character from his last master. Mr D. Framji replied very politely, saying that John's opinion of the man would have great weight and that the case would be carefully inquired into.

I thought the answer was characteristic of the difference between Indian and Egyptian officials. At Ramleh our man, Achmet, once was in trouble. A man had got into his house at night and there was a quarrel. Finally the trespasser was sent to prison. Then came a letter from the *kadi* (the magistrate) telling John that the culprit was in prison, and asking 'His Excellency how long he wished him to be kept there?' and adding, with servile politeness, 'that of course whatever His Excellency wished, would be done.' No law evidently bound him as to the term of imprisonment, in comparison with any wish of 'His Excellency'.

Our *mali* told us that some of Miss Pechey's servants were present when he went back to remonstrate with the *marwaree*, but they refused to go with him to the court. We could not make out whether it was from fear of the *marwarees* that they refused, or that they really had not seen the quarrel. The servants, generally, are so much in the power of these moneylenders, no wonder they are afraid of them.

An English officer in an Indian regiment, Major Carter, was telling me the other day of a striking case of their tyranny. In the regiment, there was a young man who had joined the army in order to get money to pay off a debt to a *marwaree*. His father had borrowed 150 rupees to buy a pair of bullocks. He mortgaged his house, and the *marwaree* lent him the money. He, the father, entered the army himself first, but when his son was old enough to join, he returned to his home. Major Carter took an interest in the boy and he rose rapidly, learning, in the regiment school, to read and write English. He became, at last, clerk to the commanding officer. I suppose originally, when the money was due to the *marwarees*, the father had been unable to pay. I do not know how that was, but I know that the father and son, for eight years, paid 40 rupees *a month* as interest to the *marwaree*.

The *ayahs* here (as well as the menservants) are often in the power of the *marwarees*. Mrs Geary told me that a friend of hers found that their poor *ayah*, a nice respectable woman, a widow, had been paying nearly all her wages, month after month, to a *marwaree*, in payment of a debt contracted by her husband who had been dead for several years. Her own *ayah* came to her in distress one day to tell her that she could not satisfy the *marwaree* from whom she had borrowed money. He had lent her some money to buy a grand sari for holiday wear, and she had gone on paying exorbitant interest ever since, till the whole sum was paid several times over. But still he would not let her off. Mr Geary sent word to the man to come and speak to him; nothing has been seen or heard of him since.

Khandalla, Friday 5 June 1885

We started at 6.30 yesterday, John's birthday, and drove to the little village of Karli, where we stopped. We left the carriage and horses under some splendid trees that threw great cool shadows on the parched ground. Here, some coolies met us, with a chair to carry me up to the caves. Six men there were, and an old rickety chair fastened to two thick poles. The men do not carry people as our Egyptian servants used to carry me — holding the ends of the poles in their hands, their hands hanging down and a rope over the shoulders to help them. Here they carry the poles on their shoulders and instead of only two men, four carry you, and two more come to relieve the others in turn. So we had six men. I believe eight would have come, only John had told them the chair was for a lady.

Well, we started, John walking and I in my chair, away across the level ground that lies between the two ranges of hills. It did not look very far to the hill where the caves are, and I thought we should soon be there, but it took us much longer than I expected to get over the rough ground — rice fields mostly — some of them freshly ploughed. The sun was very hot, though it was only 7.00 o'clock (sun time). John went on at a steady pace, rather ahead — the men carrying me were continually changing with each other, which they did as they went along without lowering the chair, or they changed the pole, from one shoulder to the other, lifting the end over their head. They were of different heights, so the chair was sometimes down on one side and sometimes on the other, as the men changed about. I cannot say I like this mode of progression. I realized, what we had learnt in our ambulance lectures, that in carrying the wounded or sick the bearers should *not* keep step. When they did step together, the motion was most disagreeable, throwing you forward in regular jerks, just like the motion of a camel. When we got some way up the ascent, the path became very rocky and steep and I got down and walked, or rather climbed, the rest. About two thirds up the hill is a little level plateau, with big shady trees, and just beyond that are the caves. As we came in view of them we saw first the top of the great arch, showing over the trees, and at the side of the rock, nearer to us, were little recesses and holes.

We did not go into the cave directly. John was very hot and tired with his climb, so was I, though I had not done much; so we sat down and rested a few minutes, and grew a little cooler, and then began our sight-seeing. It was not like what I had expected, somehow, though I have seen photographs. I knew from John that there were columns, and figures and arches, but I thought there would be more beauty, at least more mystery, within the great cave temple. It is very wonderful, there is no doubt about that, but you cannot in any view get an idea of the size or of the workmanship. There is one long hall hewn out of the rock; two rows of gigantic pillars divide this room into a nave and aisles, but the pillars are so close together that as you stand looking down towards the inner end, which is formed rather like an apse, you see only a close mass of columns hiding dark aisles on either side. In the apse stands the *dagoba*, or holy shrine, where some relic of Buddha is supposed to rest. The *dagoba* is like a huge beehive of solid rock, and on the top of it is a large green umbrella, very old, almost as ancient, some people say, as the temple. The roof is very curious, for the rock is nowhere seen. John says the builders are supposed to have wished to imitate an ordinary building and so hid the rock whenever they could. All over the roof are arches of wood, deep planks, not beams, that are fastened edgeways to the roof of rock, the roof being cut in the shape of the Moorish arch.

Over the entrance too there is woodwork, which must of course have been exposed to changes of weather. I wonder what wood it is. It looks like teak. By the entrance there were figures carved in high relief of dancing girls, one of them is said to express the idea of motion very well. So it does, but the face is not beautiful, nor is the figure graceful. The elephants, which are carved against the side of the entrance yard, are exceedingly well done. You see the head and ears and great trunk, only in one the trunk is gone. There are four enormous pillars at the entrance, or there were four; one is quite gone excepting the base and another partly gone. I do not know how they have fallen. These pillars taper towards the top. The columns inside the cave are eight-sided and have very heavy capitals. The capitals are too heavy, even for the massive pillars, and are so intricate in shape that, as John said, you had almost the feeling that the capital was not firmly supported. We hope to go again next week, and then I shall make some drawings, and I can then show better what I mean by giving some sketches of what I saw. Yesterday we could not stay long enough. It was a very hot day and, as John was tired and as by mistake we had not enough umbrellas for protection against the sun, my wish was to get down again before the day was much hotter. It was a still day, hot even for an Indian June.

After we had examined the interior, I went up to the little cells on the hill above, where Hindu ladies were sitting. To get up, I had to mount on a heap of fallen rock, and then I could reach some broken steps cut in the rock, the lower end of this rock having fallen away. When I emerged in the room above, I found it was a square apartment, the whole front open to the air and view. Round the other three sides were cells, cut back into the rock, and in one of them was a stone dais about as big as a bed. It was meant, John said, for the god's bed. In the great temple there were four beds for the Hindu god, or Deva, who is worshipped in a modern, whitewashed, intrusive little temple that stands right by the great ancient Buddhist cave, almost as out of keeping as the khedive's chalet that is built close to the Pyramids and the Sphynx — not quite though, for these modern worshippers at Karli are at least the descendants of the old believers in Buddha, while the chalet at Ghiseh is thronged with English, Americans, and all the other Western people, and is the scene of unromantic picnics or dinners to great men. A round red-faced god, a Hindu god, was seated on a throne in the little new temple, with a dim light burning before him. As we passed the door again, on leaving the caves, we saw that they had decorated the god with flowers — white of course, they are never coloured apparently — loose flowers stuck about him and thrown over him. John said it was in honour of us. There was a large family, or two or three families perhaps, living among the caves and temple. Four or five nice looking, dark-eyed little children ran out of the temple and held up their hands, with a beseeching 'Sahib! Sahib!' They looked merry over it, however, not at all like poor beggars. We would not give them anything, then, but I gave them some oranges and a few annas when we left.

We just fixed upon a sketch, to be made when we could return to Karli, and then set off down the hill. I walked down, preferring the fatigue to a journey in the chair, going backwards too, while the men climbed and slipped down the steep descent. Over the hot, baking, dry plain I, however, was glad to be carried in the chair, John going on ahead again, too hot to speak a word, only feeling that this space had to be got over before the trees that we could see in the distance, with their cool shade, were reached. When we did reach those trees — my men, almost running in their eagerness to set me down and rest — it was delicious to feel the great dense green mass above you, defying the sun altogether, and to look out from our cool resting place on the glaring country we had just passed through.

I got out my sketchbook and began to draw the men and the chair — I thought the children at home would like to see what my conveyance was. I was just finishing a rough sketch when John called out, 'You had better leave it — one man is ill.' I had not noticed that one coolie had stepped aside and was lying on the ground. We went to him and found that he was in great pain; he could not move, but lay on his face. John thought it must be cramp or cholera. We had, of course, no medicines with us, but we had a little whisky in the basket. John took it and poured it down the man's throat, his companions agreeing to our proceedings. I got the mustard pot and emptied it onto the man's stomach and made the others rub him well. I thought the heat might do him good and we had nothing else. After a little while he was able to sit up and we wrapped him in one of the horse cloths and took him, in the carriage, back to Khandalla. We meant to take him to the dispensary — to Dr Field — but he objected and said he wished to go home; and as he was evidently better we did not press him. When we got home we gave him some chlorodyne and some flannel, for a belt, and sent him to his own home.

Then, after he had gone, I found Ethel had just sent for Dr Field, having persuaded Miss Pechey to see him. I was very glad, for certainly doctors are very bad physicians for themselves. As Ethel says, 'Doctors ought to be made so that they are never ill.' I don't know what Miss Pechey would say if she had such a refractory patient. However, she consented to stay in bed, with the concession that she might just come over in a dressing gown and lie on a sofa, on the veranda here, in the evening. She gets downhearted when she is ill, so we are very glad to have her here among us. I read aloud in the evening, generally, after dinner — one of our dear old books — we are in the middle of *Northanger Abbey*, and even Miss Pechey was obliged to laugh over John Thorpe and Isabella.

Saturday 6 June

The day is looking up — Miss Pechey is certainly better. Ethel had a pleasant change from nursing this morning, for she went with John to the 'Dip', that is a part of the hill, near Lanowli, where the level summit absolutely ends, in a fall, almost perpendicular, of 900 feet. The road there is too rough for driving, and you must walk about three miles. I doubt if I could manage it. I have lost my power of walking so much here. However, John had a good healthy morning in the fresh cool air, for a strong wind was blowing. It was better for walkers than it was for me. I was sitting by the road, painting, and the sand drove into my eyes and onto my palette. The *patel* had to hold the screen all the time, or it would have fallen on my back.

A few days ago the barber brought the news that a large cow had been killed by a tiger in the night, a little way from the hotel. We doubted at first, but found it was quite true, a poor cow had been killed, and half eaten. John and Ethel were walking quite near the place at 6.00 o'clock the next morning. That was last Wednesday. On Thursday, Ethel and I went up to the hotel, to pay some calls there, and we heard that Major Lyon, the landlord, had shot the animal the night before. It was a large panther. He watched, near the dead cow, and towards midnight he saw the panther appear. He was up in a tree, and he waited there till the panther had eaten well and was quiet, and then he fired and killed it with one shot. When we got to the hotel he had just skinned it, and sent the skin as a present to Sir Jamsetjee. The animal was seven feet six inches in length, from his nose to his tail.

When I came out onto the veranda this afternoon after my siesta, John called to me to come and look — 'the men had just found a snake in the tent.' John had been sitting there half an hour before. It is a long, very narrow snake with a flat head, which looks like a dangerous snake, but it may be harmless. The men killed it, and now Ethel has it in a bottle to preserve it. When the men brought the snake, I ran over to the little bungalow to call Ethel. As I came back I had such a start, for there, on the veranda, with its back towards me, stood a panther! John laughed, and I saw, of course, it was the stuffed skin of the panther that had been shot, and Sir Jamsetjee had kindly sent it for us to see. We sent for Bracken, who was not here when the creature appeared, and it was most absurd to see Bracken's behaviour. He ran at it straining at his chain, for of course we kept him fastened for fear of his injuring the skin, then poor Bracken got more and more excited, and at last was quite furious when Ethel moved the huge creature and Bracken thought it was coming at him.

We have another dog here just now, Pompey, a pug belonging to Mrs Yorke Smith, Ethel's friend. Pompey is stout and calm and, though he snarled and growled, did not excite himself much even on seeing a panther. Pompey is in the charge of Mr and Mrs Gurney Fox, who have taken the Yorke Smiths' house for a time, but Pompey was ill in Bombay and Mr Fox sent him up to Mrs Fox at the hotel. As there were other dogs there, Pompey's presence was not desired and he would have had to return to hot Bombay, only we said we would have him here. He looked very poorly, poor old fellow, and puffed and panted, and reminded me of the old story in the *Parlour Printing Press* of the lady taking her pet dog to the doctor, and the picture of the doctor with a whip in his hand making the dog run round and round the room. Pompey, like the lady's lapdog, had been overfed. He is recovering fast, with a little starving, and Bracken, with his fun and tricks, acts the part of the doctor.

8

July–12 October

*Nasik, an old leech woman, Gunpattis, Hindu
friend wins her case, a girls' high school*

Nasik, 25 July 1885

Bᴀʙʏ, Ellen and I came up to Nasik two days ago, and already the
change of air has done Baby good. We left Bombay at 7.00 o'clock,
John coming with us to the railway station. The *chobdar* had come back
a day or two before we left, after a fortnight's absence. He is here, with
us, and I hope the bracing air will do him good also after his illness. We
were fortunate in having fine weather for the journey. The country
looked very wet, and in many parts the fields were under water. Near
Kallian, we passed over the place where the line had been washed away.
Men were still working at it. As we began to ascend the Ghats, the scenery was very beautiful; the teak trees are in full leaf and the feathery
flowers still in bud. The hills are so much more wooded than those
towards Khandalla, that the scenery is quite different. There were
beautiful waterfalls and rushing torrents — one stream reminded me
very much of the river in Savoy, that you follow for so long in going
from Chambery to Modane and Mount Cenis. We went through a great
many tunnels; the water was running down the sides in some of them;
there have been one or two landslips and I was glad when we had done
with the tunnels. We had no light in the carriage; I suppose, as the
tunnels are short, the railway people think it does not matter.

There was a crowd of natives at the Nasik station, some hundreds, I
should think. I was surprised at seeing so many people, but Mr Baker
tells me there are always a great many poor people waiting for the train
that we came by, and for another going in the other direction at the same
time, as these are slow trains and a fourth class is put on. The fare is

111

very low, but the fourth-class carriages are sometimes detained for a night or day, for the convenience of traffic. The sacred year, too, is not quite over and consequently pilgrims are still coming and going in greater numbers than in ordinary years. A little while ago — last March — there was an outburst of cholera in Nasik, and it was no wonder. At Trimbak, the holy place where all the pilgrims congregate, there is a sacred tank where every pilgrim must bathe before doing *puja* — worshipping the idol in the temple. This tank is only 40 feet long and 8 feet deep, and after the poor, dirty people have bathed in it, the water is like mud. Not only must they bathe in it; every pilgrim must fast for 24 hours, then bathe, and then drink this horrible water, and then perform *puja*. After this they may eat, and no wonder if they eat ravenously half-cooked rice, or unripe fruit, or anything they can buy.

Nasik, 8 August 1885

When John was here he told me of an incident in the great caste case going on — the Cutchi Memon case — which was curious and I wrote it down as he told me. A number of witnesses of the Cutchi Memons were giving evidence as to their community having retained Hindu customs, although they had embraced Muhammadanism. The dispute on this point has caused a great deal of ill blood, and the community is divided into very hostile factions. The orthodox party, who hold that a Muhammadan, by religion, must of necessity be a Muhammadan in law, also say that the other party are very wicked in daring to deny this, and in setting up any other kind of law than that which the Koran lays down. All the Muhammadan priesthood, of course, support the orthodox party, and equally, of course, are the objects of much reverence to both parties.

The orthodox party determined to utilize this reverence in support of their case, and one morning when John walked into court he saw the five front seats behind the lawyers occupied by five venerable gentlemen in green robes and green turbans, who were the chief Muhammadan priests of Bombay. When the witness came into the box, these five dignitaries all bent their eyes sternly upon him, with a glare that plainly intimated that their displeasure in this world and hell in the next would be his portion if he persisted in stating what he was brought there to say. The witness, however, was not intimidated, and stood firmly by his Hindu law. The counsel for the Hindu side, Mr Starling,

RIGHT. Portrait of Nora
Scott by Guido Schmitt

BELOW. The Drawing-room
of the Scotts' house in
Bombay

ABOVE. Bullock-carts in the hills near Khandalla

BELOW. Pilgrims' Gate at Nasik

ABOVE. Camels in the Cavalry lines near Poona

BELOW. Camel troops on manoeuvres near Poona

ABOVE. An Indian highway

BELOW. Mysore oxen

ABOVE. The eternal India

BELOW. Commissariat elephants at Khandalla

ABOVE. View of Bombay from Malabar Hill

BELOW. Toddy-palms by the sea

RIGHT. Lithograph of Sir
Rowland Hill, the
author's uncle and crea-
tor of the Penny Post

RIGHT. Portrait by Ellen
Hill of Frederic Hill, the
author's father

ABOVE. Photograph of the Scott family in 1890, reunited after the parents' return to England from Bombay

BELOW. Photograph of the author and her sisters with their father

applied to the court for the summary ejectment of these *mollahs* (priests) on the ground that the sole object of their being there was to frighten the witness and to stifle the truth. John then asked the witness whether the presence of anyone in court prevented him saying, freely, whatever he thought. The witness promptly replied 'Certainly not,' and John then refused to disturb the *mollahs*. Mr Starling, however, was quite equal to the occasion. He at once had all the five priests served with summonses to appear as witnesses, and then asked for the application of the rule, which excludes coming witnesses from listening to those who precede them. John said: 'I can't do that unless you tell me that you are really going to call them. I can't have the public excluded by a mere dodge.'

Mr Starling: I undertake, to call them all, my Lord.
John: Usher, order all witnesses out of court.

The *mollahs* did not move until this order was communicated to them individually and then, one by one, they stalked slowly and majestically out of court.

I have not seen Mr Baker's court yet, but I shall go one day when Mrs Baker is better. Yesterday a German lady, one of the missionaries here, dined with us. She can go out very seldom on account of her work and especially just now, as another mission lady is ill, so as she had arranged to come yesterday we would not put her off. She told Mr Baker that a native family had asked her to speak to the 'Judge Sahib' about a young Hindu lad — a minor — who owns property. The family seem to wish to keep the estate together, while the trustees propose to sell it. Of course Mr Baker would have authority over the boy and his affairs if he has been made a ward of the court, but not otherwise. It may come to a lawsuit. In that case, of course, Mr Baker cannot listen to anything from either party before it comes on for hearing. But you cannot make people understand that.

Just before I came up here we had a similar instance. A native lady has a case coming on, extremely important to her. It is down for hearing in John's court. Miss Pechey told me she had had a letter from the lady asking her to use her influence with the judge. Miss Pechey called upon her and explained as clearly as she could that it was impossible to comply with her request, and tried to make her understand our ideas of

113

justice and the impartiality of the judge. In spite of all Miss Pechey said, a few days afterwards I had a letter myself from the lady, asking me to speak to John for her. Of course I did not answer the letter. Some months ago this case was put down in Mr Birdwood's list, and then the lady got a friend to write to a cousin of Mr Birdwood's to get him to use his influence. Directly Mr Birdwood heard of it, he refused to try the case and got it transferred to another court. Miss Pechey knew of this, and she told the Indian lady that the same thing would happen again if she tried again to make an appeal to the judge. I do not know what John will do about it, but perhaps as the appeal was only made to Miss Pechey and to me, and she was told nothing could be said to the judge, he will not think it necessary to refuse to try the case.

Mr Baker was telling me that at one town where he was appointed as judge, there was a long list of arrears in the court. He set to work to clear off the cases and had got through a good many when a native official came up to him, saying: 'Sahib, if you go on working like this, the *sirkar* will say no judge is wanted here, and they will abolish your post, and then where will you be?'

Sunday
There is a good deal of opthalmia about in Nasik. It is supposed to be caused by small flies, which get into the eye and irritate it. There is quite a plague of these flies; they are so tiny that you can scarcely see them; you have the feeling that you are seeing wrong — black specks in front of your eyes. There was a curious incident two days ago, at least curious to me. The doctor had ordered leeches to be put to Mrs Baker's head. I supposed that Ellen and I should have to put them on, but Mr Baker said a 'professional woman' would come. At the appointed time there arrived an old woman, very dark, with thick grizzled hair, but not a bad-looking old body. She had a blue cotton jacket, with short tight sleeves, and a red cotton sari over her head and wound round her. She had silver bracelets on, and a nose ring and earrings, and also anklets and heavy silver rings on her toes. She came up to the back veranda with a little bundle in her hand — an old rag full of leeches. When we were ready for her, she came in with her leeches: 24 had to be put on, and the old woman got them all on and made them bite in much less time than I remember I took to get one to bite when Conny had face-

ache; and when Leslie had mumps in Egypt and was ordered leeches, we did not get them to bite at all.

The old body must be like our old servant, Mrs Collins, who had such wonderful power over all animals. Mrs Baker's head was very bad, and while the leech operation was going on the old woman shampooed it, pressing it in a peculiar way with her fingers, which Mrs Baker said gave great relief. If only the old lady had clean hands and new clothes, she would make a good attendant in a sick room, for she was very quiet and gentle in her manner. The doctor told me they do not keep any leeches at the dispensary; if leeches are needed, he always sends for one of these leech-women.

Nasik, 21 August 1885

I hoped to have gone out sketching this morning and was ready at 7.00 (6.30 sun time), but the morning which looked so bright and sunny at 6.00 had clouded over, and a thick mist and drizzling rain hid all the landscape. I am afraid it is hopeless trying anything but hurried drawings in this monsoon. Yesterday evening Etta and I went down the road towards the town and began to draw a pretty view of the lane, with a peep of the town, and in the foreground a great banyan tree. Mrs Baker drove us there, and then left us, and went on to have a drive and pay some calls, taking Ellen and Baby with her. The rain came on, however, and went on most of the time; I suppose Mrs Baker (being rather deaf) did not hear the rain and was unaware of our watery position. But we had cloaks and umbrellas, and we got under the banyan tree and were pretty well sheltered. I made a pencil sketch of a little Hindu shrine that stands by the road near to the great banyan tree. You see these little wayside shrines everywhere about the country. Sometimes, instead of a figure roughly carved, it is only a stone of some curious shape, chosen because of its peculiar form, and painted red. Scarlet is the sacred colour. Sometimes you see a few dead flowers lying before the old stone; rice or any other kind of food may have been offered but is, I suppose, soon found and eaten up, not by the god, but by some animal, as Odda's cake was in *Feats on the Fiord*.

On rising ground across the road, not 200 yards from the Hindu shrine, is an *idgah*, or praying place, of the Muhammadans. It is only a single wall, made firm by small buttresses on one side, and on this same side a flight of steps against the wall, on which the priest mounts on certain days twice a year and gives his sermon. I must draw the *idgah* and put it in my diary with the sketch of the Hindu shrine.

The other day we dined with Mr and Mrs Fergusson. Mr Fergusson is government engineer for irrigation works. He was going off the next day to some place, Wagard, 14 miles away, and to get to it he must cross the Godavari. The river was swollen and difficult to get over, and it was not safe to cross it at night. There is a ferry over the river. A rope goes from side to side, and a clumsy boat is pulled across by the ferrymen by means of this rope. He went off very early in the morning and was home again by the evening. People do not think much of distances and rough journeys here.

Mr Fraser, one of the assistant collectors, was at the Fergussons'. He only came out from England last November. He was at Oxford, at Balliol, but junior to Maurice. We were talking about some people I had had to sketch — Mr Fraser is fond of drawing himself. He told me if I wanted to see characteristic-looking natives, of all races, I ought to be at the *katcherri*, the collector's office, on the first of the month, when all government pensioners receive their money. There is a document he says giving a description of each man, with a view, of course, of securing the right man for the pension. This description is read out to the man. In the case of one pensioner the statement is: 'Eyes like a cat's and a deceitful expression.' The man hears this description of himself read aloud with the greatest complacency, pockets his money and walks away, to return next month and hear the same flattering words again.

Bella Vista, Thursday 17 September 1885

We have had a night of pouring rain. I had just gone to bed, when down came the rain, with such a noise that it seemed just as if a waterfall was outside our windows. All night it went on — one continuous roar. There was not any wind however and so I hope the sea was still calm where the *Cathay* was. She must be about 450 miles away from Bombay by now, and beyond the reach of our local storms.

It is dear Ranee's birthday today — she is three years old, so my little baby girl that I left in England is gone. I can never see the little first tottering steps, or hear the first attempts at words. Baby, here, is now what Ranee was when I left her — like her too in the face — but not quite like her. When will the little sisters meet? I hardly realize that that will ever be — nor can I realize that John is on his way to the children now, that after the long three years, after the new life, at first so hard, in India, he is really going to England — that he will actually look on the children again, with living eyes — that he will feel their sweet arms round his neck.

Yesterday I went to a little party at a Muhammadan gentleman's house, given for his daughter who had lately arrived from Jacobabad with her husband, Mr Ali Akbar. Mrs Ali Akbar (I forget her own name) speaks English very well, and is extremely advanced in her ways for a Muhammadan. Her husband is a civil engineer, whose work has made him travel a good deal in India, and his wife has accompanied him — on camel back. She sang an English song rather nicely, at least without affectation and in tune. There were about 15 Muhammadan ladies and some children, and five or six gentlemen. At one time, four of the brothers were sitting together on a divan. They looked very well, I thought, in their Muhammadan dress clothes.

I arrived very late, and as I am generally rather early in going to their parties I was attacked on the subject, and had to explain my lateness many times. We had started from home in good time, but I had not allowed time enough for mischances on the road. Major Willoughby was with me and was to get into a street carriage, when we came to one, and go to the Byculla station. However, we did not find any buggy near the part of the town where the Futti Alis live, and while we were looking about we were stopped by a procession coming along the street — a crowd of Hindus, a cart in the middle, and singing, clapping and clashing of instruments going on. I could not think what it was. In the cart was a high pole, standing upright, and clinging to it was a brown naked figure. All round the cart were men carrying little plaster images. '*Gunputtis*', exclaimed the Major and I at the same time. So they were — funny little clay figures — pinkish or yellowish — they always give their gods fair complexions. This god *Gunputti* has a long elephant's nose and the dress was of gauze and tinsel. One *gunputti*, larger than most — 18 inches or two feet high, was surrounded by little clay figures of women — dancing girls, I suppose — that were made to spin round and round. Some of the very poor people, who could not afford even these cheap little gods, carried a chair aloft — an ordinary cane-bottomed armchair with paper hands cut out and stuck on the ends of the arms, which gave it an odd human look.

117

Procession after procession carrying *gunputtis* came along the streets. It was nearly 6.00 o'clock and I suppose the devotees were all on their way to the sea — to dip the *gunputtis* in the water. Only a few of the most zealous worshippers throw the god in altogether and lose it — most of them think it enough to dip him in the sea and bring him back to serve for another year.

Wednesday 23rd

Yesterday judgment was given in the High Court in Rukmabai's case. I had heard that the case was being tried last Saturday before Mr Justice Pinkey. It had been down on John's list for a long time, but was transferred to Mr Pinkey's court, I suppose, as John had gone away. The judgment is for the defendant — Rukmabai — the plaintiff's suit is dismissed with costs. I will put the report of the case in my diary. Directly the case was over, I wrote to Miss Sakharam and I will quote her words in her answer: 'Thank you for your kind note. I am so thankful to God that He has heard our prayers and saved me from the perpetual misery, and brought the truth to light at last. — With kind regards, Yours affectionately, Rukmabai.'

I see by the newspapers this morning that the husband, Dadajee Bhikajee, is going to appeal. I was sure he would. If he had brought the suit for damages instead of claiming his wife herself, I should think it would have been difficult to decide altogether against him. The marriage had been quite legal according to Hindu law; no contention was raised by the defendant that it was not binding. What a relief it must be to Rukmabai; it is difficult for us to imagine — for the last year the dreadful idea that she might be forced to go to a man she hated has hung over her. It was the one trouble that embittered her good stepfather's last hours — almost his last words to her were upon this subject. He blamed himself for not having collected more evidence about the man — he was leaving her alone to fight the case — 'You must trust to your friends,' he said, 'Mrs Scott and Miss Pechey and Mrs Curjel.'

But I could hardly show her even sympathy, for directly John heard that the case was on his list, he said of course that I must not go to her house or ask her to come here. Then, poor girl, when she wrote to me asking me to speak to John, I could not even write to her, or see her at Miss Pechey's house, or anywhere else. Miss Pechey had tried to make her understand that no party in a suit must attempt to influence the judge, but it was impossible to make her see it in an English point of view. I am certain she did not mean to do anything the least dishonourable.

Khandalla, Friday 9 October 1885
The country is looking lovely, so wonderfully green, and the water course in the ravine is full and all day long the sound of rushing water comes up. At this minute it is the only sound I can hear, excepting a distant growl of thunder. I hope a bad storm will not come. If we had a lightning conductor I should enjoy the storm, but not as it is. Our doors and windows have all warped in the monsoon and some of them we cannot shut at all. I don't know what my mother would say to living in such a lonely place and not being able to barricade her doors. I do not know that there is another English family in the place, except the hotel people one and a quarter miles away up a very steep hill, and on the other side of us there are English people at Lanowli two miles away. The 'season' has not really begun yet; soon there will be several English people. My friend, Miss Bell-Irving, will be with us in two days. I hope she will paint a good deal. Her portrait of 'Lal Khan', the *peon* at Nasik, looked very well at the Poona exhibition. I hear it is sold.

I must go back and tell about my doings at Poona. I had not time to write much diary during my visits. Last Monday I went into the city to see the native high school for girls — the school that Sir William Wedderburn had done so much for. Mrs Wordsworth told me that her coachman could not find the place, and she herself could not even if she could have come with me, so I was wondering how I should discover it when a friend of Mrs Wordsworth, Mrs Kirkham, offered to go with me. Mrs Kirkham's husband is inspector of schools and so she knows all the schools. We got into the native town and found our way down crooked streets until we stopped outside a sort of courtyard. We walked under a gateway and across the courtyard and then, on a stone terrace, we saw a number of girls having a lesson. Miss Hurford, the head mistress, came forward to meet us. She is a slight elderly woman with a thin, delicate face, as if she had done hard work in India, and the most sweet expression.

Miss Hurford asked me if we would like to hear the English lesson, and then the girls began a story from the First Reader. A tall young woman read first — in a slow child-like way, '*This is a cat.*' She read two pages, and then the next began; six or seven read, but what was so curious in this class was that the pupils were of such different ages. It was the lowest class, Miss Hurford explained, and newcomers had to begin there. The eldest pupil was a Brahmin woman of 29 who had come to school, and her little child with her. It was very touching to see mother and child beginning at the same time to gain knowledge. The little girl was about four years old, at least we thought so; the mother was very uncertain as to her age. Her name was Tara, 'star'. She was learning in a little infant class at the other end of the terrace, recently added to the school. Then there was a Brahmin widow, aged 20, who seemed very attentive and anxious to learn. Then there was a handsome young Brahmin woman, married, whose husband had sent her to school all the way from Jubbalpore. We went upstairs next, and into the large classrooms. The house is a beautiful old Brahmin house lent by the owner for the school until the new schoolhouse is built. There are dark ceilings and columns and archways, all dark wood and all beautifully carved. It made a grand background for the graceful figures of the girls and the bright colouring of the dresses. In the central part of the long room that went from one side to the other of the house, there was a deep recess, with slight columns and little archways dividing it from the rest, and the floor raised a foot above the floor of the large room. There, no doubt, the family had performed *puja* and held all their sacred festivals.

With his back to this recess sat a Brahmin professor, 'Shastri' or 'Shastra', Miss Hurford called him. He was a stout gentleman, all in white, excepting his large red turban and his gold earrings in his ears. He sat on a chair in European fashion, but his bare feet were resting comfortably on a stool in front of him. He held a book in one hand; it was evidently a lesson about minerals he was giving, for he was asking the girls questions about rubies, pearls and other stones, as Miss Hurford explained to me — it was all in Marathi. This professor teaches Sanskrit, Marathi and mathematics. I believe he is the only man allowed to come into the school.

Then we heard some of the children sing an English song, and also an Indian song. They pronounced the words well. Though I had no book with the words, I could hear a good deal of the English words. It was a flower girl's song. After that Miss Hurford asked two sisters to sing a Marathi song together. They had been properly taught, she said, and their singing was different to the common music. They had learnt to sing

120

many more notes than are used in the ordinary music of the unlearned. It was a curious song, a good deal like the Arab music, over and over again the same weird refrain — at intervals rather a high note came in. I asked what the song was about — 'On the duty of dwelling constantly in our thoughts upon God,' said Miss Hurford.

One little girl was sitting in this class between two other children about her own age. She was stout and round faced with dark eyes, but she had a wistful expression compared to her companions. 'She is a widow,' Miss Hurford explained, 'Her name is Godu Bai Deshpandi. She is only ten years old.' I asked Miss Hurford if she thought the child was treated kindly at home, and she thought she was, but anyway it is a sad lookout for the child. The children, big and little, were in face and costume, naturally, unlike English girls; but apart from that there is a great variety of types in an Indian school. Miss Hurford told me (as I believe all teachers of Indian children say) 'that it is the easiest thing to keep discipline among the pupils.' There does not seem to be the spirit of fun, or love of mischief, or the impatience of restraint, which is inherent, I suppose, in English children. But there is not, either, so far as I have seen, or very rarely, that dull, apathetic look that one sees on some of our English children's faces when the lessons are evidently only a task to them. In the high school, the marked attention to what was being taught was very striking. From the grown up women, one would expect it, as their coming to the school at all shows a real desire to learn, but all the children seemed attentive, and they were ready to answer questions, though not always correctly of course.

We looked at some needlework done by the children, some of it was quite English work. They like our knitting and crocheting very much, and we saw a number of knitted hoods made for the various babies at home. To cover up a baby's head is the first thing of importance with a native. In this hot climate, they wear much more on their little heads than our babies do in England. Some little jackets for girls were very neatly made, the funny little jackets that only come half way to the waist. After looking at the needlework we came away, passing again the beginners' class with the grown women, and the teacher a Eurasian girl younger than some of her pupils. On each side of the steps that led onto this terrace were large *lotas* (or jars) full of water, and a brass drinking cup by each of them. There were four altogether, I think. These *lotas* and cups, were for the various castes. The one just by the steps was for

121

the Brahmin girls. If any child belonging to another caste were to touch it, it would be polluted. It must be difficult for very young children to remember the rule, I should think.

Saturday Evening

We have been able to go out this afternoon, for though the sky was covered with threatening clouds, it did not actually rain. The carriage and horses had arrived from Bombay, so Baby, Ellen and I went out for a drive. First we drove to the railway station, for I wanted to see the station master and get his advice upon a matter that makes me rather anxious. Today we have caught two snakes in the compound, one, the men say, is a young cobra, the other is a little green tree snake — venomous, but I believe not very bad. Both the snakes were found in the stables. I am afraid that at night, when the men are asleep, one of them may get bitten, or one of the horses. The place is still so damp, and the long grass everywhere is such a hiding place for the snakes that we must keep a sharp lookout. I thought the station master would be likely to know what was best to do. He said the grass should be cut down all round the stables; that we can easily do. At Bombay we put down gravel (if you can call it gravel) made of fine shells from the shore; snakes do not like passing over anything rough and scratchy. Here there is no such gravel. I suggested putting down cinders all round the stables and the station master thought that would be good, and he said he was sure the company would let me have some sacks of cinders. It would take a cart load, I think, to make anything like a sufficient barrier round the stables. I must write to the railway manager, Mr Shipp, tonight.

The *hammall* caught a most curious beetle yesterday. I do not know at all what it is. It has extremely long antennae, and long front paws like lobsters' claws at the end. We must send it home, to the children.

Monday 12 October (Dear Arthur's birthday)

It is 9.00 o'clock with us in Khandalla, and so at Burghfield it is half-past three. I fancy dear Arthur very happy, having his father with him on his birthday — all the others very happy too. It is too late in the year for the children to have their favourite birthday treat — a picnic. I dare say the little things will prepare some entertainment for John. I hope it is a bright fine day at Burghfield. Perhaps this time next year I may be on my way to England. How strange John's and my life is — partings and meetings and living constantly separated from one or other of those dearest to us. We thought we should live in England, near London, and never be far away from our families, and then everything changed and the hope of getting back to England dwindled and dwindled. But now at least we are hoping to have a happy time all together in England when John takes his furlough in 1887.

Miss Bell-Irving came here yesterday, having travelled all night. She is full of zeal for her art, and we have arranged for a model to come tomorrow — the adopted son of the contractor, whom I sketched once before. The old barber, too, is to stand for her. We are sitting on the veranda just now, under the light of a hanging lamp. The light attracts the insects and we have quite a natural history exhibition going on round us. Moths of various kinds, beetles and grasshoppers, but we have not all the insects we had at Poona. There, evening after evening, we had beautiful creatures flying about, long and elegant in shape, with a greenish colouring shading into red and gold. Mr Wordsworth warned me not to clap my hand suddenly on my face if one settled on me, for if you smash one it raises a blister directly. Mr Wordsworth said that once, after sleeping in a house where these flies abounded, he woke up in the morning and found his neck swollen from ear to ear — one huge blister. He should hardly have known himself he said when he looked in the glass.

9

18 October–4 February 1886

Account of a riot, a servant's money stolen,
Christmas at Khandalla, a prize from the
Simla art exhibition, SPCA hospital

Khandalla, Sunday 18 October 1885

THE last few days have been given up to painting, for our old friends of last year — the performing bulls and their keepers — have appeared in Khandalla, and Etta and I began to sketch them directly. Etta was so anxious to begin, that she only saw a small part of their performance. We have had the assembly of men, boys and bullocks here each morning from 7.00 a.m. till 1.00 o'clock. They came very punctually at 7.00. It was rather a long morning, even with the interruption of breakfast and housekeeping. I got through housekeeping as quickly as possible, sometimes handing over part to Ellen, but I could not leave things undone, as since our housekeeping troubles I have been myself giving out stores, so that I might tell from my own knowledge what quantity of things we really used. It was rather tantalizing to know the 'sacred bulls' were waiting there, in all their wonderful trappings, saying to me 'Come draw me,' for so many things — people and animals and landscapes, so many more than I can find time to do — are always saying to me, 'Come draw me.'

Yesterday evening we drove out past Lanowli along the Poona road, and we saw the bulls grazing on the common; the whole encampment was there, about a dozen little tents and a great many people, men, women and children. They come to the same place every year. Ellen saw a hammock slung in one tent, and a child was in it. People are as fond of swinging beds or chairs in India, as they are in Lancashire of rocking chairs.

Today is 'Dusera Day', the festival for horses. In honour of it, the coachmen and *garawallahs* appeared this morning leading the horses all decked out with flowers; they were followed by the *bheestie*, leading the bullock, and last came the *mali* (the Bombay *mali*, who is still here) bringing up the cow and her little calf. We all laughed when the cow appeared, for she was dressed up in the *mali's* grey blanket, and her head was smothered in flowers and she looked very funny. The little calf was also decorated. We gave the horses, bullock and cows some bread, which they liked; even the little calf took it quite well.

Tuesday
Yesterday was the last day of the festival of the *Mohurram*, the anniversary of the death of Hussain, the son of Muhammad's daughter Fatima. He was murdered just after he had been invited to become the imam (ruler) of Islam. In Bombay, the festival is a very striking one. I wish very much I could see it there, but each year we have been away from Bombay at the time of the *Mohurram*. Up here, in little Khandalla, there is not much to be seen, but still the sight of the *taboots* is interesting. I saw a grand one yesterday, with a little dome on the top in imitation of a Muhammadan mosque. I think I made a sketch of one from memory last year, but I will try and get a *taboot* brought here so that I may draw it properly. The *taboot* (or tomb) is carried aloft by men and followed by a crowd of people, some playing on rude instruments, some clapping, all shouting and wailing, mourning for Hussain and for the little children that were left fatherless. In Bombay, three children are led about on horseback following the *taboot*, dressed in blood-stained garments, and there is a figure carried on a bier which represents the murdered man. There is still a very large body of Muhammadans who maintain that Hussain and his descendants are the rightful heirs of Muhammad; they are called the Shiah Muhammadans.

22 October
On Tuesday Etta and I set out in search of *taboots*, for the *patel* brought word that they would not come here. We drove down to the village, and just at the entrance we saw a crowd and heard a great noise of music and shouting. The horses were rather restive, and we stopped. Etta and I got out and took up our position on a bank by the roadside; Ellen and Baby turned back and went for a drive.

Just as we thought we would begin a hasty sketch standing there and seeing what we could, a Hindu came up and asked us in good English if we should like chairs, or if we would come over to the other side of the road and sit on a little terrace of a house. We accepted his offer and went over to the terrace; and he gave us a bench and there we could draw very comfortably, barring the noise of the clapping and music, and guns going off every few minutes. Quite a crowd pressed up against me, for I was close to the edge of the terrace, but no one disturbed us. The Hindu who had befriended us stayed all the time we sketched, and waved off with a commanding air anyone who he thought came in our way. This vigorous gentleman is the chief constable here. He said he should be most happy to do anything for us at any time. He told me his name, Rab Samkar, or something like that. Whenever I thanked him for anything, he replied promptly, 'Don't mention it.' He kept the *taboot* for half an hour while we drew it. The *taboot* men were quite satisfied with a present of half a rupee. It was a curious scene; the *taboot* showing white against the houses opposite and the gay coloured crowd; some men were dancing wildly, some shooting, others singing and shouting. Women and children mixed in the crowd, some of the women carrying tiny babies. It seemed to be a holiday all through the place for Hindus as well as Muhammadans.

Khandalla, 24 October 1885

We had such a misty night and morning — I was glad Etta was not sleeping in the tent. The damp seemed to penetrate everywhere. Little Rupert was sleeping in the outer room of the small bungalow. We had hung up a cloth over the lower part of the lattice work, which forms the front wall of the room, and Mrs Ollivant did not disturb him to move his bed into the inner room.

The long grass looked lovely this morning, silvery white with the dew — most beautiful when we looked across it towards the sun. I was wandering about searching for a subject to paint, and though it was all lovely everywhere in the ravine and in our compound, I could not find anything that would quite do for what I wanted. Etta says I am greedy — like a child with a bun in one hand and a biscuit in the other taking a nibble at each. I suppose it is true, there are so many things I want to sketch. At last I went out along the road, and a very little way from our compound I found that a turn in the road would make a nice sketch with one of my favourite bullock carts going along.

I took a sketchbook and made the roughest drawing, just to try the effect, and as I was drawing the road, a bullock garry and driver came along. The *patel* who was with me asked the man to stop, which he did directly. I only kept him about ten minutes, or a quarter of an hour, and at the end I gave him a little two-anna piece. He was a fine, tall young man and looked very well in his red turban. He looked at the money when I put it into his hand, and I thought perhaps he was not satisfied. Then suddenly he stooped right down and kissed my feet. He evidently thought it a large sum, poor fellow, and wanted to express his gratitude.

Yesterday evening, driving home from Lanowli, we passed a number of bullock carts halting for the night. They looked so very picturesque. The bullocks were standing about and some lying down; they had been taken out of the carts, and the poles of the carts were propped up by two pieces of bamboo that rested on the ground. It was getting dark and the men were wrapped up in their blankets and preparing for the night. There was a little fire lighted here and there. I suppose the men were going to cook their supper. We mean to start early this afternoon, and perhaps I shall get an hour's sketching. But it grows dark very rapidly here after the sun sets, and I am afraid the bullock carts do not halt till about sunset.

Sunday

I was telling Mrs Ollivant yesterday about John's being in Alexandria at the time of the massacres. 'We were once in riots in a small way,' she said. 'It was in 1877. We were living in Surat; my husband was assistant collector. The licence tax had just been put on and there was great discontent and excitement in the town, especially in the Muhammadan part. The collector had left for England the day before.'

Mr Ollivant (who is here now for two days) told me that he saw plainly there was a very angry feeling among the people. His friends urged him to telegraph to government, but he said, 'No, I will manage it myself, if I can.' He doubled the guards on his office (the collector's) and saw that the troops in the citadel were all in readiness to give assistance should they be wanted. This licence tax was a tax on all trades, and the shopkeepers were the class aggrieved. They all closed their shops, and consequently there was no grain, for food, to be bought. It was feared that this would cause a rising among the poor Hindu population. Mr Ollivant sent out into the districts and had grain brought into the town, and had booths run up during the night just under his office windows. By this means the poor people were able to buy food, and were quieted. But the shopkeepers, principally Muhammadans, were furious.

Early that morning, Mr Ollivant and a friend, Mr White, were out in the town. They were dressed alike, in white with sun-helmets on, and they both rode large Australian horses. Mr Ollivant, seeing what the state of the town was, and that he should be hard at work all day, left his companion for a few minutes to ride back and tell Mrs Ollivant that he should not be home till night. Turning back then probably saved his life.

Mr White rode on till he got into a street thronged with an angry crowd. The crowd was most dense in front of one building — the public dispensary. It appeared that the constable had driven down this street in a bullock cart, with a number of handcuffs ready to put on the rioters. These handcuffs were in full view of the crowd, and the sight maddened them still more. The constable took refuge in the dispensary. As Mr White came up, he was hustled by the people, and brickbats were thrown at him. The steps up to the dispensary were few and Mr White rode up them, and he too sought shelter, and also had time to consult with the constable as to what they should do. The storm grew louder and the stones flew faster. The only thing was to get to the citadel and call out the troops.

All round the small compound of the dispensary was a strong, high iron paling. It was impossible to get out through the entrance, where they had come in; the crowd had filled all that side. The only way was to get over the paling at the back of the dispensary. The distance to the paling was not more than 10 or 20 yards. There was no room for his horse to get a run, but Mr White said, 'I'll try it.' He rode down the steps and put his horse at it, and with a great bound horse and rider cleared the rails, but the horse caught his hoof on one of the spikes at the top and fell on the other side, Mr White getting his head knocked; but the horse was up again in a moment and, amid a shower of stones and blows from those close by, Mr White galloped off to the citadel.

The troops were marched out at once, and reached the scene of disturbance in an hour, when Mr Ollivant had also arrived. The people were most furious against Mr Ollivant and had mistaken Mr White for him, from their being dressed alike. Mr Ollivant says his horse could not possibly have leapt the railings — it was a quiet, old horse, that Mrs Ollivant generally rode. When the troops came, they were told *not* to fire. Mr Ollivant and Mr Macpherson, the judge, were anxious to avoid all violence, but at the same time to restore order at once. However, the soldiers (who were all natives) got excited and fired into the crowd, killing some half dozen persons.

Quiet was restored, and then Mr Ollivant insisted on the merchants opening their shops. The people, still angry, were alternately threatening Mr Ollivant and expostulating with him about the tax. He told them he was ready to send up any remonstrance they liked to government, but that he should insist on the tax being levied according to the law. One man, a very disreputable character in Surat, a Muhammadan *bohra* (tradesman), vowed that he would kill Mr Ollivant. He said he knew him perfectly well by sight and that he would never rest till he had killed him. He said this before many people at the Surat railway station, where a disturbance had broken out. For a time, Mrs Ollivant says, she lived in great anxiety. The judge, Mr Macpherson, asked Mrs Ollivant to come and stay with him, with her little girl of two. Mr Ollivant had to live in the castle, and for five days they were living in this way. Mrs Ollivant was very ill afterwards.

Thursday 12 November

I meant to have written a good many letters and to have sketched this afternoon, but a disagreeable occurrence has kept me occupied in a different way. Yesterday morning, just as I was leaving the pantry (i.e. the tent), the new *garawallah*, Ganoo, came up with a very doleful face and told me that he had been robbed of all his money. He had gone to bed, he said, with it quite safe; he had put it in his coat pocket, and hung up the coat on the wall of the stable. In the morning, when he took down his coat, it was all gone — 11 rupees that I had given him for his wages, and four annas besides that he had remaining from his last month's wages. But this had happened on Monday night, and instead of coming to me at once, when he discovered his loss the next morning, he waited till Wednesday morning. In that time of course the robber, whoever it was, could have easily hidden the money. He says he waited to make enquiries among the men before coming to me.

I sent off for the chief constable, but he was away at a distant village where there had been a robbery. So a subordinate policeman came yesterday, who could not make anything of the matter, and only this afternoon the chief constable appeared. He has examined all the men's boxes and clothes, and can find nothing. Two men, Ameer and Chouty, are away on the road to Bombay; they started with the black horses early Tuesday morning. The *garawallah*, Ganoo, suggests that one of them is the thief, though when Mrs Ollivant and I questioned him yesterday morning, he said he could not think of anyone, only he had lost his money. Now, the constable says, he must examine Ameer and Chouty, so he is starting off by train tonight to catch them upon the road, and Ganoo has to go with him. It is most painful to me to think of these men, whom we like so much, being stopped tomorrow, accused by Ganoo, and examined by the constable. We have found them perfectly honest, and they are so obliging and nice. It has grieved me very much. I do not in the least believe either of them did it, but I cannot refuse to have them searched. The men, who sleep in the stables, are the two coachmen, the two *garawallah*s, the *mali* and Rupert's *tattoo-walla* (pony-boy). The only one who, as we know, has been dishonest once, is the *mali*, who was selling our cow's milk in Bombay. The constable has now taken the *mali*, Vitaldas (the coachman) and Ganoo off to the police station, to examine them further, I suppose. But though suspicion may fall mostly on these men in the stables, anyone else might of course go in while the men are asleep and commit the robbery.

We cannot go home on Saturday, I fear now, as I must wait till the constable returns here. If nothing is found on Ameer or Chouty, he will leave them at Bombay; if either was guilty, he would bring that one back here. We could not go out this afternoon, at least I could not leave the house while the constable was here.

Bella Vista, Saturday 19 December 1885
I will begin my diary early this week, as Leslie tells me to do with my letters to him. I am alone this afternoon, and at present undisturbed by visitors. Miss Sanderson has gone out, arrayed in visiting style, to pay some calls. It is a proof of our climate doing her good that she should be able to go out today, for she had a fatiguing expedition yesterday. She and I went down to the fort to see the collection belonging to the Natu-

ral History Society. I think I mentioned in my last diary that I had arranged with Mr Phipson for us to go yesterday.

The rooms are large and airy — so lofty, light and spacious that one does not seem to be in a museum as we think of museums in London. From the windows there are pretty views over the town and harbour, with its shipping. Through Mr Phipson's office, which is close to the rooms, we saw an alcove full of beautiful tropical ferns. As he sits working at his table, he must see many of his beloved specimens through the open doors. It is a romantic office, as I told him. He, and the Jardines' cousin, Mr Anderson, are the great workers in the society. The specimens are all arranged most beautifully. They are displayed in a way that you see them so clearly. My experience of museums is not great, but I never saw a collection so well shown before.

The fish are in bottles of spirit — some 200 different kinds, all from the harbours. Each fish is suspended by a fine wire from the gills, which is attached to a little bar of wood fixed across the mouth of the bottle. Some objects — the lizards I think — were in a cabinet, with red curtains over the glass doors. Mr Phipson said the colouring of these creatures was evanescent, and would fade if exposed to the light. He said the red colour of the curtain prevented the lilac rays of the light, which were the injurious rays, from affecting the colours. There is a good collection of wild birds — mostly contributed by Mr Anderson — only they have very few parrots, as yet. There are several specimens of the brilliant little honey suckers, that we used to think were humming-birds.

There are snakes in plenty — a very fine specimen of the Russell's viper, that was found on Malabar Hill. It is a very deadly snake — not so large as the cobra — but with a powerful head and jaws, and dreadful looking teeth. Then there was a little green tree snake, poisonous, like those we find at Khandalla. One or two specimens of snakes were from our garden there. In a very large glass jar there was a sea snake alive — very poisonous. It was about a yard long. Mr Phipson took hold of its tail and drew it partly out of the water; I begged him to be careful. He said he was always very cautious, but it seemed rather risky.

Almost the fiercest animal in the collection was a little vampire bat. Its large double ears and wizened face, and its crooked wings and sharp claws give it a really demoniacal look. I thought of the words of Hawthorne's little daughter when she was looking at a hermit-crab (which seemed very fierce to her, I suppose), 'I hope God did not hurt himself when he made it.'

Sunday 20 December
We had a stormy day yesterday. By the evening, when John and Bertha and I went out to dine at the Birdwoods, the wind had risen quite to a gale. The wind made it very cool, and John was glad of that at dinner. I was fortunate, too, for I had Mr Birdwood on one side, and he is invariably pleasant, genial and also interesting in his talk; and on the other, Mr Watson, minister of the Scotch Church here — also pleasant and with plenty to say. He has been in many parts of India. For some years he was at Simla, and then in Karrachee (in Scinde). He is not one's idea of the typical Scotch minister — he is a sportsman, but greater than his love of sport is his love of natural history. He was talking about falcons (some one had spoken of 'hawking' in India) and he told me he had trained many hawks, and that it was most interesting work.

'It is always the peregrine falcon,' he said, 'that is used in hawking; they are the same wherever you find them. I have had hawks from all parts of India, from England, from the north of Russia — they are all alike, their plumage just the same, and the same warlike nature. It is the king of birds,' he added enthusiastically, 'it is afraid of nothing — it would go at an eagle.' I was telling him about Khandalla, and how interesting it was to me to be on a great highway and see the traffic that was passing all day along the road — the bullock carts, buffaloes, pack-horses, donkeys, laden with the belongings of a whole village, travellers of all sorts, from an Indian prince, in his carriage like a lord mayor's coach (a rare occurrence though that is), to the hundreds of poor half-naked peasants, plodding along their 20 miles a day.

And then he told me of Simla, and the road sights there. The great highway to Tibet passes over the Himalayas, and through the village of Simla. Simla *is* a village, though it is the seat of government, and means, to us, the viceroy, council, and all the official life of India. Mr Watson says there you have quite a different scene. The road, though a good road at Simla and for some miles from the town, further away becomes a rough track, and at last, when it winds over the passes of the Himalayas and stretches away to Tibet, is a mere sheep path. 'So,' he says, 'all the merchandise coming to Simla and going from Simla to the north is brought on sheepback.' Flocks of sheep are constantly coming in — 200 or more, with two, or three men at the most, to drive them, and every sheep has its two little panniers filled with goods. From Tibet, they bring down wool and grain and various things; from Simla they take back salt, which Mr Watson said was very precious in the interior far north, and was only obtained in this way. The men and their flock travel about 20 miles a day, sometimes 30.

Khandalla, Sunday 27 December 1885

We are at our little house in the hills again. John and Bertha have been here since Wednesday. Baby and Ellen, and I, came up on Friday, Christmas Day. We had a morning of hurry, with preparations for a journey, arrangements for our invalid and Christmas doings.

Bertha had put up some Christmas decorations, and 'A HAPPY CHRISTMAS' on the wall, in green leaves, faced us as we came in. John had some thrilling news for us — a tiger had been shot the night before on the hills a mile from this house. Another piece of news was that a house was being built near to us. It is on a little hill on the other side of the road, and will not interfere with us, excepting that the inhabitants will command a full view of every person and everything that goes in or out of our compound. A Parsee is building the house, and it will be a big house with a great many very small rooms. The Parsees make their houses so, to contain several families. My mother would think any neighbours an advantage in this lonely place, even if they did overlook your compound.

A third piece of news John had was that he had promised to give away the prizes at Mr Summers' little Sunday school. I think I spoke of Mr Summers and his work before. He is a retired officer — an engineer I should think — of the Indian Navy. He has a small pension from the Indian government, and the good man lives here and spends his life in looking after the poor people of Khandalla, combined with a small trade in rice, hay and cows. He holds a little Sunday school every Sunday morning, and he has also a small dispensary, and gives out simple medicines to the sick.

Ethel came up to us yesterday — Saturday. She and Bertha went off for a little walk with John this morning, as it was not yet time to start for the school, but John returned without them, and they continued their walk. Bertha says they felt very guilty deserting our school distribution this way — they just went a little way up the road, till they saw the carriage safely out of sight, and then returned (I might say 'sneaked' back) to the house.

John and I were to be at the school by 8.00 o'clock. We drove to the railway station, and there the stationmaster told us the way to go — across the line and along a tiny footpath to a little bungalow among the trees on the slope of a hill. The little school, however, is not held at the house; we were taken to a barn on the hillside, or rather a haystack, for Mr Summers explained to us that the erection of poles, and a roof on which was piled a quantity of hay, was his haystack and school combined. There were no walls of any kind, only on one side a trelliswork with an opening cut in it. The ground was cleared and levelled, and the pupils were all sitting on it — most of them cross-legged. Near me, was a boy, rather a big boy, his brown legs bare, one thigh shrunk and withered. Further on was a child, blind of one eye — then a woman, blind of both eyes — then a lame person. I looked at the good old man by us, living here among these poor hill folk, and I thought he was caring indeed, for 'the maimed and the halt and the blind.'

There were about 50 present, not all children, however; some mothers with their babies were there, and three or four old women and two old men. We sat on chairs at one end of the barn, with a table in front of us on which the prizes were laid — all clothes, cotton petticoats for the girls and shirts for the boys; I forget the right name for the white tunics. There were dark cotton saris for the women, and white cotton *dotas* for the men. The prizes were given simply for regular attendance at Sunday school. There is no teaching, except religious teaching; the Bible is read to them, and the children learn hymns and texts by heart. Mr Summers pointed out an old man to us who was a most regular attendant. He had a fine face and grey beard, and with his tattered garments and his staff in his hand, it seemed as if an Indian 'Edie Ochiltree' was waiting there for his accustomed alms.

The proceedings began with a hymn. The children sang pretty well, though in a harsh voice, led by Mr Summers. Then a boy stood up, put his hands together, and repeated the Lord's Prayer. Others followed him, and then Mr Summers read a chapter from the Old Testament about Adam and Eve. He read and explained as he went on, all in Marathi. We could just tell he was speaking of the various nations —

English, Parsee, Mussulman, Hindu, all came from Adam and Eve, we were all one family here. Then there was more singing, and finally the prizes were distributed. The children came first, then the women, young and old, and lastly the old men. One poor tottering old woman was helped forward. I had often seen her in the road; I dare say she is not more than 60, but she looked 80 or 90. Everyone was delighted at receiving their garment. About 40 pupils altogether, including the old people, received prizes for regular attendance. There were several children there who had been very seldom to school, or who came yesterday for the first time; of course, as Mr Summers said, he could not give them prizes. John, however, asked him to let everyone present have an anna, and we produced what money we had in our pockets. There was great excitement and crowding round, but at last we got away and followed Mr Summers to his house.

As the school place might be called, by courtesy, a barn, so the living place might be called, by courtesy, a house. It was a tiny stone building with apparently two small rooms. Mr Summers showed us into his sitting room and with kind hospitality asked us to sit down, and then brought out from a cupboard a Christmas cake, which was very good. The room was bare, but perfectly clean — earthen floor, whitewashed walls, dark wooden table and chairs, old English in make, as you often see here. On the walls were one or two little pictures, prints, from magazines. The place, poor as it is, must give the people an idea of something better and higher than their own mud huts, and dirt and darkness.

Khandalla, Sunday 3 January 1886

It is very cold again this morning. I am writing in the nursery, which is the only warm place in the house. Last night we had two blankets on our beds, or rather a blanket and rug or shawl, for we do not possess two blankets apiece. Baby is very well in spite of the severe cold, the thermometer having gone down, even in this room, to 64 degrees.

We had an excursion yesterday morning, John and Bertha and I. We went to a place among the hills that people call the 'drop'. There is a valley between two ranges of hills that slopes upward and ends abruptly in a precipice. We set off from here before half-past six o'clock. It was bitterly cold and almost dark when we dressed and took our early tea. We were wrapped up in cloaks, shawls and rugs, and even then we grumbled at the cold and could hardly believe that in three hours' time, as John said, we should be crying out against the sun. We drove through Lanowli and a long way along the new road that leads to Sukha Patha. We passed within a mile or two of a large tank near which a tiger had been seen the day before, and that morning Mr Shipp, the manager of the railway, had gone off in pursuit of it. A poor bullock had been found, half-eaten. Some natives had seen it; there was no doubt it was a tiger. We had to leave the road after four or five miles and go across the moor. John had sent on some men with a chair for me, as it was further to the drop than I could walk. Before we left the carriage the sun had risen, and the country looked very beautiful as one peak after another caught the light. I was glad to walk the first half mile, to get warm. The *shikarri* had come with us as our guide, and went on ahead, a striking-looking figure with his huntsman's dress. His coat, greenish-brown, was decidedly English in make, but the broad white scarf (*dota*) wound round his waist and his large white turban, were Indian. As he stalked on before us, I thought, in spite of his turban, he looked very like 'Hawk Eye' in *The Last of the Mohicans*. By this time I was in my chair, carried by four coolies, two extra men close behind to relieve any of the four bearers when they were tired. But it was easy work for them, as the ascent is very gradual and I am not very heavy. John and Bertha followed; last of all, behind them, came the cook's boy, with a coolie carrying our breakfast in a basket.

The first part of the way was through level fields, or common, with large trees here and there and a stream of water that at first was quite narrow but ended in a pond. Bamboos grew on each side, their graceful feathery branches looking very fairy-like in the tender morning light. Further on we came to a large pool covered with water lilies. The leaves were like the leaves of our English water lily, but the flowers were quite different, pointed petals all soft and downy, like tiny ostrich feathers, as Bertha said, and the centre of the flower was deep yellow. It is not a large flower, about an inch and a half across. We did not stop, however, then, on our way to the hills; we wanted to get to the precipice while there was still the effect of the early morning light.

The country became wilder as we went on, and we had to go over rocks and across some water. The men carried me very well, only now and then on the slope of a bank slanting my chair rather, but there was nothing like the climb there is at Karli. Within half a mile of the 'drop' we came suddenly in sight of the distant mountains. From my height (above the men's heads) I had a good view of everything as we came along. When we had almost reached the precipice, I got down from my chair and waited for John and Bertha. We went together onto the rocks and stood on the edge, looking down a sheer fall of 900 feet. The *shikarri* stood by, ready to give a hand to anyone who might feel giddy. Below, at that depth, no sunlight had reached it, nor would reach it for some hours to come. The view was very wonderful — range upon range of hills stretching away, rocks and trees and withered grass in the foreground; below, far away at the bottom of the ravine, jungle that might be the home of any wild animals, so lonely and undisturbed they would be there. As far as we could see, in every direction all was wild, open country; not a sign of anything human, not the smallest hut, not the roughest path was to be seen. John told the men to get some big stones and throw them over the precipice. They brought stones so huge they could only just lift them. They hurled them, one after another, over the edge. It seemed quite a long time before we heard the crash below, but even then they had not reached the bottom; they had struck on some projecting rock, and we heard them strike again, and again, among the debris below.

Bombay, Friday 22 January 1886

There is not a great deal this week to tell about; Bertha and I paid a visit to a Muhammadan family last Friday, and we went to convocation at the university last Tuesday. But I have described convocation before, and also a previous visit to this Muhammadan family.

However, the visit was somewhat different, as there was only the family themselves, with the addition of a niece who came in while we were there, and consequently we were more at home with them and saw more of their usual life. We drove along through crowded streets and came to a queer-looking yard, or rather alley; you would doubt if there could be any good house in such a place if you did not know Eastern towns. There we turned in, under a gateway and up this alley, and finally went through another gateway, and then we were in a pretty little front garden with a tall house and a porch in front. The children were waiting there for us, and they took us up to their mother who gave us a warm welcome. The drawing-room is a splendid room, 100 feet long, with a long row of windows overlooking the tank. The room opens onto a wide veranda, where they have made a badminton court. Bertha asked little Nazali (the third daughter, I think she is) whether she could play badminton, and thereupon a game was proposed, and Bertha and the little girl played for an hour. The dear old grandmother and I and the mother sat and watched the game — they were much amused to see Bertha playing with Nazali. They were a curious contrast — Bertha, the tall English girl, prettily dressed, but ready for business, and Nazali the little dark Muhammadan maiden with her brilliant red silk skirt, gauzy jacket and embroidered cap, her long plaits of hair flying out as she darted here and there in the game. Nazali has been at school, a day boarder at a convent school at Mazagon and, as her mother told us with pride, she is in the fourth standard.

The convocation took place last Tuesday. John was not there, as his throat was still troublesome. It was a pity he could not go, as Bertha wanted to see him march in with all the judges in their scarlet robes in the procession. It was a brilliant scene and Bertha was as much struck as I was the first time I saw it, and as I am indeed every time I see it again, by the wonderful variety of races and the one object drawing them all together. As the candidates went up for the degree, and were presented by the dean of the faculty to which they belonged, it was very striking to see the various races represented. Three young men went up together (engineers I think they were), one a Hindu, the next a Parsee and the third a Eurasian. Then came up a good many together (for medicine), Hindus, Parsees, Eurasians and four or five Scindis, men from Scinde. You can tell them at once by their peculiar headdress.

I do not know if I mentioned that my prize came some weeks ago from Simla — a very substantial prize — a cheque for 150 rupees. I felt very rich, for I never earned anything like it before. Then I have had the pleasure of settling how to spend it, as Conny and I used to do with our money box, for I am not going to 'practise what I preach' sometimes to the children and save my money. I bought first a present for John — a large scrapbook in which I put some sketches I have done here and in Egypt, then of course the children must each have a present out of it, and two other people — one Binnie Cross, whose dear father taught us drawing and made us love art so long ago, and then dear Miss Grant, at whose school we learnt drawing with Mr Grant still longer ago. How we enjoyed those lessons, though we children could only ask him questions by writing on his slate that hung ready at his side, for he was quite deaf.

Then I thought a share ought to go to the bullocks, at least to their race, for it was drawing my poor patient bullocks, at Khandalla, that won me the prize. And so I am in correspondence with Mr Shroff, secretary of the Society for the Prevention of Cruelty to Animals, upon the possibility of setting up a branch at Khandalla. I think the head constable will be the agent there very likely.

Sunday 24 January 1886, 7.30 a.m.

John and Bertha and I dined yesterday with Mr Fox and Mr Macpherson. There were only a few guests, and it was a pleasant, friendly party. Mr Newcome Fox told us that he had been away shooting for the Christmas holidays in the Central Provinces. He was in the jungle, camping out most of the time, with his fellow sportsmen. At one village where they halted they saw a curious instance of the working of the local government bill. The elections for the municipal board came on, but the voters could not be induced to go and vote. There is no law, I suppose, to compel people to vote, but the members of the municipality could not be appointed without votes. The polling officers devised a curious expedient. In the night, when the villagers were in bed and asleep, they went round the village and carried off the shoes of all the voters. Then they proceeded to the polling place, and waited for the morning with all the shoes piled up in a great heap. When the villagers woke up and found no shoes, great was their consternation. It is *the* mark of a respectable man just above the coolie caste to wear shoes when out of doors. So they were obliged to betake themselves to the polling booth and beg their shoes from the officers. There they were caught, and had to vote before their shoes were restored to them. What would people say in England to such a mode of forcing an election?

I do not think I ever finished the history of our *garawallah* and his lost money — the money that he declared had been stolen from him at Khandalla last November. When the loss was discovered our head coachman, Ameer, and the *garawallah*, Chouty, were on their way back to Bombay. The chief constable, taking Ganoo with him, followed them and overtook them just as they arrived in Bombay. Ameer had only a few annas on him when the constable searched him. He had had ten rupees from me for the journey, but had spent it nearly all. His wages, he said, he had left in Simon's charge. That was what Simon told us before the constable and Ganoo started. Chouty had all his last wages with him, 11 rupees, and about eight rupees besides. His explanation was that he had not spent any of the money which I had just given him and that he had saved the eight rupees from the month before, and that that was what he always did, and then every few months he sent money to his wife in the country. The servants at home corroborated this statement when the constable and Ganoo returned. I was very glad that there was no reason to suspect Ameer or Chouty. As they had left Khandalla before the accusation of robbery was made, it was probable that, if they had taken the money, it would still be on them.

The chief constable then returned to his first idea, that Vitaldas, the second coachman, who slept in the stable with Ganoo, was the man. But there did not seem to me any more reason for suspecting him than any of the others. He was taken again to the police station and examined, but nothing more could be ascertained. Ameer and Chouty told the constable that they believed it was Vitaldas, that they saw him that night put his hand into Ganoo's pocket, but as we found that Ameer and Chouty, and I believe also Ganoo, had been drinking in the bazaar that evening after having their wages paid, their testimony was not worth much. If they were both awake at the same moment and saw Vitaldas do such a thing, they should have spoken at the time and roused Ganoo. We shall never know how that money did go if it really was lost. The chief constable was able to talk to us in English, but I did not consider his knowledge perfect, as he addressed me in all our conferences as 'Your Honour,' or 'Mother.' I told Mrs Ollivant of this last style of address, but she would not believe me until one evening she was standing by me and the constable came up and gave his account of the expedition to Bombay and addressed us both, by turns, as 'Mother'. Then Mrs Ollivant was so inclined to laugh that it was all I could do to look grave.

3 February 1886

Since I sent my last diary, there have been two or three incidents worth telling of. First of all we had a visit from some Muhammadan children last Friday — the children of the *nawab* and *begum* from Hyderabad whom I have mentioned. The English governess, Miss Boyton, brought them. The eldest was a little girl of seven, the next a boy of six, then another boy of four, and then the baby girl, a year and nine months' old. The eldest girl had a sweet little face and nice manners. She seemed very fond of Miss Boyton. The little boys, as well as their sister, spoke

English and understood readily all we said, although they had only learnt the language since Miss Boyton had been with them, and that was only ten months. Their father is very anxious that his children should learn English ways, and insists on their always eating as we do, with knives and forks and spoons. One day, Miss Boyton told us, he came into the room when the children were having tea and the little girl was eating a piece of toast, which she held in her hand. He exclaimed with horror, 'Why do you eat like that?' and turning to Miss Boyton, 'Why has not she a spoon?'

We had tea, coffee and cakes set out in the dining room, and we all sat down round the table, Mrs Jardine's little girl and boy with us, and also Mrs Birdwood's boy. The little Muhammadan boys were dressed in red velvet and silver braid, made in imitation of English boys' costumes, but they had their native embroidered caps on. Baby was captivated by their appearance and put her fat white arms round their waists. The baby had a red jacket, brilliant yellow silk trousers, an embroidered cap that came down over the ears, just like the helmet did in some of the old suits of armour. Round her neck was a heavy gold circlet, made of one piece of gold and quite stiff; on her little ankles were thick gold bangles, and on her wrists little bangles of glass and lac. She is a year and nine months old, but she cannot stand yet, and has only two teeth. I think she must have some delicacy of constitution. Our baby looked so big and strong by the little fragile thing.

The elder girl wore her hair in a long twist down her back. The hair was entirely covered with gold and silver braid, so that when you lifted the hair it felt hard and stiff. She had a long cream-coloured tunic, which hung down to her ankles, a necklace and earrings, but not much display of jewellery. 'Sabzahida' they called her, but that was a pet name — her real name was Dildan Conissa, Begum. The eldest boy, they called 'Budhamia', but that was a pet name. After tea 'Sabzahida' repeated some nursery rhymes to us very readily as if she liked them.

'Little Bo Peep' and 'Baa Baa Black Sheep' and one, 'Pretty Lips', which I had not heard before, and in which there was some action too, for she kissed her hands repeatedly. She and the baby were taken into Miss Sanderson's to pay her a visit. Then Bertha proposed a game in the garden and Willoughby Jardine and Dick Birdwood were delighted, and started a game of Fox and Hounds, and when I came out from Jane's room I saw all the six children in full play, running about, and darting in and out through the arches of the porch. Miss Boyton says they never play in their garden at home. They seemed to take to it very naturally here, and a few days ago whey they went to tea at Miss Pechey's they played at Blind Man's Buff with the greatest zest. I asked the children to come again to see us. It is very pathetic to me to look at little 'Sabzahida' and hear her careless happy little voice, and to know that in less than a year she is to be shut up in the harem — taken away from the kind Miss Boyton and doomed to live all day with a violent tempered mother and ignorant slaves.

Thursday 4th

Last Monday, Bertha and I went with John to Parel to see a hospital for animals that has been established by the Society for the Prevention of Cruelty to Animals. The ground has been presented by a rich Parsee merchant — Mr Dinshaw Petit, and the hospital is named after his wife, the Bai Sakarbai Dinshaw Petit Hospital for Animals. There is a large house in the compound, that has also been given to the society by Mr Petit and which is to be made into a veterinary college. The hospital was opened two months ago for the admission of patients, i.e. bullocks and horses, but I think other animals are to be taken in when there is more accommodation.

The payment for each horse per day is six annas; for that the horse is fed and doctored. I should think large numbers of horses will be sent to the hospital for treatment as the place gets more known. There were a great many bullocks in the bullock shed — 60. They were ranged along in two rows, and there was just space to pass along easily between the two rows. But the bullocks were not tied like the horses by their back legs; only round their heads there was the usual rope, which was fastened to a ring in the wall. As we walked along, close to the rows of hind legs, the manager told John that some of the oxen became very *musti* (frisky) with the good food and rest, and that the men could hardly hold them. John says he had to smile and look pleased, but thought he should not be sorry when we had got through the 60 bullocks. I do not know what the charge for the bullocks is, probably less than for the horses.

10

9 February–April

Bassein (and a longer visit later), another big party for Indian ladies, Parsee wedding, power of mothers-in-law and sad plight of widows, a case in the Criminal Court [Nora Scott away for 18 months in England]

Tuesday 9 February 1886

LAST Friday, after our mail letters went off, Bertha went over to 'the other bungalow' to help Ethel write invitations to Indian ladies for the party on Monday. Bertha was a long while away, so I concluded many letters had been written, until I got a note from Ethel in which she said, 'The invitation cards have not arrived, I am thankful to say, so we are spared for today.' So Bertha and Ethel were amusing themselves instead of working in the cause of social progress. (However, the cards *have* arrived now, and Bertha has gone over to write them at last).

The next day, Saturday, we were to draw little Miss Budrudeen Tyabjee. I had, as usual, various notes to write and people to see, two of the servants ill and arrangements to make for them, a man from one of the missions with a subscription book, the old butler wanting directions for finishing the repairing of the drive, and the new butler just arrived and wanting general instructions for everything. Well, I got through all these little matters as fast as I could, and my housekeeping, and was ready for the little girl when she appeared at 11.30.

Then soon 'callers' arrived, and my drawing came to nothing. I had invited Saraya's elder sister to come to luncheon and take her little sister home. I think it must have been the first time they had had a regular meal in an English house. I knew that they might not like all our

143

dishes, so I begged them to leave anything they did not like. Bertha came home for luncheon and between us we kept up conversation. The girls were shy and did not talk much, but when Bertha was alone with Miss Tyabjee she was more communicative. Bertha asked her how long she should remain at school, and she replied, 'About a year, and then I shall go into purdah.' And when Bertha asked her if she should be glad to be grown-up, and live as her mother and the other grown-up people did, she burst out, 'I hate the purdah.' Then she laughed at her own warmth, but it can be no laughing matter to her to give up her present free life.

In the evening, John and I went for a drive and took little Baby, who sat most contentedly on my knee, and then on John's. We passed a group of Hindus who had just been before John in a lawsuit. They smiled as we passed, I suppose at seeing the High Court judge carrying his baby.

We all went to bed early that night in preparation for our early journey next day to Bassein. I was awake at 4.00 o'clock, and at 5.00 o'clock we got up and found our tea ready for us on the veranda. It was all dark and cold excepting that one candle was alight on the table. By a quarter to six we were off. At the station we found Ethel waiting with Moidin, her nice Muhammadan servant, who always goes with her on journeys with the camera. Miss Pechey could not come at the last moment, as some patients were very ill, nor could Miss Ellaby. The dawn was come now, and as we left Bombay in the train it was very pretty to see the light growing clearer on the city, and the palm woods, and the sea. It was not the line we travel on to Khandalla; it was the Bombay and Baroda Railway that goes to Ahmadabad and the north. But first it runs south to Thana, as it must do, indeed, to get out of the Island of Bombay. We went through Bandra and Mahim, seeing the beautiful Mahim woods under the early morning light, and then on through pretty country and rich vegetation till we crossed the Thana Creek, by a long bridge, and saw in the distance, right on the edge of the creek, the ruins of Bassein. It was too far off to see more than the outline of woods and buildings standing out against the morning sky. We could just make out the deep wall that bounded it on the sea side. Once there was a wall all round, I believe, but it is in ruins now. The train took a long time winding round the creek, and we crossed another branch of it on another long bridge before we came to the station for Bassein–Bassein Road.

When we got out we found the subordinate judge waiting for us, with two or three other men. (I think I said John had written to the judge, and he had kindly made arrangements for us.) We went through the little station to the road on the other side. There all the policemen of the village — about six — were drawn up in line to salute the High Court judge, and here some carriages were waiting for us, very queer carriages they were to us. One was a very old and very high chaise with a hood and a white horse, which was evidently intended for John. The other was a much queerer thing — a bullock dummy. It is something like a cab, only the door is at the back, and you have to scramble over the back seat in entering. There are only two wheels, a pole for the bullocks and a little space in front of the carriage for the driver. Ethel, Bertha and I got into the dummy, and were effectually shut in when the door was closed. John went on in his chaise and was soon far ahead. Then there was besides a bullock cart for Pedro, Moidin, the luncheon basket and the camera. We set off at a trot, but soon our driver began urging the bullocks to a canter, crying out, hitting them and pricking them with the goad. The dummy swayed about and the motion was horrible, and besides the poor bullocks were suffering, especially the right-hand one which was smaller and did not seem so strong as the other. We called to the man to stop, and when he took no heed, we touched his shoulder through the open window, but still he only went on hitting the bullocks and shouting to them, and all he would say to us was, 'Sahib,' and pointed ahead to where John's chaise was. He meant evidently that he was to catch up the 'Sahib' and thought, I suppose, that as we were only women our orders were nothing. We poked him back, or rather hit him, and at last I made him understand that we would not give him any money if he did not stop hitting the bullocks, and go slowly. The poor little black bullock was bleeding from the goad. We went on better after this, and though we shook and jolted were able in the intervals to gasp 'How pretty,' or 'Is not that picturesque?' as we passed through the pretty country.

Mr Romane had kindly put the courthouse at our disposal for the day, which was very nice for us. He was on circuit and was holding his court at some other place, but had returned to Bassein for the day to meet us. We went upstairs, through the court, which was on the first floor, and up another staircase to the living rooms above, where we found a very comfortable sitting room, furnished with old English furniture and English carpets. On a side table were piles of fruit — a present to us from Mr Romane — bananas, oranges, pomegranates, pineapples, coconut and locust fruit. It was just 10.00 o'clock by the time Pedro and Moidin had prepared the breakfast and we were hungry, for we had been travelling since a quarter to six o'clock. It was 11.00 o'clock before we got to the ruins.

The bullock dummy had disappeared when we came downstairs, and another very comical sort of chaise or buggy, only holding one person besides the driver, had come in its place. John got into this, and we three into the old chaise with the white horse. The driver held the old reins — half leather, half rope, loose in his hand. He never guided the horse in any way that I could see, and we had various narrow escapes of collisions as we trotted through the town. The streets of the new Bassein are very picturesque, as beautiful, I thought, in their way as the ruins themselves. The houses had a great deal of wood carving about them, and the upper storeys projected like the old half-timber houses in England. The shops in the lower storeys were gay with bright colour. The shop people looked cleaner and more prosperous than those in the poor parts of Bombay, and the people we saw in the streets seemed healthy and comfortable as far as I could tell.

When we got near the ruins, we left the road and drove over the turf (if you call dead yellow grass turf) and stopped before a modern bungalow. On the little veranda were three very English looking dogs — a bulldog and two terriers. 'There must be people staying here,' said John, 'at the travelling bungalow.' A man came out of the house in English dress and greeted us: 'Would you like to see the place?' he asked. 'Yes,' said John; 'Those are nice dogs. Are they yours?' 'Yes, they are good dogs,' and the gentleman proceeded to unloose them, though they were so wild with excitement that they would hardly let him get hold of their collars.

We all set off through the jungle to the nearest ruin — a great church — the Church of St Francis. They say the saint lived there himself at one time. The roof was gone, but the lofty walls stood up, towering above the trees, grey against the hot blue sky. Creepers had grown over parts of the lower walls and saplings were growing out of crevices in the walls here and there, while along the edge of the walls and on the pinnacles dead dry grass waved yellow against the deep blue overhead. Outside the church there are cloisters with beautiful round arches. The walls and the columns must have been coloured in old times, for a deep red still clings to them here and there. The cloisters form a square and the centre space was once, I suppose, a pretty garden. Now it is wild confusion of grass and shrubs and long creepers, and one beautiful mango tree that stands leaning towards the arches, a witness that all the beautiful Gothic buildings were foreigners in a strange land. In the great silent church, cool and dim, as we came from the hot cloisters, we saw on the altar two candles burning. A woman had come and lighted them and gone away while we were in the cloisters. It was a poor fisherwoman, Mr Littlewood told us, who comes every Sunday and lights two candles, and leaves them burning on the high altar. I wonder what her story is?. We wished that we had many hours, instead of only three, to spend in the place. Bertha and I made some little sketches, and Ethel took a photograph and then we went on to see other ruins.

John and Ethel had gone on while we were drawing, and found another beautiful subject for a sketch — a Hindu temple by the side of a pool — huge mango trees behind it, and beyond the grey ruin of another old church — the church of St Paul. We sat down in the shadow of a third great church and drew as fast as we could, but it was nearly as much pain as pleasure to see the beauty before you and know that you had but half an hour to draw. John gave repeated warnings and at last announced that it was time to go, so we shut up our sketchbooks and came away, along another route, along what had once been a principal street of the busy thriving Portuguese capital, past the courthouse, where in old times there had been bustle and business — suitors and barristers, attorneys and clients jostling each other as they do now in the Bombay High Court — now so silent and peaceful and beautiful, with big-leaved creepers and feathery grasses.

We looked down the narrower side streets, and at the ruins that had once been private houses where the Portuguese noblesse lived, and fancied how the fine ladies used to come out into those narrow streets, where carpets were spread for them to walk on and where attendants carried grand umbrellas over their heads, while every Hindu they met had to prostrate himself before them. No Hindu who was not a Christian was allowed to come within the walls of the city, and no Hindus were allowed to pursue any calling higher than that of *garawallah*s (grooms). The Inquisition was fearful in Bassein. But they had their grand qualities too, those old Portuguese men and women.

When the town was besieged 100 years ago by the Marathas, the defence was splendid. The siege lasted for months. At last only 600 Portuguese were left, and 16,000 Marathas were outside the walls. The city fell, but the Marathas gave good terms to the enemy. The Portuguese marched out carrying their arms with them, and then Maratha chiefs reigned in Bassein. Hindu temples were built and the churches decayed, the houses were deserted, the streets unused, and silence and desolation fell on the great city. One might fancy the Germanic curse had fallen on Bassein, the curse with which the harper cursed the wicked king who slew the old harper's grandson, that his name should be forgotten, that he and his race should vanish in oblivion, not that he should be thought of and remembered as a great fierce, mighty warrior — hated and feared, but that he should be nothing — *nichtigkeit* should be his lot, his very name should perish.

We left the silent city and came across the burnt grass to the bungalow we had started from.

Wednesday 17 February
Last Saturday Bertha and I went to the Muhammadan girls' school, which is in connection with Mr Squires' church and mission. Some time ago the mistress, Miss Davies, had asked me to give away the prizes, but it was so long now past Christmas that I thought the prize-giving must have taken place while we were away. Miss Davies told me the school was such a difficult place to discover that I had better send our coachman to her own house one day before the prize-giving came off, and she would take him with her, and show him the street and the house. I did so, and when Bertha and Miss Ellaby and I set off, Ameer drove us without any difficulty straight to the place.

We knew the distribution would be a quiet affair, the only Englishman likely to be there was Mr Squires, and probably only a few English ladies, so a suggestion John made to me was not as alarming as it might have been. He said he thought I ought to say a few words after distributing the prizes; very little I need say, but just something of congratulation to the prize winners and encouragement to the others. I saw at the prize-giving at the American school how flat the ending was when no speech at all was made, so I thought I would try.

The school is held at the top of a high old-fashioned house. We went up a dark staircase, passing two or three floors. On one landing there was an opening through which you might easily tumble down into the yard below. Up we went, in the dark, till we came to a sort of attic; then another staircase led up in another direction altogether, and finally we came up and out into a very large square room with windows round three sides. The pupils, all assembled and seated on rows of benches, the schoolmistress, Miss Davies, and several other ladies were there, and a Hindu teacher, a Brahmin, who gives some of the lessons. He sat meekly at one side and did not speak. Miss Davies told me he was a great talker generally, but had a very discordant voice and consequently he had been ordered not to talk. After a time, a Muhammadan came in, the father of one of the children, I suppose, and another Hindu, and finally, after we had waited some time, Mr Squires. He said he was sorry that he was late and that he had kept us waiting, 'But,' he remarked to Miss Davies, 'I hope next year you will ask me to discover the source of the Nile — it would be much easier than finding your school.'

Then the proceedings began. Some of the elder girls sang a hymn, and then some of the little ones. Then there was a short examination in Scripture history, all in Hindustani. It was curious to hear the familiar names, only pronounced differently. The children knew their history well and answered very readily. Then there was a little examination in arithmetic. The children said the multiplication table, but in such a sing-song voice that at first I thought they were singing. Miss Davies told me that they were extremely clever at arithmetic, and would go up to any numbers in addition or multiplication; quite little children would rattle the tables glibly off, giving instead of 3 x 8 or 5 x 8, 3½ times, 5¼ times and so on, and many of the children (the elder ones I suppose) would count up till they got to 90¼ x 90, till Miss Davies herself, and Mrs Deimler, could not follow them.

I thought, as I sat listening to the entertainment, that I knew my little speech all right, when Bertha suddenly whispered to me that there were prizes for everyone, no distinction was to be made. Well, this was dreadful. I could not now congratulate specially the prize winners and I could not condole with anybody. When there was an opportunity, I asked Miss Davies about the prizes, and she told me that it was so, there were prizes for every child. The prizes were only for attendance, and only in case of very irregular attendance was a prize not given. But, she added, next year she should change this system; she had only had the direction of the school for a short time and had not liked to change the arrangements at once. So I had to alter my speech and say that 'next year there would be special prizes and that then every girl could not win a prize, but that all could try,' and so on. A lady who knows Hindustani very well, and who works in the school, stood by me, and at the end of every sentence translated what I had said.

Saturday 20 February 1886

I wrote my last week's diary rather irregularly. I told about Saturday's doings, and Tuesday's, but left Monday's untold. Miss Pechey and Ethel gave their grand ladies' party on Monday, and I could not tell about that in a hurry. It was a great event because the party was given in the evening, an innovation in ladies' parties. Hitherto they have been always given in the afternoon. Miss Pechey thought they could make the entertainment a prettier one in the evening, as the house and garden could be lighted up; it was also a more convenient time for Miss Pechey, and it turned out to be more convenient to some of the Indian ladies. Some Arab ladies, whom Miss Pechey invited, replied that they should be very glad to come 'if they could come in the evening, but that their purdah was so strict they could not drive out in the daytime for fear of being seen as they got in or out of the carriage.'

Bertha spent the day with Ethel, helping her to prepare for the evening. I sent over big-leaved plants to decorate the hall and landings — crotons, lilies, ferns — and sketches and books for the ladies to look at. I could not go over and help them, as Jane was suffering very much that day with her arm and I could not leave her. In the afternoon we had three doctors here — Miss Pechey, Miss Ellaby and Dr Arnott — and Jane's arm was operated upon. The operation was quite successful, and as it was done under chloroform, Jane did not suffer at the time. Though the pain was bad afterwards, Jane felt it much more bearable than the previous suffering, because there was the prospect of recovery. The doctors all agreed that the pain would soon lessen. Miss Pechey and Miss Ellaby were so glad that the operation was all over before the evening.

It was a strange day of illness and gaiety, but a party for Indian ladies does not seem to me like an ordinary festivity; one hopes it is doing some good; it is certainly hard work for those who give it, and the more anxious one is that every Indian lady should enjoy it, the harder the work is.

At 9.00 o'clock Bertha and I set off. The guests were invited for half-past nine, but Ethel wanted us to be there in time to receive them. One Parsee family had already arrived; they had appeared before 9.00 o'clock. We stood on the veranda, talking to the guests and watching others arrive. It was very pretty looking down on the garden and the drive, which were brilliantly illuminated. Rows of little *butties* lined the drive on each side and there was quite a mass of little lights on the pillars of the gate. Every border in the garden was marked out by these *butties*, and above in the trees were hung Chinese lanterns. It was wonderfully pretty. I thought the prettiest sight of all was the coconut palms lighted by the lanterns that hung to their huge leaves. Then, nearer the house than the palms was a tall pine (a Norfolk Island pine) on which were numbers of lanterns. It looked like a Christmas tree for giant children. The tree is 80 feet high, and even the agile Hindu boys could not climb nearer than eight or ten feet to the top. Captain Briscoe told Ethel (when he saw her in the morning) that she would be taken up for manslaughter if she urged a boy to go up any higher, for the Norfolk Island pine grows weakly here. It shoots up in our tropical climate three times as fast as in its own home, and the wood is brittle here and breaks off with any pressure.

Well, the guests arrived rapidly, and carriage after carriage turned in at the brightly lighted gateway and came up to the hall door, where Ann, the English maid, was stationed to receive the ladies. About 100 or 120 Indian ladies came, and about 40 English. The Arab ladies were the most wonderful in costume; they wore large black silk cloaks that went over their heads, which were cut square and hung straight down each side of the face in old Egyptian style. On the edge near the face, the silk was embroidered thickly with gold thread. The ladies were not handsome, but they had striking faces, dark eyes and dark complexions, darker than most of the Indian ladies here, and strong features. I wish I had had more talk with them.

There is certainly, as Miss Pechey says, a great change in the manners of the Indian ladies in one respect since we gave our first entertainment.

They are far more ready to be amused, and far more ready to talk to each other. A Hindu lady will recognize a Parsee whom she has met at these parties and speak to her, or a Muhammadan will talk to a Hindu or a Parsee, not as at first, only to the English or to ladies of their own race or caste.

Sunday 21 February 1886

Yesterday was a hard day of pleasure — a Parsee wedding in the afternoon, a Hindu wedding entertainment in the evening. At 4.30 a friend of ours, Mrs Curjel, whom I had asked to go with me to the wedding, came here, and we went down to a house just below us, where a Mr Tarachund lives, the father of the bridegroom.

As we drove up to the gate, we saw that the garden was crowded with Parsee gentlemen, all in white, and that the whole place was prepared for a *tamasha* (festivity). One of the gentlemen, brother of the bridegroom, I think, came forward to meet us, and escorted us through the garden to the house. We walked up the drive. There were rows of chairs on each side, on which were seated Parsee gentlemen robed in white. The ladies of the family and their friends were in the house. We were taken upstairs to the drawing-room, where the ladies were, and we were glad to find our friends, Mrs Cama and Miss Manochjee, there ready to introduce us. It was such a wonderful sight, the crowd of ladies in their brilliant gala attire. I had never seen such a large number of Parsee ladies together before. When we were at Mr and Mrs Mehta's party, there were a good many ladies, but gentlemen also and English people and Hindus. *Here* there was not a person who was not a Parsee, excepting ourselves and four other English people.

The dress of Parsee ladies (with the exception of that of widows) is gayer and lighter in colour than that even of the Muhammadans, and much gayer than that of the Hindus. The mother of the bridegroom was a pleasant, comely looking woman, dressed in pure white silk, with just an embroidered edge to her sari. I told her I hoped I should look as young as she did when my eldest son was old enough to be married.

We sat round the room, talking and listening to Gujerati songs sung by some women who sat just within a bedroom that opened from the drawing-room. I asked what the songs were about and a lady told me they were all wedding songs. It was not a cheerful kind of music, very harsh and monotonous. We saw two trays on a side table, on which were piled some clothes and in the centre of each tray was a conical shaped object covered with silver paper and decorated with flowers, paper flowers, I think they were. We were told these were the presents for the bride and bridegroom given by the bridegroom's family. Besides the clothes, there was a coconut on each tray, and several envelopes. The envelopes contained bank notes. The conical shaped things were sugar loaves; they are given in token of plenty. The clothes for the bride were beautiful. The sari was of fine Chinese silk with a border of gold and silver embroidery, then a thicker silk for the loose trousers, and another kind for the bodice, very fine white muslin for the headdress (under the sari), white muslin, or rather net, for the shirt that is worn under the sari, and embroidered slippers. Miss Manochjee told me that the white shirt made of cotton must be worn by every Parsee woman. 'It is part of our religion,' she said; 'it must be white and it must be made of cotton; it cannot ever be silk; it means humility.' The coconuts are given for good luck; they are also a sign of plenty. Though they are still given as presents from old custom, they are not kept by the persons to whom they are presented, but are given away to the lower servants or poor people. The *lotas* are for real use, and though, as in this case, when the family is rich they may be made of real silver, they will still be used as common water jugs for the bathroom.

Then came sounds from below of bustle and welcome, and one of the ladies told us that the procession from the bride's house was coming. We went out onto the balcony, over the porch, and we saw a number of women, gaily dressed, coming down the hill, preceded by a band which, however, was not playing. By some mistake, they had not obtained leave from the commissioner of police to play in the streets, and consequently they could only march in front of the procession. There were only two men accompanying the procession of women. One carried a silver *lota*, and the other a tray of presents. They all came into the garden; there the men stopped, but the women came upstairs.

The principal relation of the bride was her aunt (her mother was dead). The aunt came first, and the bridegroom's mother went forward to meet her and received her with a little ceremony. The invitation was given to the bridegroom to come to the bride's house, accompanied by his parents, relations and friends. The aunt was a nice looking woman; she had a pink sari and pale yellow silk jacket below, but as the pink was rather a lilac pink, the colours did not look amiss together. After a

153

little visit, the bride's friends went away again, and soon after the bridegroom followed, and all the rest of us. As we came out of the hall door, a gentleman came up with wreaths and nosegays. He hung a garland round my neck and round Mrs Curjel's, and gave us each a nosegay. The wreaths were made, as usual, of little white sweet-scented flowers and silver tinsel; the nosegays were flat and straight in shape like small cricket bats, and were made of roses and marguerites.

The bride's house was only half a mile away, just by the Gowalia tank; it was the bride's house only for the day, however; it was large and conveniently near to the bridegroom's, and had been lent to them for the occasion. When we got near, we saw that the house and compound were brilliantly lighted. There were a great many gentlemen sitting on chairs or walking about, dressed in white. Sir Jamsetjee was on the veranda, in white also. Mr Sarahjee Bangalee too, who has done so much for the cause of the medical women in India, and several others I knew. We went into the house and were welcomed by the aunt of the bride and other relations. They were in a long room that was in shape like an indoor veranda or corridor. It went round three sides of a large square room in the centre. There were sofas and chairs arranged against the walls, and a great many ladies and children sitting on them. We were taken to two chairs, opposite to which were arranged two little tables and two chairs, for the bride and bridegroom, we were told.

The presents to the bride from the bridegroom's family were presented, and the bride received them at the other end of the long room, but I could not see whether the bridegroom or his mother presented them. A number of ladies crowded round the bride, and helped her to change her dress and put on the beautiful garments that had been given her. Meanwhile, the bridegroom had taken his seat on one of the chairs. When the bride was ready, she joined him, and sat down on the other chair nearest to us. She did not look very happy, I thought, though she smiled now and then. On her neck and on the sleeves of her white jacket she wore a little orange flower, artificial, I think it was.

The two priests now came up and stood in front of the bridegroom. One of them was the high priest, a fine looking man. They were both dressed all in white, with white turbans that were rather like the Parsee hat in shape, only the high priest carried on his shoulder a fine cashmere shawl, folded up; that was the only difference in their dress. The high priest began the service, reciting in a sing-song voice passages from their holy books. Every now and then the other priest joined in, and they both spoke together. There seemed to be no pauses and there was no change of expression. After about 20 minutes, some of the guests retired into another room. Miss Manochjee Cursetji told me they had gone to the feast, and asked me to come and look at them. I hesitated, as it did not seem very polite to the priests or the wedding pair, but Miss Manochjee Cursetji got up and beckoned me to follow, talking all the time, not hearing my expostulations, and so we went too.

We found a great many ladies seated on benches by narrow wooden tables. There were no tablecloths on, or dishes or plates. Before every lady was a large piece of plantain leaf. There were too many guests for plates and knives and forks to be provided for all, and so none were used; the ladies eat very daintily as they do in Egypt, using a small piece of bread as a help. The menservants carried round trays with various kinds of food on them, and with a large spoon put down a portion of each dish onto the plantain leaf. I stopped and spoke to one lady, Mrs Jamsetjee, who was much amused at our seeing her eating in this primitive fashion. 'We wash our hands,' she explained, 'before and afterwards.' 'We have a proverb,' said Miss Manochjee Cursetji, 'which says fingers were used before spoons and forks.' I told them we had a saying, 'Fingers were made before forks.' Then we were called away into a little inner room where some refreshments were laid out on a table — plates, knives and forks for the few English guests. We were asked especially to taste 'the wedding pudding,' it was just a custard pudding flavoured with Indian spices; it had not a wedding appearance, being quite plain. Then we were offered some wine, and we drank it to the health of the bride and bridegroom.

By this time it was 7.00 o'clock, and as I was to go out again in the evening, I said goodbye and came away. I was sorry not to see the end of the ceremony.

Bassein, Sunday 7 March 1886
We have been living among the ruins for the last five days — that is Bertha and I have been here all that time. John could only stay two days, then he had to return to Bombay — but yesterday he came back again, and Miss Pechey and Ethel came with him. I hardly thought we should really carry out our plan of coming again to Bassein and staying

several days, and yet here we really are, sketching all day, and photographing too when Ethel is here. We think Bassein as beautiful as we did the first time we saw it; and now we know all the place, the ruins seem familiar — like friends — and the look of them, as we have seen them every day in the morning light, or evening glow, with the palms and the creepers and the deep shadows, is laid away in 'some odd corner of the brain' to give us pleasure when we shall be thousands of miles away from the silent city.

I was just finishing the last sentence and Bertha had gone off to bed, when I heard sudden cries outside. They seemed to come from the jungle, quite near the house, and the cries grew louder and louder. I ran out onto the veranda, calling for the *chobdar* and Pedro as I went. Bertha followed in a minute, and Pedro, and then the *chobdar*, who came pulling on his tunic; he had gone to bed I suppose when I called.

Then we saw dimly a number of people — struggling and fighting. The *chobdar* and Pedro ran past us, and reached them; in a minute they had seized a man and were wresting a long pole from his grasp. It was all so confused, in the dark night with just a lantern for a light, that at first we could not make out what had happened. A girl ran past us, and on to the road, and disappeared in the darkness. Then the *chobdar* and Pedro dragged the man between them, up to us. A wild man, almost naked with black hair. He struggled so fiercely, I thought almost he was going to rush at us. Another man, as wild and much taller, was pursuing him, and some half dozen other people — all Hindus. The shrieks we heard had come from the woman, the man was beating her with the pole. He had hurt her, evidently, for there was blood on the *chobdar's* coat.

The man poured out his account of the affair — which, being interpreted by Pedro, meant that the girl was his daughter and that she was running away to the bazaar where she meant to dance, and that he was a Maratha (a high caste) and would not let her. But the others gave a different version, and said the man was a bad man and had been drinking. Bertha says he smelt strongly of spirits. I did not notice it. I asked, where the *nazirs* were — they would know where the magistrate was, or chief constable, but they had gone away for the night and no one knew where they were. We ought to have learnt where they lived, and where also the *patel* of the village or some other official was, to whom we could apply in case of sudden need. What could we do? We could not let the man go on in pursuit of his daughter. Bertha secured the stick, and we have it now safely here.

At last, while we were considering what was to be done, the girl came back and into the house. I told her to stay here, and then told the servants no one was to tell the man she was here. Then I wrote a letter to the chief constable asking him to protect the girl, and telling him what had happened. I told the *chobdar* he must take the offender and my letter and find the constable. Of course I sent another man to help him, and they both had sticks. I expected the wild man to refuse to go with them, but he had grown quiet, and when they told him he must come, he got up and went with them. Then we saw to the poor girl. She is hurt mostly on the face, and her mouth is very much cut about and swollen. She was trembling all over, but able to walk and speak to us. Pedro has given her some food, and she has cooked it for herself. When I offered her tea, she shook her head; she could not drink or eat anything prepared by our hands — she was too high caste for that, being a Maratha.

Bella Vista, Bombay, 11 March
We are at home again, in Bombay, but before I speak of our return I must finish the history of Sunday evening at Bassein. I told the girl to stay with us for the night. Then we waited for the *chobdar's* return. I began to write my diary — for the evening's excitement had quite waked us up, and I had better make use of the time. In the daytime sketching left me no time for writing. Bertha laughed at the idea of my writing my diary just then, and declared that 'she knew if a hyena walked in and began to eat her up, I should begin my account of the catastrophe before he had half finished his meal.' Why Bertha fixed on a hyena I don't know, as they are not in the habit of attacking anything larger than small dogs, as far as I know, and Bertha is decidedly bigger than a small dog. I told her she had a most tragic effect as she swept about the veranda in a long pink cotton dressing gown, and in a commanding voice addressed the man with, 'Give me the stick!'

Presently, back came the *chobdar* with three policemen; the man was left safely locked up, but the girl must go and show herself to the police doctor and tell her story, and then she could come back for the night. So we called the girl and she went off with the policemen, with no reluctance apparently, as I thought she might have, to accuse her father. I gave the policeman the pole with which the girl had been beaten, as of course it would be wanted in evidence.

Then Bertha and I retired, at last, to bed. We thought everything was settled now for the night, but before I was in bed there was a noise again in the darkness outside — voices, and people moving about, and I put on a dressing gown and went out to see what it was. There were the three policemen back again with two *toddy-wallahs*, i.e. the men who climb the palm trees for toddy, and another man, a Parsee to judge by his clothing. The toddy men, wild enough in appearance, nearly naked, and with their great leather thongs over their shoulders, were quite calm and stood looking on unmoved, but the Parsee rushed forward and threw himself down on his knees before me, imploring the 'Memsahib' to say that he should not be taken to prison. I asked the policemen what he had done. They had found him, they said, hidden in a bush near our house, and one of the policemen crouched down and imitated the posture of the hiding man. The other man said that this Parsee gave drink to the father of the girl, and a woman, who had come out of the house and was standing near us said, 'Yes, it was so.' The Parsee denied it, though he admitted he had given spirits, once, that day to the culprit. Pedro had to interpret mostly, though we could make out a little of what they said and one of the policemen spoke some English. I told the Parsee he must go with the policemen, that he could tell his story, and if he had had nothing to do with the affair he would not be punished. So, at last, they all went away, the policemen, the *toddy-wallahs*, the Parsee, and some men and women, who, I suppose, had been in the first fray and were interested in the proceedings.

Then we went, again, to bed and this time we had no interruption. I don't know what my mother would have said to our insecure doors, after such adventures. One door, onto the veranda, would not shut at all, and the other, though there was a hasp, was a crazy structure of broken planks that held together apparently only because it was not moved. We kept a lamp burning in the little bathroom next to us, but we are fond of darkness, and so we had no light in our own room, only a candle and matches close to us. Outside, it was very dark, for there was no moon-light. The tiny crescent moon, one day old, had set long before, but now and then a ghostly light flashed on the opposite wall and 'flickered across into the night,' as one or other of the men carrying a lantern passed by our old, broken door, with its many cracks and holes.

We were up early the next morning and at work at our sketches. Bertha, who was drawing near the house, was to send for me if I was wanted, but the girl was safe in the house and her father locked up, so there was no need to stay away from our drawing. We had noticed an Englishman one day, while we were drawing near the Hindu temple, and in walking a little further on we passed his tents and saw a lady and a baby. We had not thought of this the night before, but even if we had we should not have disturbed him at 11 o'clock, unless there was something very alarming. However, as we were to leave Bassein that afternoon, I thought it would be well to tell the Englishman what had happened and ask his advice, as he would probably be staying a few days at least, and would probably know Hindustani. So, though I was not 'got up' for a call, I went off to the tents. On my way, Bertha appeared, and joined me, though at first she declared she could not pay a call in such a 'painty' dress. However, we walked up to the tents with great dignity, and introduced ourselves.

We had learnt from the *nazir*s that it was an 'engineer sahib named Gibbon.' So I began, 'Mr Gibbon, I think?' 'Fitz-Gibbon,' he observed, and we went into the tent with Mr Fitz-Gibbon and his wife, and told them what we had come for. Mr Fitz-Gibbon was very friendly and ready to help us. He promised to see the chief constable and let me know what was to be done. It was a cosy little tent, with carpets, and chairs, and tables, and a little couch at one side, on which lay the baby — such a fat merry little thing — only four months old. On a table on the other side of the tent, breakfast was set ready; it all looked very comfortable — a little home scene in the midst of jungle and ruins. Mr Fitz-Gibbon is an engineer, his headquarters are at Thana, but for many months of the year he and his wife are travelling — living in tents, staying a few days here and a week there as the work requires it — now accompanied by the baby, 20 or 30 miles perhaps from the nearest doctor — the life of many a young married couple in India.

We drew as much as we could that last morning. John wanted a sketch of the house itself, with the ruin showing beyond, and I managed to make a hasty drawing, just in pencil, sitting out at midday in the shade of a palm tree. Bertha and Miss Pechey went about Bassein one day at 12.00 and 1.00 o'clock, looking into ruins and crossing hot open glades as if they were in England, and declared that they were quite comfortable.

We set off in good time for the train; we did not mean to lose it this time and travel again in a goods train. When the train came in we found there was only one first-class compartment and that was filled by a family of Parsees, who, besides shawls, cushions and parcels, had brought two large boxes into the carriage, which filled up a large share of the floor space. There was no compartment for ladies alone, so we were obliged to get in and take the small amount of room left for us. Further on, however, when we stopped at a station, the guard did have the boxes taken out. The ladies had no shoes on, nor did they put them on when we got in. There was a little child, with a very dirty face, and their manners were not pleasant. I do not mean towards us — they were polite to us, excepting that they should have made more room, or apologized for their boxes, when we got in. One of the men spoke English. I do not mind what race my fellow travellers belong to, but I do object to being forced to travel in a small carriage with people whose customs are not nice.

They reminded me of a little Italian teacher of languages who used to come out to us at Ramleh to talk Italian with John. He was engaged by the month, but one day, before the first month was nearly gone, as John and he were sitting talking in the little drawing-room, he spat on the floor. John was so horrified, he jumped up and told the professor he found that he should not be able to go on with his lessons for the present, paid the month's salary and bade adieu to the gentleman. The little man did not know of course that he had done anything amiss, and must have wondered at the sudden termination of the engagement.

We reached Bombay at about 7.00 o'clock. John was at the station, and then we drove home along the very familiar road, and up Cumballa Hill, in at our white archway and along the drive — our drive that Miss Pechey says is 'the prettiest bit of Bombay' (perhaps our friends would not all agree) — and up to our porch. On the veranda was little Baby and Nellie by her — but baby would scarcely notice us at first, turning her little head resolutely away, as if on purpose to tease us.

Bella Vista, Bombay, 26 March 1886
I have had such a busy week that I have not been able to write any diary, and now I am not sure that I shall get enough written to be worth sending. Last Thursday night John and I went off to Khandalla. Bertha was not able to go with us as she had caught cold, and a night journey

would not do for her. So we left her in Miss Ellaby's and Miss Sanderson's charge. Miss Ellaby had come to stay with Jane while we were away.

John and I started from the Byculla station at 11 at night, feeling much more inclined to go to bed than to get into a railway carriage, only that there was our dear little peaceful Khandalla at the other end. The moonlight was very lovely when we came to the Ghats and saw the great hills standing out, black and white, in the light of the full moon. John saw more of the scenery than I did, for I fell asleep for two or three hours, but John slept very little; he does not sleep well in the train. We arrived at Khandalla at about half past four o'clock — the early dawn was just beginning to lighten the sky in the east, and the moon was setting, large and yellow like a harvest moon in England, as we walked from the station to our little house. The birds were beginning to chirp and twitter in the garden, and all the Khandalla world would very soon wake up, but I suggested that we should go to bed, and we did and John got a few hours sleep.

When we got up and came out onto the veranda, there was bright sunshine and the air was hot. But it feels quite different to the air here — at Khandalla it is dry and exciting, not moist and enervating. That afternoon I worked at my sketch of bullock carts — John wished me to finish it, but I was out of heart with it and did not think I could make anything of it. I seem to have got on just far enough in art to see how defective my drawings are and how very much better they might be done. However, by the end of the afternoon my sketch did look a little better. If I could have had another day at it, I could have corrected several of the faults, I think, but the next day, Saturday, we had to go over to Lanowli, to the distribution of prizes at the railway school, and the next day John had to return to Bombay.

We had engaged a *tonga* for the afternoon and at 5.00 o'clock we were ready and waiting for it, but no *tonga* appeared. At last John said he must set off and I must give up coming — it was too far for me to walk. Just then, however, an old *tonga* was descried coming along from Khandalla. It was an extraordinary old vehicle, but there was no choice. We got in and set off, but once outside the gate, the ponies declined to go on. One began to jib, but at last, by dint of the driver dragging it by the bridle and running along the road for some way, it was prevailed on to set off at a gallop; the driver clambered in, and we rattled and jolted and shook, up hill, and down dale, till we arrived at Lanowli. I felt very trembly and anything but calm and dignified, as the distributor of prizes should be.

We found the school decorated for the great day and the schoolroom quite crowded with the relations and friends of the school children. First we had a little musical entertainment and the children did very well, one girl, of about 14, played, really, extremely well. Then the report was read. It was an excellent report, the inspector describing the school as the best railway school in his division.

Then I gave away the prizes and the entertainment was over. We did not need to return to Khandalla in our shaky *tonga*, as our friends, Mr Shipp and Dr Field, drove us back in their dogcarts. It was such a beautiful evening that John and I sat on the veranda enjoying the lovely moonlight, only regretting that we must go back to Bombay so soon.

Monday 12 April

I had not time quite to finish the history of the last week's doings before I had to send off my diary. Last Monday I went to see a neighbour of ours, a newcomer, Mrs McLeod Campbell. Mrs Campbell had invited several friends to come and take tea with her and hear a paper read by a Hindu lady, Miss Powar, on her work in the *zenanas* among Hindu ladies in Bombay.

Miss Powar is very earnest in her wish to devote herself to the reform of the social life of Hindu women. She hopes to go to England eventually to 'tell the people in England about her Hindu sisters,' as she says. This little lecture to us last Monday was meant as a trial, on a small scale, of speaking to a public audience. There were about a dozen of us present, all ladies. We had tea first and talked for some time, till I wondered whether we were to have any lecture at all. At last, however, Mrs Campbell proposed that the paper should be read, arranged a seat for Miss Powar, and we all sat down, Miss Powar also sitting. Perhaps it was less formidable for her than standing, and with such a small audience it was easy for everyone to see and hear her.

Miss Powar began by telling us that she had been saved from the miserable life of a Hindu woman by her parents becoming Christians. 'God, in his love, helped me,' she said, 'or else I might now be married to a bad husband, or I might be a miserable widow, or I might be the victim of a cruel mother-in-law.' Then Miss Powar told us she would

162

read some extracts from her diary. This was a large book in which she kept a regular history of all her daily visits among Hindus. Most of the stories were sad, a few were very terrible, and a few were cheering, as showing what comfort and pleasure an educated friend might bring into a dreary, commonplace life. To Mrs Campbell and to some of the hearers the tales of suffering were new, especially the instances of the cruelty of mothers-in-law. They were not new to me, but it made me realize the fact that these stories are really true when Miss Powar told us of friends of her own who had actually gone through the hardships described.

One girl she knew, was married and lived with her husband and his mother not far from her house. The poor girl was ill treated by the mother-in-law to such an extent that she fell ill. She was then sent home to her own father and mother and under their care recovered her health. As soon as she was well, however, her husband came to fetch her home, or sent for her, I do not remember which. She implored her parents to keep her with them and not send her back to her husband's home and the dreadful mother-in-law, but her parents told her they had no power to keep her; she must return to her husband. Then she begged them to let her run and say goodbye to her dear friends, the Powars, who were so near. The husband (or his messenger, whichever it was) agreed to this and the girl ran round to her friends' house. Miss Powar told me she came up to them hurriedly, saying she could not wait, she was going away, back to her husband, and then as she ran off out of the house they heard her call out again, 'Goodbye.' Some time afterwards, going into the compound, they found the girl in their well, drowned; she could not face the return to the mother-in-law.

Another young woman Miss Powar knew was fearfully ill-treated by her mother-in-law; for the smallest offence, such as falling asleep when told to sit up, she was beaten cruelly. At last the girl destroyed herself. She leaped from the top of the house, which was four or five storeys high, and was so injured by the fall that she could not live. Miss Powar went to see her. The horrible mother-in-law came into the room where the dying girl lay. The poor girl started up in bed when she saw her mother-in-law, exclaiming, 'You cannot hurt me any more. I am out of your reach now.' And soon afterwards she died.

It seems inexplicable in a country where women are so downtrodden that such absolute power should be allowed to the mother-in-law. Over a son the mother has great influence, if not power, but over the daughter-in-law her rule is unquestioned.

No doubt such cases of brutality are rare among the upper and more civilized classes, though Miss Powar's friend who drowned herself was a high-caste Brahmin. But even among the most educated and enlightened of the Hindus the tyranny of custom remains. A Hindu neighbour of ours, of high rank, has two widowed daughters. One of them has been a widow for seven years and, though her life is different from that of her sisters whose husbands are living, in that she eats coarser food and wears commoner clothes, still she enjoys a good deal of liberty and is, I think, tolerably happy. But the other sister, whose first year of widowhood is not yet over, is condemned to a very sad existence. She lives apart in one dark room and can see no one, nor speak to anyone excepting her parents and brothers and sisters. Mrs Birdwood, who knows the family well, told me the mother, who is very affectionate to her children, feels this treatment of her daughter extremely painful. She cried when she spoke of it to Mrs Birdwood, and said she had no heart to go out herself while her dear daughter was shut up in darkness.

Bella Vista, Saturday 17 April 1886
Last Thursday Charlotte and I went to the court to hear a trial. We drove down with John, and when the carriage stopped at the steps of the Courts of Justice, John's arrival was announced by the blowing of a horn. We went up the winding staircase in the 'Judges Tower' and then, while John went to robe himself, the old *chobdar* conducted Charlotte and me into the Criminal Court and onto the Bench. We sat down on two very heavy and imposing looking chairs and waited for John. Several barristers whom we knew were in court and we saw amused smiles on their faces at our appearance there. Then John came in, preceded by the macebearer, who carried the great silver mace and laid it down on the table before the Bench. Everyone rose as the judge came in and the court crier called out 'Oyes! Oyes!'

Then the jury were sworn in. It is very striking, the appearance of a jury in India, especially here in Bombay where we have such a variety of races. First an Englishman, the foreman of the jury, was sworn. He was a very English-looking Englishman, with a smooth face, shrewd expression and reddish hair. Beside him sat a Hindu, a comfortable stout man with a heavy turban and the *dota* or scarf over his shoulder which denotes high caste. Then came a Jew, then a Parsee, two more Englishmen and a Muhammadan, and two or three more Hindus. The clerk of the court swore them all in, but the form of the oath varied according to the race of the juryman to be sworn; the Bible was only offered to the Englishmen; the others were asked 'to affirm solemnly before Almighty God that they would well and truly try the case between the Queen–Empress and the prisoner to the best of their power and ability.'

The case to be tried was a curious one. The prisoner had been arrested on the charge of having in his possession tools for making coins. In England, John says, it is sufficient to prove that the offender had in his possession tools for making coins of the realm, i.e. current coins, but here in India it must also be proved 'that the accused used these tools to make counterfeit coins and with the intention to deceive.' In this case the prisoner was found in possession of a great many tools for making coins. Three dies were produced in court; they were the only dies for making coins that were current coins, the coin made from these dies is a Turkish coin called a *ghazi*. It is still current in the Turkish dominions, but the last issue of the coin was more than 40 years ago.

Mr James Jardine was counsel for the prosecution. He spoke well, as he always does, giving one the impression that he is an able, conscientious lawyer, straightforward and honest in all he does. He called as his first and principal witness Mr Brewin, the superintendent of police for a certain district in Bombay where the prisoner has his shop. Mr Brewin gave his evidence very well, speaking in a loud, distinct voice. You felt that he was telling you the truth and that nothing would shake him in his statements. His evidence was that, having heard from a man one of the witnesses called that coins were being made and sold by the accused, he, with five or six native policemen under him, entered the prisoner's shop one afternoon three months ago and found some dozen men and one woman at work making gold and silver coins. He described the contents of the shop and of a room out of it. There were a great number of tools for making coins and there were bars of gold and silver metal. He left two policemen in the shop and then went upstairs to the third floor where he was told the prisoner lived. There he found similar work going on, and a very much larger number of coins. He seized everything. There were some *ghazis*, I forget how many, but there were more than 1600 *mahjors* — another coin that is said to be current in parts of the Turkish dominions. Excepting the *ghazis* and the *mahjors*, the coins were all fanciful pieces of gold and silver, some in imitation of coins once in circulation in India but not current now, that are used so largely here for ornaments worn by native women.

Mr Brewin did not suggest, and no one else did, that the current coins, the *ghazis* and the *mahjors*, were made of base metal. It did not seem likely therefore that anyone would take the trouble, and run a risk too, to make coins of exactly the same value as those he was imitating. In cross examination Mr Brewin admitted that there was nothing hid in the manner of making these coins, that the lower room in which the work was going on was quite open to the veranda, which was open to the street in a busy part of Bombay.

Mr Lang was counsel for the defence and he did his part well. One witness was a Muhammadan, an Arab from Baghdad, now living in Bombay. He told his story that one day the superintendent of police came to him and showed him a small coin, a Turkish *ghazi*, and asked him if he could get some coins made like that. He took the coin and went to the prisoner's house and gave the prisoner an order for 40 *ghazis*. They were all ready by the next day. When he had told this story quite glibly and easily, Mr Lang suddenly changed his tone and turning to him said: 'And how long have you been a spy employed by the police? How much were you paid for this transaction?' The man looked perplexed and answered: 'Nothing, I was not paid anything.'

'And what did you take all this trouble for then? Are you a friend of Mr Brewin's?'

'No,' said the witness, 'I never saw him before that day when he brought me the *ghazi*.'

I believed him; he seemed to me to speak honestly. Mr Jardine wanted to press the point of the 1600 *mahjors*, but they were not included in the charge and so John could not allow them to be put in, in evidence. I cannot say the prisoner had a very innocent face. He looked quite capable of doing a good many dubious things if they were to his advantage. But I felt sorry for him as the police did seem 'to have pounced down upon him in a very arbitrary way,' as Mr Lang said in his speech to the jury, and his shop had been shut up for three months.

After the final speeches of the barristers John made his charge to the jury. He had been talking that morning to me about the case, but by the time he came to deliver his charge he had changed his opinion very much. He told me afterwards so much fresh evidence had come out in the trial that the case was quite different to what he had thought it. The jury took only about five minutes to consider the case and then the foreman gave their verdict, 'Not guilty.' The prisoner was told he could go and away he went, out of the prisoner's dock, down the steps and out of the court. How delighted he must have been.

11
November 1887–June 1888
*A prize-giving and a bazaar, Institute for Deaf
Mutes, tableaux vivants for author's
purdah party, a Parsee ceremony,
Matheran, a stay at Poona
in the cavalry lines*

Bella Vista, 19 November 1887

JOHN has had a curious case before him, which he decided on Thursday. It was an action brought by some young men who claimed a share in certain property left by a Muhammadan tradesman, who died about two years ago. The plaintiffs said that this man was their uncle and had been partner with their father, who was also dead now; that all the property belonged to the two brothers, in common, and that they therefore should inherit a share of the property as well as their cousins, the daughters of their uncle. The defendants, these daughters, on the other hand, maintained that the young men were no relations of theirs at all, that their respective fathers were not brothers, but only friends living together.

The plaintiffs brought witnesses to prove that the two men came to Bombay, accompanied by their mother and sister, that they all possessed a burial ground in their native country — Scinde — that since they came to Bombay, many years ago, they had all lived as one family, in one house — holding all they possessed in common. What was strange was that the plaintiffs had not put forward any claim when the uncle died. At that time the sister was still living, who would have been an important witness. Now, when they make their claim, there is no witness in a position to speak with certainty as to the relationship.

168

Both plaintiffs and defendants belong to the large tribe in Afghanistan and in the North West Province of British India called Pathans. The Pathans are divided into clans (like the Highlanders) and everyone belonging to one clan bears the same name. So that these two men coming to Bombay from the same village and having the same name seem to have been looked upon as brothers. An old woman was brought up as a witness for the plaintiffs, who stated that she 'knew all about the relationships as she was "invitation bearer" to the caste, that she had never doubted that the men were brothers.' But then it was proved, on the other hand, by other witnesses that there were two separate fathers in the village in Afghanistan. John decided that there was no proof of relationship, or partnership, and gave judgment in favour of the defendants.

Bella Vista, 11 December 1887
It is a hot still day — the sea is very calm and the fishing boats, with their great pointed sails, come sailing along near the shore. It is a day when you feel very idle, when you think you would like to lie on a sofa and read poetry, while the silent Hindu pulls the *punkah* for you — nearly asleep himself, all the time. 'All round the coast the languid air did swoon, Breathing like one that had a weary dream.' The little sounds in the garden, the hum of insects and the low chirp of a bird here and there, seem only to tell you how silent it is — for how else could you hear such tiny sounds? The bare-footed *mali* creeps about with his noiseless tread, picking flowers to make the house gay, and filling his basket with the red hibiscus, sweet scented chumpa, white gardenia, yellow alimanda, blue bougainvillea, red and white oleander, and other Indian flowers whose names I do not know. The variety of flowers seems never ending. I wish I had time to paint them all — even all we have in our garden. My mother would have liked to see them. I think the great beauty — in Bombay, the beauty of the flowers and trees, and, above all, of the many palms, and of all the tropical vegetation, and the beauty of the scenery — the peerless view of the great city, with the sea and the islands and the distant Ghats — this daily, hourly feast of beauty, helps us through the Indian life, the time of exile from our beloved ones.

Thursday 15 December

I am writing under difficulties. The sun has set and I must have a candle by me for light. So mosquitoes are attracted and, as I write, I cannot easily defend myself, and my left hand, which is still, is being stung all over. (Happy thought — put on gloves.) John is very late this evening, for he has to attend a meeting of the Byculla Schools Committee — rather tiring after a good day's work.

Next week John is to give away the prizes at St Peter's schools and he will have to make a speech. I am to give the prizes to the girls and John to the boys. Last week I had to examine the girls' needlework and adjudge the prizes. Nurse will be amused, I think, at the idea of my judging needlework. But really it was very difficult, for so many of the specimens of needlework were almost exactly equal in excellence. I had to examine most minutely, the little stitches were so neat and regular. In the lower standards, where there are a large number of children, I am giving some little extra prizes. Tiny children of four and five years old had hemmed their little handkerchiefs very neatly. I should doubt if any of our infant schools in England could show better work. The needlework in the eighth standard was first rate; babies' pinafores, beautifully made, such pretty stitching and buttonholing. I have to write a little report on the children's needlework. The prize distribution at St Peter's is to be on Thursday 22nd.

On Wednesday I am to give away the prizes at a very different school — a school belonging to the Church Missionary Society here. Miss Myers is the mistress. It is a quiet unpretending school, but, I believe, is well managed. There are children of all races in it, as is usual in our schools here. I had just written to Miss Myers and to Sister Gladys about these prize-givings when I had a letter from the secretary of the Scottish Orphanage, asking me to join the ladies' committee of that institution. I have agreed, but I cannot undertake to be a very active member.

Yesterday we had a little dinner party. A learned Frenchman and his wife have come to Bombay, Monsieur Senart, the oriental scholar, and they have brought letters to John and Mr West. We expected an elderly and somewhat sedate personage in the great French savant — but he is neither elderly nor sedate. He is very genial, very natural and very merry — as good company as Monsieur Trayer is when just the friends he likes are round him and he is in his happiest mood. Another savant was here, Dr Stein, the Hungarian Orientalist, whom we met last summer at Rose's and Florence's house. He came to call on us in the afternoon, and we asked him to come to dinner 'to meet Monsieur Senart.' Mr and Mrs Peterson dined with us, and Mr Peterson confessed to me, that he had suggested to Dr Stein that he should call on us, adding, 'Then perhaps we shall meet you tonight.' So it was fortunate, we fulfilled his prophecy. Monsieur Senart speaks English well, but not so fluently as Dr Stein. He and John talked French mostly. John always enjoys a talk in French, and does not often get an opportunity here. We are planning an expedition to Kenara to see some ancient caves with remains of temples. It will be very interesting to go with such learned people.

Bella Vista, Bombay, 21 December 1887
How different the shortest day is here in India. I am sitting on the veranda — just below me a garden full of flowers and away beyond a sunlit sea. John is writing in his study, with the *punkah* waving, though it is only 8.00 o'clock in the morning.

Yesterday morning I had a visit from a Hindu gentleman and his wife, who had arrived in the P & O mail on Monday. They had come from England, where they have left two children to be educated. Miss Manning had written to us about Mr and Mrs Munmohan Ghose. We met them once, two years ago, when they were staying with the Wordsworths. They are very intelligent agreeable people. I asked them to dine with us, and they came, and we had a very pleasant evening. Mr Ghose was dressed entirely as an Englishman in an ordinary dress suit. Mrs Ghose had a simply made English dress, but over it the Hindu sari, which gave her a pretty, graceful appearance, and I thought looked nicer than the completely English costume she wore in the morning. John asked Mr Ghose how he had managed the 'caste' question when he first went to England some years ago. He said that he did nothing at all.

I thought that the best way was not to stir up the question, and I never asked them to admit me again to caste. If I had they must have said 'no'. So I never paid any fine or went through any penance. I waited, and after some time they began asking me as usual to come to the different ceremonies. Once, there was a

171

difficulty. While I was in England my father died, and when I came home I could not perform the religious ceremonies, because I had been across the sea.

We asked him about the position of widows on his side of India. 'They are much better off with us,' said he, 'than they are here in Bombay.' 'Can they wear the same clothes as other women wear?' I asked, 'and can they eat the usual food?'

No, they would not want to do so, but they are kindly treated, and often they are thought a great deal of in the family. An aunt of mine was a widow at 14, and she lived to the good age of 87, and from the time she was a widow, she never ate more than one meal a day.

We all exclaimed with surprise at this. 'What time did she have her meal?' 'Between 1.00 and 2.00 o'clock.'

And I remember very well when I was a little child, going with my brothers and sisters and standing outside her door when it was time for her dinner (we might not enter her room because she was a widow). Then she would come to the door and hand out some of the food — she made very nice dishes with fruit and milk.

'But what did she eat?' we asked. 'Uncooked food. She must not use fire. But the food was very nice — milk and rice and fruit. I don't remember her ever being ill for an hour. She was very kind to me, we were very fond of her. I think we loved her more than our mother.' Then we talked of the seclusion of women, and how Calcutta compared with Bombay in that respect. The first Hindu lady who went to Government House there was the wife of Mr Tagore. (The Tagores are people of high caste and good position.) It was 20 years ago at a 'drawing-room' at Government House. When she came in and walked up the room towards the viceroy's party, all the Hindu gentlemen present, some 50 in number, marched straight out of the assembly and went home. 'India is ruined,' they said, 'if this is what our women are going to do.' Now, Mr Ghose says, things are changed. At every drawing-room, there are at least a dozen, or perhaps 20, Indian ladies and nobody objects.

Mr Ghose's son, a boy of 16, is living in London, studying with the well-known 'crammer' Mr Wren. I think the Indian boys, and English boys too, need more care than they seem to get in these great brain-filling factories, where some 200 or 300 youths are worked up for examinations. In this case the boy is all right, as Mr and Mrs Ghose arranged for their son to live in the family of one of the professors. The daughter, a girl of 14, is at Richmond, in a very nice school, and very happy.

Friday 23 December

Yesterday and Wednesday were busy days. On Wednesday I went to Girgaum to give away the prizes at a school there belonging to Mr Squires' church. Miss Myers, the headmistress, told me that there was no printed report of the school, that they worked in a very quiet way, but that they liked to have a little ceremony at the prize-giving. The parents of the children and a few friends come. I had been to a similar entertainment at another school two years ago, and that was so very quiet and private in its character that I did not mind making a little speech, five minutes long, to the children. Well, I thought this would be the same, and John advised me to think of something to say in case it was wanted. I wrote down a few sentences, which John said would do, and learnt them off by heart. Mrs Turner went with me to the school, and Nellie.

When we got there I found a large room full of people, the school children, 130, and about 70 or 80 grown-up persons. We sat down; a table in front of us was covered with the prizes. Soon the entertainment began. There was some pretty singing and some very fair playing on the piano, and one or two pieces of poetry were recited. After that Mr Squires gave a report of the school, and part of his speech was rather solemn, for he alluded to one poor class, one entire standard, that had no prize for good conduct. He encouraged them to behave better, in a very nice, kind way, but still it was rather dismal, in the middle of the entertainment. He ended by speaking of his little son of eight years old in England, and of the pleasure it gave him to hear of his doing well at school. Then I gave the prizes — a great many — and it took a long time. When it ended I began my speech. Perhaps it was Mr Squires' speech, or giving the prizes, or my nervousness — I don't know what it was — but when I was half way through, everything went straight out of my head and I could not remember a word more. It was very horrible for a second or two. Then I said to myself, 'I can't sit down having failed utterly,' so I said 'Well, now I will just tell you — for the younger children here — a story of my little boy of eight, as Mr Squires has spoken of his little boy of eight,' and so I told them the story of Johnnie's going to bed one Saturday night with all his clean Sunday clothes on. The reason was he had been blamed for being late Sunday morning so he thought he would go to bed all ready dressed. The children laughed and people clapped, and I sat down safely.

Bombay, 20 February 1888

When I sent off my diary last week, I had just finished telling about the bazaar. The fair was over on Monday 13 February. But we stallholders had still some busy days before us, making up our accounts, getting in payments, sending things to people who had not taken their purchases away, and so on. I sent Mr Phipson (the secretary), as the result of my art stall, 1400 rupees. I have now about 30 more to send him, and that will make the sum just £100. It is much more than I expected to make; I did not think so many people would care to buy pictures. I could have sold more watercolours than I had, especially figure pieces. I have repaid myself for some of the expense I incurred, such as frames for the engravings Ellen sent me, and the etchings and other things that Mary Clover bought for me; we could not afford to spend a great deal of money on my stall. Twelve sketches of my own doing I sold, large and small, and made 320 rupees by them; I did not expect it at all. Ellen was cashier, as I said, and kept the accounts most exactly. Every evening when we left the tent she carried her heavy money box with her. It reminded me of old days when Constance and I saved up our pocket money and our earnings: and then we had a great emptying of our money box and counting up of our money, and then went off with glee to the old 'Pantheon' to spend it on birds and birdcages.

There were many funny little incidents during the fair. One man, a corn merchant, asked the Duke of Connaught for a photograph of the duke and duchess. The Duke gave it to him, telling him the price. 'Will you write your name on it?' the man asked. 'Certainly, that will be four rupees extra.' Oh, then I won't have the name,' replied the man.

Another Indian asked the duke for a small article that was one rupee. 'One rupee! why, I can buy it in the bazaars for eight annas.' 'Yes, but you see,' said the duke, 'you have all this nice tent to buy it in, and here am I to serve you, and a nice carpet to walk on.' 'I don't care anything for all that,' was the man's reply, with a contemptuous gesture of his hand.

24 February

Last Wednesday John and I went with Dr Porter, the Roman Catholic Archbishop of Bombay, to see the Institute for Deaf Mutes. The immediate cause of our going was that John had been asked to preside at the annual meeting, which will take place in about ten days, and Dr Porter offered to show us the place and explain the system of teaching.

This institution was founded by Dr Meurin (Roman Catholic bishop) who left Bombay two years ago. An institution of this kind was very much needed, as there was, before its establishment, no education whatever in this presidency for the deaf and dumb. There are about 20 boys at present in the school, but there are 100 more ready to come in when the funds will allow of it. An Englishman, Mr Walsh, is at the head, and he is a professor of the art of teaching the deaf and dumb, his system being the 'oral system', as he explained to us.

The boys were divided into three classes, not according to age, but according to the time they had been learning and their proficiency. Most of the boys were Parsees, two were English, and one was Hindu. There were no girls. Mr Walsh proposed to show us what the boys could do, beginning with the lowest class. A large blackboard was put on an easel in front of the children. On it were letters — or rather combinations of letters representing sounds. Mr Walsh pointed to the letters 'oh,' and a little boy, about eight or nine years old, said 'ooh' in a queer prolonged way; then 'ah,' and so on through the vowels, and then to syllables, a great many with the same vowel — cat, mat, bat. The little boys spoke better than the big ones. Two Parsee boys, brothers, big fellows of 16 or 17, evidently found it very difficult to make the different sounds of the letters. Mr Walsh said these boys, who had only entered the school a few weeks before, were just learning to make sounds; sometimes it took a boy several months to learn to say 'ah' or 'oh.' None of the boys in this class had any idea of the meaning of the shortest sentence when written, but they could understand some very short directions when spoken by Mr Walsh, such as 'come here,' 'give the pointer to A,' but then Mr Walsh helped them by pointing out the place or the boy. They could make each other understand their wants by signs. But in the 'oral system' signs are discouraged. The object is to teach the children to read and write the ordinary language. Mr Walsh says in the 'sign system' language is compressed as much as possible, and when a boy has learnt the signs and then afterwards attempts to speak or write ordinary language, he finds it a most difficult task. 'If I said to them on my fingers,' said Mr Walsh, '"I went yesterday to Bombay," I should say "Bombay I go," with a sign meaning the past, yesterday.'

In the next class the boys read some short sentences, and they evidently understood the meaning. 'Have you seen the cat?' 'The cat has caught a mouse,' 'Where is the dog?' and so on. Mr Walsh pointed to the words, and one after another the boys read a sentence. Then he pointed to separate words, not connected with each other, and generally the boys knew them. Mr Walsh tested their knowledge by writing a sentence wrongly. One sentence was 'a cow has two horns'; Mr Walsh wrote on the board 'a horse has two horns.' A bright little boy saw the mistake at once and pointed to it. Then John told me to draw a horse, and a boy on it — which I did (not very well though) and Mr Walsh wrote over it 'a sheep.' Most of the boys saw this mistake directly. Mr Walsh told a little boy to write on the board what it was, and he rubbed out eagerly 'a sheep,' and wrote over it, very clearly, 'a horseman.' Mr Walsh gave his directions to them verbally; they watched the motions of his lips. It was of course immaterial whether he made any sound or not. I spoke to them too, using the simple words they knew, and they understood me. The archbishop told us that one day he asked a little boy who is very bright and the most advanced of the pupils, if he had *heard* from his mother. 'No,' answered the boy, 'I am deaf. I cannot hear.' So Mr Walsh said, 'You must give the most literal and exact meaning to the words you use.' 'Have you got a letter from your mother?' said Dr Porter then. The boy still looked puzzled; 'got' to him meant 'fetched,' they are told to 'get' something in the sense of 'fetch'. It was very curious to see how Mr Walsh made them produce the different sounds. When a boy, for instance, pronounced 'goat' as 'coat', Mr Walsh took one of the boy's hands and held it against his throat, while he put the boy's other hand against his, the boy's throat. Then Mr

Walsh made the sound of 'K' very distinctly, and then 'G', and the boy felt that the vibration was different as he gave the different sounds, and after one or two attempts he made the sound of 'K' quite well. Mr Walsh showed the boys how he spoke, how he held his lips, how he moved his tongue. Sometimes he put the boy's lips into the right position himself. The boy watched him closely and then tried to imitate him. Mr Walsh has a keen intellectual face and very mobile features, thin and sensitive lips and no moustache or beard. His hands are thin, and he has narrow pointed fingers that were always moving as he spoke, illustrating or emphasizing what he said. His whole heart is in his work; you see that directly. We made some remark about his needing a great deal of patience in his profession.

Yes, he said, that is true. You must be quite patient, however slow the pupil is in understanding you. If you lose your patience for a moment, it is all over with you. The deaf and dumb are very nervous, and if you speak the least impatiently to them they get flurried, and then they have no power to think of anything.

John asked him if he thought the theory was true that a child who was deprived of one sense was endowed with great keenness in some other sense. He said it was not so at all, as far as he could tell, rather the other way. The children, who were deficient in one sense, were often inclined to be deficient in others. He supposed the physical cause that made one sense feeble tended to make the whole body and brain feeble too. He pointed out two boys who were wearing spectacles; their sight was weak. He said that one sense would often become keen from constant use, the sense of touch, for instance, or the power of observation.

The boys in the highest class were much more advanced than the others. They read aloud, quite nicely, a story written up on the blackboard. The story was about two sailors on a ship who saw a white bear on the ice with its cubs. They got their guns and shot the cubs. 'The poor mother licked them, and tried to make them well; she was very sad.' We asked the boys questions about what they read, why the bear was sad, and so on. They seemed to understand it. One boy answered our questions very well; he would not be beaten, even when he did not know a word we were using. The archbishop called the ground where the bears were the 'dry land'. That was an expression he had never heard before. Mr Walsh explained it to him, making him see that it was the same as ground, the contrary to water. In the lower classes, when a boy did not understand a noun, Mr Walsh showed him what it was, when he could, by a picture. He had a number of plates at hand, with coloured pictures of different objects. I had taken a basket of flowers with me for the children, and they seemed to like them, especially those that they could smell. I offered a flower to one little boy, who did not look more than five or six years old, but he did not understand what I meant. He was dressed in better clothes than the others and had come with a servant. He was the son of one of the officers of the High Court, and it was his first visit. I hope Mr Walsh may be able to train him, as he is so very young.

We came away very much impressed with all we had seen. It is very wonderful to see the gateway of knowledge being slowly and painfully opened to these poor lads. Through the unwearying efforts of such men as Mr Walsh, the lives of the deaf and dumb may be completely changed. If these children remain long enough with Mr Walsh, the whole world will be to them entirely altered. From a dull, vacant existence, hardly better than an animal's, they may rise to a life of reason and intellect. To them also (to all whose minds are not hopelessly enfeebled by illness or disuse) knowledge may yet 'unroll her ample page.'

'Goodbye, Mr Walsh, we wish you Godspeed with your noble work.'

Khandalla, 29 March 1888

Well, my purdah party came off last Friday; Marian, Nellie and I worked hard for ten days before. We had rehearsals and, what people never have in England, rehearsals complicated by one of the actors being a purdah lady and purdah arrangements having to be made. I thought it would be a nice thing to have Indian children as well as English among the actors. I had ten children, six English, two Parsee and two Muhammadans. It was an experiment to have children to whom anything of a dramatic nature was totally new. But I risked it; I wanted very much to bring the Indian children in, and that they should take their part with the English in entertaining the guests. So I invited Sakeena and Saraya Tyabjee — daughters of Mr Budrudeen — and the two children of the Jehangirs, Coomi (girl) and Kallu (boy). Four Petersons and two little Pottingers made up the number. Mrs Pottinger acts capitally herself and her children are naturally good actors, and they were most easy to teach. Of the others, the Tyabjees were equal to any — indeed Sakeena was, I think, the best among them.

We had simple subjects, hackneyed to English eyes perhaps, but that did not matter. I arranged the tableaux chronologically and I tried to make the dresses as true as I could to history. Queen Elizabeth was the most striking. Sakeena looked well in a flowered silk skirt over a great hoop, yellow satin body and enormous sleeves, and great white ruffles. The tableau that was pronounced the prettiest was the one of Charles I's children, taken from van Dyck's picture. The two little Pottingers, with their fair skins and yellow hair, and little Kallu Jehangir, with curly black hair and black eyes, were the royal children. We had two dogs, a brown china pug and a white china spaniel, the nearest approach we could make to Charles I's spaniels. Little Irene Pottinger is only five and a half. The last tableau was taken from dear Mr Cross's picture of little Lady Lucy, in black velvet and her fair hair hanging down, as it does in the picture.

The guests were invited for 9.00 o'clock, but Lady Reay was very late, and at last, after waiting some time, we had to begin the pictures without her. I arranged just a few seats in front, for Lady Reay and some Indian ladies of rank, among them the little niece of the Aga Khan, a tiny bright-eyed little maid who came with two attendants and kept awake till 11.00 o'clock. Mrs Sheppard (the commissioner's wife) had kindly come from Coorla, where they were in camp, to help me, and most helpful she was. I could not stay to receive all the guests, as I had to arrange the tableaux, and Mrs Sheppard took my place. Marian was in the green room (i.e. Nellie's room) helping to dress the children, as she knew just how they should be. I stood by the stage in front and gave a description of each picture before the curtain was drawn. Then Mrs Cotterell-Tapp repeated it in Hindustani and another friend in Marathi. So I think the guests understood something of what it was about. It reminded me of our old acting days to be standing up before a roomful of people making my little speeches. We had about 110 or 120 Indian ladies, and 50 or 60 English, as nearly as we could count.

After the tableaux were all over, we went into the dining room for supper, and while the ladies were all there our men came in and cleared the drawing-room of the stage and chairs. People did not stay long, however, after the tableaux were over. We had just two songs from

179

Lady Morland, and then everyone went away. The day before we had a dress rehearsal for the wives and children and relations of our servants. Mr West's servants all came, from the wives of the dignified *chobdars* down to the families of the low caste *garawallahs*. They all came so neatly dressed, some quite grandly. One little woman, in red silk and jewels, remarked to Mrs Tapp (who was explaining it all to them) that 'she had been to a great many *tamashas*, but never in her life to such a *nautch* as this.'

Another day we had a dress rehearsal and Mr Budrudeen and his brothers came to see the tableaux, and they were much amused at seeing Sakeena and Saraya in such novel circumstances. As a great concession, John was allowed to be present, but when Mr Peterson looked in for a minute on his way to a dinner party, to see *his* children performing, Mr Budrudeen did not approve.

Khandalla, 30 March 1888 (Good Friday)

We are a large party in our little house today. Mr Woodward and Colonel Willoughby are with us, and we expect Charlotte Ellaby this evening. The colonel arrived this morning, having travelled all night. He left his regiment on the march, rode to Ahmadnagar, and came thence by train. He looks very well, very brown and sunburnt. He says they have had great heat by day, but generally cool nights. At one place, however, the night was very hot, and he says the men were all lying on the ground outside their tents, stripped to the waists.

There are regular resting places where regiments halt on the march. I, in my ignorance, thought they chose the most shady, comfortable place they could, but the colonel says that a regiment means a body of about 1200 people, besides sheep, dogs and, in the case of a cavalry regiment as his is, about 600 horses and baggage ponies besides; and it must halt where supplies can be got, and that is near a village. At these halting places there are regular 'lines' marked out for the accommodation of the men. The village people bring in supplies for the regiment, the *patel* (headman) of the village arranging for the food for the horses. But he says he is very careful to see that the men who furnish the fodder are paid directly for it. For in several cases he found when he paid the *patel* for the whole supply, the money never reached the men who owned the hay or grain. Long after the regiment had left the place, demands were sent to him for money which he had given to the *patel*. These *patels* are very useful men in their villages, but there is of course always the risk of their abusing their power. The custom of one man being the headman in the village is of very ancient origin. I do not think it is known when it began.

The regiment will reach Poona on 6 April. The march from Neemuch to Poona takes nearly two months. The longest march in one day is 20 miles. That is not very much for the men and officers on horseback (it is a cavalry regiment), but it is quite as much as the camp followers can manage.

1 April 1888

One day the week before last Marian and I went to the house of some Parsee friends, Mr and Miss Bhownuggree, to be present at a Parsee ceremony, called the *najote*. Miss Bhownuggree had asked us to come, as she thought we should be interested in seeing it. The *najote* is the ceremony of investing a child with the white cotton shirt and white woollen cord, emblems of his religion, which henceforth he must never be without. The white shirt is made of cotton, and is generally thin, like muslin. It is the sign of humility. The cord is made of the finest white lamb's wool, and is made in a threefold twist. It is the symbol of innocence, in being made from a lamb, and the threefold cord is the emblem of their religious precept. 'Pure thoughts, pure words, pure deeds.' A child is about ten years of age when he or she goes through the *najote* ceremony. It seems to me that the *najote* is to Parsees very much what confirmation is to us. Perhaps it is something between baptism and confirmation. The child is not exactly admitted into the Parsee Church. Their theory is that every child born of Parsee parents is a Parsee, but he is confirmed in the principles and dogmas of the Parsee religion.

When we arrived at Mr Bhownuggree's house, we walked up the steps and were just going to enter the drawing-room when a Parsee gentleman came hastily out and stopped us. Then Mr Bhownuggree followed him and he explained why we had been stopped. The service had begun, and while the service was going on no one but Parsees could be in the drawing-room, as only Parsees might tread on the carpets whereon the priests were sitting. He said he would take us round by another way. So we went down the steps and then up a steep wooden staircase onto a veranda at the other side of the drawing-room.

181

As the windows were all wide open, we could see and hear everything that went on.

In the middle of the room was a little platform, only about a foot above the floor, covered with a white cotton cloth. On this dais sat three children, one girl and two boys, with their backs to us. They had white sheets or towels wrapped round them, and looked as if they had just come from the bath, which was the case, for the children must bathe immediately before the *najote* ceremony. They had little round caps on their heads and the ordinary loose Parsee trousers, but we only saw the little dark heads above the white covered bodies.

Opposite to the children, and facing them, sat three priests, all dressed in pure white. They were all talking very fast, reciting the service in the Zend language, which no one present understood. There were six other priests in the room, sitting on the carpet near the children. One priest was feeding a little sacred fire with sandalwood. The fire was on a silver brazier and had been brought alight from the Towers of Silence. There were also flowers, placed near the children, some in little wreaths, some just the separate blossoms without stalks or leaves. The wreaths were hung on little erections (I don't know what to call them) in the shape of a cone, that looked like sugar loaves made of silver. A cone is the emblem of good fortune. There were also two dishes on the carpet near the priests, full of what looked like sweetmeats, but it was really chopped-up coconut, almonds, raisins and pomegranates.

After the priests had gone on reciting the service in a very sing-song voice for some 20 minutes they stood up, each priest came close up to the children and, saying some words in Zend, threw the shirts over the children. Then the priests took up three white cords and, holding the cords in their hands, they turned the children round so that they faced us and had their backs towards the priests. Each priest took hold of both hands of the child in front of him and made the child hold the white cord with him — just as one holds a baby's hand to make it write a word. Then the priests recited some more texts from the shastras while they held the cords and the children's hands high up; and then they passed the cords round the children's waists, winding them three times and tying them in front in a loose knot.

It was an impressive sight, very impressive — the three children standing there, each one in front of a tall white priest, the strange religious sayings in the long-dead language, the mystical clothing of the child in the shirt of humility, and the threefold cord of pure thoughts, pure words and pure deeds. When the tying of the cord was finished, they all sat down again, priests and children; and the priests went on talking, and while they spoke they took up handfuls of the chopped coconut, rice and almonds and threw them over the children until the dish was empty. The fruit is used at the *najote* as at a wedding; each kind of fruit has its special meaning. The coconut (like bread with us) the staff of life, the pomegranate plenty and prosperity, the almond amiability (the oil in the almond signifying the wheels of life running smoothly), the raisins kindness (from the sweetness of the raisins).

Then the service was over. All the nine priests and the three children stood up, the white cloth on which the children had sat was taken away, the parents and friends of the children came forward, and there was much kissing and congratulating and shaking of hands. The little brazier with the sacred fire of sandalwood was carried away and would be taken back, still alight, to the fire in the Towers of Silence. Then presents were given to the children. The little girl had some very handsome jewellery given her, and they all had presents of money, some friend giving ten rupees and another as much as 50. I said it was very kind of friends to give her such nice presents, but Miss Bhownuggree told me that it was quite understood that when the children of these friends went through the same ceremony, presents of equal value, or in the case of money with a few rupees in addition, should be given by them in return. My father would say this supports his theory that presents are often a trouble, instead of a good, to the receiver.

The ceremony being all over, we went down to the garden, and there we sat down in the pleasant shade. Toddy was handed round; not hot steaming Scotch toddy, but cool refreshing Indian toddy. At first when Mr Bhownuggree offered me some I hesitated, and so did Marian, and so (very much) did Miss Stevenson, and so did Miss Pechey, but having bravely taken the first mouthful we went on and ended by all liking it. Mr Bhownuggree said they were all so fond of it that they missed it when the toddy season was over. The taste is very curious, slightly acid and slightly effervescing. Marian says it is like 'milk and champagne with a little yeast in it.'

Monday 16 April

I am expecting a visit today from Miss Sorabji, the young Parsee lady who took the degree of BA at the last convocation. I call her Parsee, but she is only half Parsee; her father is Parsee and her mother Hindu. They are all Christians, however. Mr Sorabji became a Christian more than 30 years ago, to the great indignation of all his relations. He often had to hide to escape from the persecution of his fellow countrymen. However, he persisted and married a Christian woman, and together they struggled through some years of great privation and persecution. Now they are living, not only unmolested, but much respected.

Mr Sorabji is a missionary clergyman. His wife has a large and successful school at Poona, to which girls of all races and religions come. She has also what we should call a 'ragged school', a day school, for the children of the very poor, who can pay nothing. It is an unusual thing, two schools of such different rank kept and managed by the same people, but it seems to work well in this instance. Mrs Sorabji, who came to see me last week, told me that she tries to make the girls in the boarding school interested in the poor little things in the day school, and that the other day a girl went home and, of her own accord, collected a little sum of money for Mrs Sorabji to spend on one of the poor children who was destitute. Mr and Mrs Sorabji have eight children, seven girls and one boy. Miss Cornelia, the BA, is now living at Ahmadabad; she gives lectures there in the college.

I did not write about the convocation last January, as I had no time just then to do so. I have often described it before, but this time there was a new feature, a woman taking her degree of Bachelor of Arts. Miss Sorabji looked very nice in her gown and cap (in English style). She is slight and rather tall, with fine dark eyes, good features, though rather large, a sweet expression — altogether a striking face. When she went up among the men and Mr West pronounced the magic words, 'By the grace of this university you are admitted to the degree of Bachelor of Arts' (as nearly as I remember them those are the words), there was great cheering. At first there was a pause, for our students here do not cheer everything as English lads do; I was longing for people to cheer and saw that a gentleman near me, Mr Grubb (the preacher), felt the same, and we started the clapping, which was taken up directly and cheering followed.

Friday 20 April

Miss Sorabji came to see me last Monday, and stayed an hour or two. I asked her about her work at Ahmadabad. As I told her, we have not in England arrived at the point of having women professors in men's colleges and I wanted to know how she found the plan worked. She said she had found it very easy, that there had never been anything unpleasant, and that at the end of the term, when the principal made a speech, he observed that the presence of a lady professor had had a decidedly good influence on the students. Miss Sorabji lectures an hour every day and assists in the examinations. For that she has 100 rupees a month. The principal wants her to apply for the second professorship, but I do not know if she will. She is very anxious to gain the 'Queen's Medal' at our university here, which gives the student two years education in England. The question is whether a woman is eligible. The original idea of this scholarship is that the winner should go to England and, on his return to India, be more fitted to do good service to the government in one of the services here. No doubt, when the scholarship was founded there was no idea of the winner being a woman. But I do not see how the government can rightly refuse a woman because when our university threw open its doors to women, it declared that 'wherever *he* was written *she* should be understood to be meant equally.' Miss Sorabji has made her application and the question is still under consideration. I believe the matter has been referred to the supreme government.

Matheran, 15 May 1888

Last Monday, 7 May, we left home, Ellen and I, and came by the afternoon train to Narel, the nearest station to Matheran. We arrived at Narel before 4.00 o'clock, and there we waited for an hour until it was cool enough to start on our journey up the hill.

Mrs James Jardine had come from Bombay by the same train, and she was on her way to Matheran also. Her husband, instead of enjoying the vacation with her, is hard at work in Hyderabad, engaged by the Nizam as his counsel in this great law suit concerning the government of the Nizam and the ex-minister, Abdul Huq. However, the heavy fees paid to the barrister must be some compensation for the loss of the holiday. Mr Inverarity, another leading barrister, has gone to England, retained by Sirdar Diler Jung (Abdul Huq) with a fee, rumour says, of one lakh (100,000 rupees). I believe, it is not so much as that, however.

Mrs Turner had kindly sent down a *tonjon* for me, and another was waiting for Mrs Jardine. A pony was ready for Nellie. A *tonjon* is a wooden chair with, as it were, two backs, but only one seat. To each *tonjon* there are eight men, four to carry it, and four to relieve them when they are tired. So we had 16 men. Then there were two more men, one for Ellen's pony and one for the *chobdar's*, as he was too old for the long climb. So with two *tonjons*, two ponies, and 18 men, we set off on our journey to Matheran.

Just beyond the station there is the little village of Narel, some dozen houses; mud huts with palm-leaf thatch and cottages (as we should call them) with tiled roofs and stone walls. Most of the houses, even the mud huts, were raised on stone foundations, I noticed. I suppose the monsoon is bad at Narel, lying low, as it does, and at the foot of the Ghats. There were a good many haystacks in the village, mounted on wooden piles some eight or ten feet high.

The road is at first quite level, but soon it begins to rise. It was still very hot when we set out, but after a mile or so we came into a wooded part of the country and then it was much pleasanter. The dust was bad; every now and then we had to shut our eyes, as clouds of dust flew over us.

The chairs are comfortable enough, but very unsuitable, it seemed to me, in one way. They are so very heavy; they are made of wood with cane seats, thick solid wood, and the poles that are fastened at each end and borne on the shoulders of the coolies are thicker than a man's arm. Why the men do not make light chairs of bamboos and cane, I cannot think. Before we started, Mrs Jardine told me that she believed these bearers are as a rule short-lived, and I did not much like letting them carry me after that. However, they are very anxious to get the work, and I learnt afterwards that men often come from long distances — from Mahabaleshwar for instance — just for the season, April and May, and earn a good sum to take home with them to buy seeds for their crops.

As we ascended the hill we had wide views over the plains. The road is very steep part of the way, quite too steep for any carriage. When we came to any specially steep place the men generally set off at a run. After travelling in this way for an hour, we came to a little thatched hut and a level plateau shaded by trees. Some coolies were resting, and one or two foot travellers, while a woman in the hut was selling lemonade and fruit. This is the halfway house. Our men put down the *tonjons* here; Ellen got off her pony; and we walked on, while the men rested a little and had some water to drink. In ten minutes they followed us with the *tonjons*, and after another hour's ride we reached the highest part of the ascent. Here the path was very precipitous, and wound round a great red rock that towered above us and came out onto a level road — level in comparison to the mountain path we had just left. Here the 16 bearers all stopped, and set up a shouting and yelling — a rejoicing at our reaching the top of the hill. Then on we went again, but as we neared a toll house, where apparently the *tonjons* going and coming are noted down, the men began to shout and yell.

After a time Mrs Jardine and her bearers left us and disappeared up a leafy path that was marked by a signboard announcing 'RUGBY HOTEL'. We went on along the high road of Matheran, past the bazaar, a collection of three or four houses, or rather shanties, with notices in English over the fronts, 'GENERAL MERCHANT', or 'SO AND SO (generally a Parsee name) LICENSED TO SELL WINE, ETC.' Then at the roadside we passed a signboard, 'GOVERNMENT TELEGRAPH AND POST OFFICE', and away among the trees, with its shady veranda and deep tiled roof was the post office. Further on again we passed other signboards, rather delusive, it seems, for the name on the board only meant that that path led to it, but in many cases it is a quarter of a mile or half a mile away. My bearers seemed so cheered at the prospect of arriving at the journey's end that they kept up a very loud song, one man running by my side (they were all running now) and shrieking out 'ha-eeh'oh!' over and over again, then bringing in queer names, one after another, names of gods and goddesses I should think. The poor fellows, they were very polite and obliging, but very ragged and very, very dirty. It was not pleasant to be carried by them. It would be much better if they wore a neat livery of some washing material and charged a little more for the *tonjon*.

We came at last to a narrow path and a board with 'UNDERWOOD' written on it. Well does the house deserve its name, for it is surrounded with a close 'underwood' of shrubs and saplings, with taller trees shading it all. A man came running towards us with a lantern and lighted us along up the steep path till we arrived at the bungalow, and the little cavalcade stopped. The tired bearers set down my *tonjon* in front of the veranda steps. Mrs Turner was on the veranda welcoming us with voice and look in the kindest manner, but unable to move, for she is lame and tied to her chair. It was delightful to find ourselves at the journey's end. I made my bearers and the pony man happy with a little present. The charge for a *tonjon* is eight rupees, a rupee for each man, but then, no doubt, they have to pay something for the *tonjon*. After half an hour there was again shouting and bustle, and lanterns moving among the trees — our luggage arriving; seven more coolies, men and women, with boxes and parcels and bundles, the boxes slung on poles carried (each box) by two men, but the parcels and bundles borne on women's heads. Poor people! they seemed so pleased when I gave them only an anna each over the fare — six annas instead of five for carrying luggage seven miles, four miles of it being a steep climb.

Khandalla, 25 May
We came to Khandalla, Ellen and I, last week, after our ten days' visit to Matheran. Before I speak of this last week and our doings here, I must finish my Matheran diary.

Matheran has been described by one guidebook writer as somewhat like a starfish in shape, and I think that is true, the hills being formed of a tableland and many promontories that jut out from it. Splendid views are to be had from these projecting hills — 'points' is the Matheran expression. For a good walker there is a great deal to see, but you must go a long way through thick woods before you are rewarded by a fine view from a 'point'. There is only one path that I know of where you walk along by the edge of the hill, and have an open view for at least half a mile. There is a lower path some way down the hill, I believe, called 'Monkey Path', which is open.

There are great numbers of monkeys at Matheran and they are very fearless, coming into the compounds and running and jumping about close to the houses. I only saw monkeys one day, when Mrs Turner and I went out in *tonjons* to pay some calls. As we went along the road near 'Underwood', we saw some monkeys on the wall of a compound — great grey fellows, with black faces and a crown of white hair over their foreheads. They ran and leaped and swung on the trees, and seemed very happy I thought. I wish one would have stayed for me to draw him, but we could not have waited then, for we had three or four miles to go, and to get back, before it was dark.

We went to two of the hotels. Country hotels in India are very unlike our country inns in England. Each of these inns was made up of four or five separate low buildings, with deep tiled roofs and verandas, all standing in a big compound. Trees, large and small, all about the houses; no attempt at a garden, except that in one or two cases there were a few pots, with straggling plants, by the steps to the veranda. In some hotels where people cannot get a sitting room to themselves, a part of the veranda adjoining their bedroom is divided from the rest by screens and matting, and serves as an outdoor parlour. We only found one of our friends at home, and after seeing her, we went on to the gymkhana, that important institution in all Anglo-Indian stations.

Down a steep slope we went in our *tonjons*, through a wood and then through a turnstile, the top of which our men lifted off to let our *tonjons* pass. There we found ourselves amid the rank and fashion of Matheran. Lawn tennis was going on, and both players and spectators were specially interested because the tournament was on. Our friend Miss Jefferson was playing, and very well too, flying about with great activity. Another lady, delicate looking, pale and prim, known for her very quiet reserved manners, was playing most energetically and making very good strokes. Some of the little village boys, dressed up in tunics and knickerbockers of khaki, the material used for soldiers' uniforms, were stationed at various points to pick up the balls, so to these little Hindu lads the 'hot weather' brings business and pleasure. It was growing dusk when we left the gymkhana, distant thunder made me anxious to start, and Mrs Turner also. We went off and only stopped once, just to look at the view from 'Artist's Point', as someone has named an opening on the rock, whence you have a beautiful view of mountains and plains and the faraway water of Thana Creek.

We were glad to reach home, for it was almost dark. Two nights before a large panther had been seen on the hill. It suddenly appeared on the veranda of a gentleman's house. The family are in the habit of sitting on the veranda in the evening and a large dog they have was always with them, always, until this evening. But when he was called as usual he would not stir, but kept crouching under a table in the dining room. No doubt it was aware of the presence of an enemy. Some of the servants went out onto the veranda, the ladies of the family being still in the house. There, to their horror, they saw the panther. They screamed and shouted, and the gentlemen of the family ran out, catching up any sticks they had, and the animal fled. Traps were set for it at once, but when we left Matheran it was still at large. A poor buffalo belonging to one of the hotels was killed one night, and two or three poor little calves. In one place the traces of young panthers were found.

I should like to have seen the 'mar forest', that is a wood entirely of fish-palms. It must be very pretty, but it was a long way off from us, too far for Mrs Turner. One morning Miss Jefferson kindly lent me her pony while she walked, and we went to Chowk Point and some other places where there are fine views. We saw a curious lonely hill standing up abruptly from the plain, the lower part joining the great Matheran Hill. A solitary tree grows on the summit and people call it 'One Tree Hill'. Up the ravine between 'One Tree Hill' and Matheran the first English lady who came to Matheran was carried. The story is that her husband first discovered the merits of Matheran as a hill station and, anxious to test the practicability of getting visitors to the place, took his wife up. She made the ascent in an ordinary chair with poles fastened to it, borne by coolies, and when they came to the precipitous ascent by One Tree Hill she was blindfolded. I think I would rather have seen the path, however dangerous, than have felt that I was unconscious of what was around me.

After a pleasant visit of ten days at Mrs Turner's, we left Matheran and came on to Khandalla. We made the descent of the hill in the early morning, and very beautiful it was. We started at half past six, by the sun, and reached the railway station at Narel at about 9.00 o'clock. Near the foot of Matheran Hill I saw a white shining crystal at the side of the path, and then I remembered having read that the rocks in the lower part of the hill were full of crystal and pretty stones. I stopped my bearers and got out of the *tonjon* and had a hunt for crystals, the pleasure of the search and the triumph of finding the stones carrying me away to our far-off happy days in the Isle of Wight, when dear Mamma provided us with geological hammers, and we children spent hours searching and hammering and splitting and smashing, and carried home at last, in triumph, an ammonite or a sea urchin or a fossil sponge. There are very pretty crystals to be found here, as well as at Matheran, but there are no fossils in these traprocks.

Cavalry lines, Poona, 31 May 1888

I did not stay very long at Khandalla, for my friends, Colonel and Mrs Willoughby, asked me to come home with them and spend a few days here, and I was very glad to accept their invitation — and here I am. It is very hot here; even those residents who pride themselves on the climate of Poona cannot deny that it is very trying just now. I do not myself remember ever to have felt heat so trying. The thermometer has marked as great a heat, perhaps even greater, at Khandalla sometimes, but then the heat lasts only a few hours in the middle of the day; the mornings and evenings are lovely. Here the heat seems overpowering by 8.00 o'clock in the morning. Cavalry lines are a mile or two outside Poona. Here the regiment (the Queen's Own Third Bombay Cavalry) is stationed. This house looks onto the drill ground, from which it is divided by a wide road with trees on each side that leads to Poona. The soldiers' houses, the school, the hospital and the ground where the horses are picketed form what are called the 'lines'. The horses have no stable of any kind; they are tethered to low posts in the ground, and there they have to stand through sunshine or rain. There are several camels belonging to the regiment; they are to have stables as they are more delicate than the horses and cannot stand rain. It is quite a new experience to me to be living among military people.

A young fellow was here yesterday with us, such a nice bright-faced boy; he does not look more than three or four and twenty. He talked of all the little daily topics and told us about their house, a little house he shares with some other young officers, and how some other 'fellows' had left their drawing-room empty because they could not agree as to the manner of furnishing, one wanting to make it 'aesthetic', another wishing to adorn the walls with saddles, guns and swords, the third proposing to make it into a smoking room. How easy and careless and happy life seemed to be to him. After he went away Marian told me that this very young officer had already obtained the Order of St Michael and St George for gallant conduct in his profession.

He was stationed near Aden when his regiment received orders to march to the relief of some Egyptian subjects who were shut up in Howrah, and kept there close prisoners by the Arabs. The regiment commanded by Colonel Hunter proceeded to Howrah, but young Peyton was sent on into the desert beyond Howrah with some Indian recruits to form an outpost. These new recruits were quite undisciplined; they had to be taught and drilled — and that was not all. Mr Peyton felt very doubtful as to whether they would stand by him in case of an attack. However, he did his best; he drilled them and taught them and, with their help, threw up a zareba (a defence formed of earthworks with hedges of prickly shrubs that are to be found in the desert). Here he ensconced himself and his men. At night the wild tribes of the Goulas came down from the hills and attacked him. His men stood firm and kept up a steady fire, and when they were within ten yards of them, the enemy turned and fled. When day came, Mr Peyton sallied out with his men and attacked the Goulas, killing many of their men and returning before nightfall to the zareba. For three days he held his little fort, the only European, with his wild recruits. Then he was recalled. Howrah had been relieved. The Egyptians had been rescued; not a shot had been fired and the short campaign was over.

At home, in the House of Commons, Sir James Fergusson spoke in warm praise of Colonel Hunter. Soon afterwards the colonel received, in due form, the Order of Companion of the Bath. A letter came also to the young subaltern from Lord Salisbury, informing him that 'Her Gracious Majesty the Queen was pleased to confer on him the Order of St Michael and St George, in consequence of his gallant behaviour in the late expedition.'

Another young officer I met who interested me, Mr Edwards, is also in the Third Bombay Cavalry. Colonel Willoughby spoke very highly of him. 'He is a splendid young fellow', said the colonel. 'When we were at Neemuch, there was a man running amok, he came on towards the lines with a loaded rifle, shooting at everyone he met. Edwards went out alone and met him and took him single-handed.' 'Running amok' is a well-known phrase in India. When a man has a sudden and peculiar attack of frenzy, caused sometimes by a sunstroke, sometimes by drinking, or sometimes by great emotion, he will start off, gun or knife in hand, and, rushing along the road or down the village street, attack everyone who comes in his way. Sometimes the man who is running amok, after having killed four or five persons 'and injured many others, will stop of his own accord and quietly give himself up. The frenzy, I suppose, is over, but his poor mind can hardly be happy if he is conscious of the harm he has done. A younger brother of Mr Edwards is living with him just now, though he does not belong to the regiment. He has come out to India hoping to find some employment.

He has applied for a post in the Burma Police Force, but does not know yet if he will get one. He has considerable talent for drawing, and has some idea of taking up painting as a profession.

Last Wednesday I went with Marian to see the school of the regiment. They had, as Marian told me, a much better building for the school at Neemuch; here they have to manage with a small schoolhouse which only just holds the number of pupils. The schoolmaster is an old Mussulman — Mahl Khan — a worthy old man, and keenly interested in his work. The outer room, into which you come straight from the road, was full of the little boys who were all learning to read or write in Hindustani. In the next and much larger room were the bigger boys. Some tall fellows must have been 16 or 17. In the first class there were only four pupils. There had been more, but as Mahl Khan told us rather sadly, one had enlisted, one had got employment at Neemuch, others had left for various reasons, and so he had only now a small class of head boys. Mahl Khan asked us what we should like to see first.

Some specimens of their writing were lying on the table, sentences in English and Hindustani. The writing, as usual in Indian schools, was excellent. Some boys had written the heading or title in green and red ink in ornamental letters; the effect was very pretty. There were various sentiments expressed, such as 'God bless our good colonel,' and 'Welcome to Colonel and Mrs Willoughby.' Mahl Khan said the boys would now read to us, which they did. It was English (*Little Arthur's History*) and they read easily and clearly, but in a harsh, monotonous, sustained tone, never dropping the voice. Marian says she tried once to teach them how to read differently, but her attempt was not successful; it seemed to perplex both the pupils and schoolmaster, and she gave it up.

The boys were asked by Mahl Khan to spell some of the more difficult words, and they did not make any mistakes as far as I remember. Then they wrote on their slates to my dictation. I did not read from any of their books, but just made a sentence or two, saying I had come to Poona and that I had often heard of the school. Most of the boys wrote it out correctly; only the words 'Colonel' and 'Willoughby' were too much for some of them. In most of the classes the boys learn poetry by heart, and we heard many poems said. One boy recited the 'Wreck of the Hesperus', and then another repeated a poem 'Little Jim', a sad story of a sick child who is dying. I never can stand pathetic tales like that, but still I would rather hear it told by a schoolboy, a white-faced English lad or brown-skinned Hindu who has learnt it simply as a lesson, than be obliged to hear it at some evening party or afternoon 'at home', recited by a would-be genius who shrieks and wails it at you, and when the tragedy is over smiles and bows and goes off with a flattering hostess to drink tea or eat ices.

The boys next showed us what they could do in arithmetic. As usual with Indian children they were very quick at this branch of their studies. Some boys worked out a difficult sum in proportion very rapidly. They seemed amused when I told them I could not have done it. Nor could I, by the proper rules, and in the time they did it. I might have made a rough calculation by a clumsy method of my own, perhaps. Next we had a little examination in geography. There were good large maps on the walls. One was taken down and hung over the blackboard. The boys were asked to point out various places. Marian and I put a few questions to the boys, but Mahl Khan seemed rather nervous whenever we did so, he was so anxious for his pupils to answer correctly. He evidently preferred that the questions should be the regular book questions that the boys were used to.

The children in the lower classes then went through their little exhibition. One little Hindu boy of six with a bright eager face is the son of Marian's *ayah*. The schoolmaster patted him on the shoulder saying, 'this is a very intelligent child.' In the lowest class the boys do not learn English; they learn to read and write in Hindustani. Though the boys are of two races, Hindu and Muhammadan, I did not see that they made use of more than the one vernacular language.

After all the children had finished their performances and as we were preparing to take leave, a tall Mussulman, black-bearded, white-coated and white-turbaned, walked into the school. He said something to Mahl Khan, whereupon the schoolmaster turned to us and asked us to stay a few minutes longer, for this man was anxious for us to hear him do his lessons. He was a *sowar*, one of the colonel's messengers and a pupil of Mahl Khan's. Of course we sat down again directly, and then this soldier read aloud a page from *Little Arthur's History*, and afterwards repeated a little poem. After that he seemed quite satisfied. Of course we expressed our pleasure in hearing him. I had taken my sketches to show the boys, and they and the schoolmaster and the *sowar* all seemed much interested, crowding around me and pointing out with exclamations of pleasure any objects in the drawings that were familiar to them.

At last we said 'Goodbye,' and came away, Mahl Khan giving the boys, at Marian's request, a half holiday. 'Only one thing I wish, Mahl Khan,' I said, as I shook hands with him, 'I wish you had a school for girls too.' That is the one drawback; the school is good and suitable to the needs of the pupils, but then one half of the soldiers' children is left out in the cold. The *ayah's* little boy is there in school, learning and enjoying his work, as his bright little mind grows day by day; his sister, two years older, is to stay at home — no learning for her, no reading or writing; nothing to be learnt beyond the task of an *ayah*, the extremely simple work allotted to an Indian maidservant. Still, though ignorant, she may be happy if her lot is like her mother's. The *ayah* is a good gentle faithful woman. Her husband died in the regiment, and ever since she and her children have been cared for by the kind colonel, and will be as long as he is stationed in India. No wretched fate of the Hindu widow is hers; safe in the colonel's house, *ayah* to his wife, she lives respected and unmolested.

Bella Vista, 21 June 1888

I am again very much behindhand with my diary. It is three weeks since I last wrote. I was staying then at Poona, with our friends Colonel and Mrs Willoughby. I left them on 1 June to come down here and meet John. His ship was expected on 2 June but it did not arrive until Sunday the 3rd. The four weeks had seemed a very long time.

I enjoyed my stay at Poona very much. The account of the school I gave in my last diary, but there was a good deal more that I saw that I thought was very interesting. One day the colonel arranged some 'tent-pegging' for me to see. I, in my ignorance, expected to see the whole tent put up and taken down. I did not know that tent-pegging was a feat of horsemanship and spearing only. Marian and I were invited to come out at 5.00 o'clock and see the tent-pegging, which was to be done by the Indian officers on the drill ground.

A number of soldiers were fixing some pegs in the ground, and at a little distance were six or eight of the Indian officers on their horses, waiting for the signal to be given. Two pegs only were driven into the ground at first. The colonel signed to an officer that the audience was ready. The officer gave the signal to the riders and two of the Indian officers dashed off; they came flying past us, urging on their horses with hand and spur and voice, their right hand holding the long lance. As they neared the pegs they bent down, their turbans almost touching the horse's neck, their right arms down lower. The lances touched the ground for a second, for a flash, and then were swung up in the same moment almost, high, high over the heads of the riders, riding upright now, dashing on, on, and there on the points of the lances were the wooden pegs, speared and carried. The officers pulled in their horses and cantered gently back again. New pegs were driven into the ground and two more officers galloped up to spear them. This time only one officer takes the peg. They ride again. Once I think both riders missed. But there was one officer who always speared his peg, a Mussulman — a fine looking fellow. But they were all fine looking, strong and warlike in appearance.

The head of the Indian officers, the Risaldar Major, who has just completed his 30 years' service, did not ride himself; he stood with us and explained everything. He will retire in a few months, much to Colonel Willoughby's regret. The colonel and Marian have a great esteem and liking for the old man — yet I must hardly call him 'an old man', he is only between 50 and 60. He began his soldier's life early. He has all sorts of honours, and a ring presented to him by the commander in chief for some special deed of gallantry. I must ask the colonel to give me the details when I go next to Poona.

Well, the tent-pegging went on. After two officers had ridden several times, four pegs were fixed in the ground and four officers rode to spear them. It was such a splendid sight — the fine men in their picturesque uniforms, the fine horses, the splendid action, the perfect union between man and horse, the rush, the colour, the excitement — it was an enjoyment to be there, spectator of it all. It is born in us English people, men and women too, the love of beautiful horses. When the tent-pegging was over, the Risaldar Major came up followed by a soldier carrying a tray — and on the tray were garlands of flowers and nosegays, and a silver vase full of rose water. The Risaldar Major took up a long wreath of pink roses and little white flowers, and hung it round Marian's neck, then he hung one round my neck, and did the same to Ellen and the same to the colonel. So then we were all adorned in the pretty Indian fashion. We thanked them all for the pleasure they had given us and said 'salaam' and walked away.

But we had not gone far when we were asked to come back again. The officer told the colonel that one of the soldiers wished to show us a feat of horsemanship, and so back we went and took our seats again. The soldier was mounted on a strong little native horse. He rode up, near to us, and threw down on the ground a red handkerchief. Then he rode away to some distance. The officers and men who had begun to stroll about over the drill ground fell back again into a little crowd of spectators. The soldier came galloping up on his active little steed, leant over as he neared the handkerchief, hung down, and made a snatch at it, but missed, recovered his position and galloped on. I was so sorry for him that he had missed it. However, he rode back directly to the starting point and tried again. Then he came, head hanging downwards on his horse's side, he stretched out his hand, clutched the handkerchief, struggled back to his proper position, and waved the handkerchief triumphantly as he dashed on. Then he performed another feat. He rode along at a good pace, clinging to the horse's side. How he managed to hold on I do not know — he looked as if he were glued by invisible glue to the side of his horse. It looked to us very dangerous, and even the colonel was glad when the ride was over and the soldier safe. The riding reminded me of the wonderful riding I saw last year at the exhibition in London of Buffalo Bill and the Wild West.

This same evening the colonel took us round 'the lines' — I was very glad to see the camp, or rather the settlement of a cavalry regiment. It is very interesting to see all the arrangements. The lines were larger, the colonel said, at Neemuch, and the accommodation for the men better. He is doing all he can to improve the little houses — some he is pulling down, in order to give others more air and light, and other ones are to be rebuilt. The word 'lines' describes what the form of the camp is. There are, as it were, little streets of huts built in parallel lines, with a space in front of the huts where the horses are tethered. Also in straight rows, trees have been planted along the 'lines' and so the horses were generally in the shade. About 600 horses were picketed on the 'lines'. They had just had their evening feed — some were still eating. They looked very comfortable and well groomed. It is rather presumptuous of me to criticize horses that are under the colonel's care. Of course they are splendidly managed. I recognized several of the horses that we had just seen tearing madly along in the tent-pegging. They were shorn of their splendid riders and fine harness and saddles now. The colonel seemed surprised that I knew them. I suppose the habit of drawing, and especially of drawing animals, makes one notice quickly what is characteristic in their appearance. The horses are tethered by the hind legs, and then a loose rope is tied round their head to a tree or a post near them. They have to stand out there in all seasons and in all kinds of weather. Only a sick horse is under shelter when it is sent to the hospital. The soldiers' huts are just 'mud hovels' as the colonel said, and the Indian officers' little houses are not much better. These cavalry lines were built many years ago. The colonel knew them in 1871 when he was a junior officer and was quartered there with his regiment — the very same that he now commands. It is a curious change, as he says, to come back after so many years to the old place.

12
July–November
*Visit to Hyderabad, Golconda, schools for girls,
a Muhammadan breakfast, paper chase,
Khandalla again and alarm from a
panther, Hindu 'punja' and
a mad musician*

Friday 28 July 1888 (In the train between Wadia and Hyderabad)

I AM on my way to Hyderabad and Ellen is with me. We are really to
see a great native state and really to live for a week in a city where it
is not safe for you to go about without an escort. We left Poona last
night taking the *chobdar* with us. If the *chobdar* had his scarlet and
gold gown, a decided air of the *sirkar* (government), it would give a
dignity and impressiveness to our appearance, but 'though in pleasure
he had a frugal mind,' and has arrayed himself in a black tunic — and
instead of looking like a *chobdar* of the High Court, he might be
anybody.

The colonel and Marian kindly came to the station and saw us off.
We left Poona at 8.00 o'clock. It was a dark day and the sky was
covered with clouds. This train is the mail train, but it takes its time
over the journey, stopping about every half hour on an average all
through the night, lingering ten minutes here and a quarter of an hour
there. We have the ladies carriage to ourselves and last night we settled
ourselves to sleep in true Indian fashion, with pillows and shawls, and
in the morning having a nice refreshing bath in the little bathroom
attached to our compartment. We have made no night journey on the
continent so comfortably. This morning early, at 4.00 o'clock, we had
moonlight, but the moon is on the wane and the light did not show us

199

the country very distinctly. Before 6.00 o'clock we had daylight, and then we saw we had come into a different land from that we had left.

The houses with brown sloping roofs and wide verandas of Bombay and Poona had all disappeared, so too had the Hindu temples. We were within 20 or 30 miles of the native territory. Everything had changed; the houses were flat roofed and whitewashed, or painted pale blue, and one we saw on a little bit of rising ground with a flagstaff on the top was so like our neighbour's house at Ramleh that it took us straight back to Egypt. Then we passed some old mosques in the distance, and close by an old gate with an archway that distinctly showed it was Muhammadan. I tried to sketch one or two of the passing sights. They are very hasty sketches — just to give some idea to the children and those at home.

Another change came directly we had left Wadia (the frontier station between the Bombay presidency and the Nizam's territory) and that was that the men we saw at the stations and walking along the roads carried arms. A fine looking man has just stopped close to us to drink some water and in his belt is a revolver. We are at a station now. The country is much prettier here than it was half an hour ago. It is more wooded and we noticed some very fine trees — mangoes and tama-rinds.

For a good many miles we went through a barren desolate country; the ground, where there was any earth, was strewn with stones. In other parts it was nothing but bare rocks. In one place, huge grey boulders lay tumbled together in a great mass — rather like a herd of elephants asleep, I thought. In another part we saw great excavations in the rocks. Perhaps there had once been tanks there — as long ago even as the great Akbar's time. It looked like massive stonework built against the rock, but we could not tell, seeing it only from the train, whether it was really man's work or only a curious formation of the rock that gave the appearance of regular layers of stone. All round were rough quarries, and the whole ground, far and near, seemed to bring forth nothing but stones. People in the Stone Age might have lived and flourished there. After two hours more in the train we are still passing through a rocky country, but it is really wooded now and the grey boulders showing through make me think of Fontainebleau.

At Wadia, when we had breakfast, a gentleman came in whose face I knew. It was Mr Inverarity, the leading counsel for Abdul Huq. He is on his way to Hyderabad. But I did not allude to the business that took him there, for John tells me in his last letter that Abdul Huq may be a litigant in his court and that I am not to give any opinion about the matter.

The monsoon has only reached this part lately and the bright green grass is just springing up over everything. We have passed a great many cattle grazing on the new grass; they look very thin, poor things. I am afraid they went through a bad time before the rains came. We have just been passing through a beautiful forest, with a valley and small river below us. The trees were most luxuriant — the fig trees with their magnificent great leaves are all in bloom, and mimosas with their tiny fluffy flowers have been sending a delicious scent into the train.

In one little glade I saw a beautiful wild peacock. It took our noisy approach very calmly. This train is a train after my own heart. It goes comfortably along at about 15 to 20 miles an hour and you can see all the country and enjoy all the sights, with the additional comfort that your life and limbs are not in imminent danger, as it seems to me they are when we tear along in our English express at 40 or 50 miles an hour.

30 July 1888 (The Residency, Hyderabad)
We have been here nearly three days — Ellen and I — but I have not until now had any time for writing up my diary. I have just managed to get my daily letter to John written, and a few letters for the English mail to the children and home. There is much to see here, so much to write about, so many things to draw that I do not know how to get everything done.

We arrived punctually at Hyderabad station yesterday at 4.00 o'clock. A carriage was waiting for us. Leaving the *chobdar* to look after the luggage, Ellen and I got into the carriage and drove off. We passed some old Muhammadan burial places quite near to the station (they had an old, bygone, forlorn, deserted look), and then the houses here and there (white and flat-roofed), and then we came to a little street of shops, the Residency Bazaar, as it is called. The houses are small but picturesque, and very like the shops in Alexandria. Some fine trees hung over the street, giving a pleasant shade. Then we came to two wide crossroads and, at the angle, the great gateway of the Residency. Over the gate are the arms of the East India Company, but I did not notice that as we drove through. I thought they were the Royal Arms of England. We drove up, through a large compound with green turf and large spreading trees and shrubs and creepers, and then the road turned, and we came into full view of the house.

The coachman drove us up so quickly, I could only just see that the Residency was very grand, as I had heard it was, and that there were great white columns, and a painted frieze, and a wide flight of steps in front of us. And then we were mounting the steps and men in white and scarlet were bowing and salaaming and another man, all in scarlet, was conducting us into the house. We were taken into the great drawing-room, but before I had time to look or wonder Mr Howell came in and gave us a kind welcome. Mrs Howell had been out hunting that morning with the son who had arrived the day before. He is on leave from his Gurkha regiment.

Mr Howell told us that this great hall was always used for *durbars* and other important ceremonies. On the walls hung the colours of various regiments of the Indian Contingent — some so torn that you wonder the tattered silk still holds to the staff. The furniture is a queer mixture of old magnificence and modern paltriness. The red velvet chairs with massive gold arms and legs look fit for the Nizam himself to sit upon. These chairs came from George IV's pavilion at Brighton. The *punkahs*, black and gold hanging on black and gold cords, the columns with gold cornices, and the painted vaulted roof are all in keeping with the historical associations of the place, and the importance of the Residency where the envoy from the great East India Company lived. Below us in stone vaults guarded night and day by sentries is kept 'the treasures of the Berars' — the tribute paid to the British government by the Nizam and out of which the expenses of the Hyderabad contingent are defrayed.

That first day I did not see much of the house; our own rooms are on the first floor, up a long flight of stone stairs, 43 steps we go up every time. Ellen and I are quite by ourselves in the central part of the house. Mr and Mrs Howell are away in a new wing; their son and a friend of his on another wing. From the gallery outside my room I can look down into the drawing-rooms. Below, in front of the house, two sentries pace up and down all day and night. At each gate there are other sentries. There is a system of signals on the roof of the house — semaphores — by which, Mr Howell says, the troops at Secunderabad, four miles away, could be summoned in case of need. In the old company's time riots were frequent and there was no electric telegraph then. It was supposed that the Household Guard could protect the Residency for a short time until assistance could arrive.

On Friday afternoon Mrs Howell took me out for a drive. We went through a suburb in the city and out to Secunderabad. The country was very pretty, undulating, with fine trees standing alone or in groves, and the rocks, as I had seen them from the train, lying tumbled together in wonderful groups. We passed several mosques, some in ruins, but very few habitations of any kind. Secunderabad is, as I have said, four miles from here. The English troops are quartered there and it is under British jurisdiction. There are some fine modern buildings belonging to the regiments and very pretty gardens, and a very palatial shop belonging to one of our Bombay firms, where you can buy anything from a reel of cotton to a statue or a horse's saddle. On our way home we went into some very beautiful gardens — the public gardens of Hyderabad. They are on the other side of the city to the fashionable quarter of the town and very few people, Mrs Howell said, seem to go to the gardens.

The next day, Saturday, I began a sketch of the house. Mrs Howell took me round the grounds and showed me the various views. Enclosed in high walls is an old-fashioned garden called the Rang Mahal. It used to belong to a house that was built, long ago, for the wife of the resident. She was a Muhammadan lady, and her husband built her a private house and garden. The house is pulled down now, and the garden is added to the Residency.

1 August 1888

Sunday is mail day here. Letters for England have to be posted on Sunday night or early Monday morning. In the early morning we went to church. There is an English church, St George's. It was a nice service with very fair singing. A choir of boys has been formed lately. The clergyman, Mr Fitzpatrick, comes from one of the missionary societies. He is very earnest and is doing much good among the poor English and Eurasians in Hyderabad. There was Communion, and I stayed for it. After the communicants had left the altar, and the clergyman had begun the 'Lord's Prayer', a poor native woman went up to the altar rails — and then hesitated and turned away. She had been waiting for the others to go first, and had not noticed when the time came for her to go up. I wondered what the clergyman would do, and was very glad when he stopped and signed to her to come forward, and then administered to her the Holy Communion. After the service, as we came out, I stopped and spoke a word to her.

That afternoon we drove out into the country to see the fort of Golconda. The very name is romance, and it seemed quite unreal to be going there. However, that is the real name — and I read it in a history of Hyderabad. We drove through a part of the city, though it was not the shortest way to Golconda, but Mrs Howell knew I should like to see the city, the native town. We went through some streets that reminded me of Cairo and Alexandria — all the houses whitewashed, or painted some light colour, and all flat-roofed. There were more balconies with little roofs over them to keep off the sun than we have in Alexandria, and there was not the fine woodwork we have in Cairo.

In one street there was a little crowd gathered before a house. Indian music and singing were going on and we heard strange cries. Some women were standing together with *chatties* (jars) on their heads, three or four of them, one above another. They seemed to be common earthenware *chatties*, and they were painted in gay colours, spotted all over in red, blue and yellow. There were some flowers and leaves round the brim of each jar, and in the mouth of the top jar of each pile there was a little fire burning. Even in the bright daylight we saw the flames. Near the women some black sheep were standing, held by some boys. We wondered what it was. 'Is that a wedding?' I asked. 'Smallpox,' said Mr Forbes, who knows the city better than the rest of us. 'They are sacrificing to the goddess of smallpox.' Smallpox, we knew, was rife in the city, and cholera too. I am afraid those poor sheep were to be sacrificed, but I did not think of that at the time.

We went on now through streets less thickly peopled, more open, more trees and peeps of country seen between the houses. We passed some mosques with pretty carving and delicate elegant patterns traced in their white walls. It is only stucco, not real stone, I was told; but I thought it very pretty all the same. 'You should see Agra and Delhi and places in the north; there all the carving is in marble. This place will not do after them.' 'Well, I have not seen Agra and all those places and I think these buildings here are beautiful.' I would give them my admiration and I maintain that the Mussulman architecture here, and in Egypt, is beautiful, however the carving may be done and however fragile and crumbling the material may be.

At last, after an hour's drive, we came in sight of the great fortress. It stands on a huge rock rising up out of the plain. Rain was beginning to fall as we drove up and the sky was dark and lowering. The trees that grow all round the base, and some high up on the rock, looked darker than any Indian trees usually do. It all seemed in keeping with the place — the mighty fort that has been the stronghold of generations of great rulers — sometimes Muhammadans, sometimes Marathas. We went up a sloping narrow road and in at the great gate. The doors were made of wood, very thick and studded all over with sharp pieces of iron. They might be spearheads — they were so large. They were to defend the gate — to prevent its being battered in by elephants. We got out of the brake here and began our climb. As we mounted higher and higher, the view became wider and grander and, easing out from among the trees, we saw more of the castle.

'Look at that pretty tank,' exclaimed one of the party, who was in front of us, pointing over the wall. We all hastened to the wall and looked over. There was a deep pool, or tank, among the rocks some 20 feet below — trees waving over it and creeping plants and grasses. 'Here are cool mosses deep, and through the moss the ivy creeps, and in the stream the long leaved flowers weep.' Excepting for the word 'ivy', these words of Tennyson's describe the little pool. Some women were down there by the tank, stooping over the edge, and others were kneeling or sitting on the grass, busy with something. 'Are they getting water?' I asked. 'It is a sacrifice, a horrid sacrifice,' cried out Mrs Howell. As she spoke I saw plainly the leg of some animal — a goat, I think, and the poor limb was decked out with a coloured handkerchief. The poor dead creature. That is what the women were busy about. We turned away, sickened at the sight. Its pain is over now poor thing! Is there another life for it to live again and be happy? Somehow I trust it will be made right.

We went on our way again, climbing up while the rain came falling down faster and thicker. Mr Howell hurried on and found a shelter for us in a little temple in the rock. We were quite protected there from the rain and we watched the storm approaching from the west, and hiding all the country as it swept over it. Away in the east we could see a stretch of sunshine lighting up the great new palace of the Nizam. After waiting 20 minutes or more, the rain slackened and we went on and climbed to the very top of the fortress.

The walls of many rooms are standing and in several the ceilings are there too. It was a palace as well as a fortress. In old times the rulers lived at Golconda; Hyderabad was the garden house, only the pleasure grounds. The walls were strongly built — beams of wood formed the tops of doorways and on these beams were built up walls of stone again. The stones were rough blocks some two feet thick, and in some cases were projecting so that it seemed as if the next high wind might send them toppling down. No mortar seemed to have been used anywhere. I was rather glad to come out of these rooms with their broken doorways and ceilings. On the very top of the fort was a smooth little terrace paved with stone and surrounded by a low battlement. I made a hasty pencil sketch from there of a bit of the fortress and the country beyond, and some mosques far below in the plain. But it was too much of a bird's eye view to be very pretty.

It was growing dark. I finished, and Mrs Howell said we should be going. So down we went. The little narrow staircase was not pleasant to descend in the dark. I steadied myself by keeping my hands against the walls, like chimney sweepers did in England in old times. Then on through the ruined halls with their tumble-down ceilings and out into the fresh air. Then down, down, down the steep path and the steps — slippery from centuries of passing feet. Some steps were so steep, and I was so tired and my knees so shaky I was afraid of falling. We were all down, at last, and very glad I was to find myself at the gate again. We mounted the brake and drove away. Our last sight of Golconda was the pale light of the sunset that was just showing through a break in the clouds.

2 August 1888

On Monday I had a good morning's painting at my sketch of the Residency. The sun was shining and the house looked very pretty. I was out by 7.30 and painted till 10.30. Breakfast is at 11.00 and dinner at 8.15, but sinking nature is revived by tea and bread and butter at 4.00 o'clock.

I made a sketch of Auberon Howell's servant, a Gurkha from his regiment; he is a curious looking fellow, quite unlike any Indian that I have seen. His face is like a Malay, with its yellow skin and slanting eyes; he is not more than five feet high. The Gurkhas are all small, but they are the bravest of the brave. A little Gurkha will attack anyone, the tallest Rajput or the fiercest Sikh, no matter, and the little Gurkha is the victor. Like some dogs, they seem born with the instinct of fighting; to see anyone not belonging to them or to their regiment is to attack them. They always go armed, their favourite knife is long and curved — a *kukri* it is called. One or two smaller knives are generally in their belt as well, handy for use. They wear a funny little cap on their head, stuck on one side like an English private wears his cap, and it gives them a knowing, swaggering look.

In the afternoon there was a meeting of a school committee at the Residency. A school for girls had been lately established in Hyderabad by the *nawab*, Umed-ud-Dowlah (Syed Hussein), and Mrs Howell takes a great interest in it. The committee met to decide upon a second mistress. We arranged with Syed Hussein for me to visit the school the next day. Yesterday Syed Hussein came to breakfast, and afterwards he took me to see the school. Mrs Gilchrist met us. Mrs Gilchrist is the wife of Major Gilchrist, who is at the head of the Bodyguard; she is one of the few English ladies living in Hyderabad itself. Their house is close to the Residency. We had only half a mile to drive, for the school is in Chuddargath, quite a way from the city.

The house is large and very airy, and stands in a large compound, which is enclosed by a high wall. It could not be better for purdah girls. There is a wide veranda to the house; the roof is supported by large white columns. All the houses inhabited by the English, and many of those belonging to Indians, have these white columns on the outside; they are quite a feature in modern Hyderabad architecture. Besides the high garden wall and the deep veranda, the house was further secluded by the trees, which were very fine and numerous. The *nawab*, of course, could not enter the compound, so we left him outside sitting in the carriage, and walked across the compound to the house.

Mrs Littledale, the headmistress, met us on the veranda. This lady is a Hindu married to an Englishman. She took us into a classroom where the elder girls were working. There were two daughters of Syed Hussein and a niece, and I think one other girl. Two of them read aloud, very nicely, but in a low timid voice. Mrs Littledale's own child came into the room and read with them; she was much younger than the others, about eight years old, but she read much better than they did, in a clear strong voice. It is the difference of training, and the English blood in her too, perhaps. Then we saw some younger children, they were learning Persian with a native teacher, a woman of course. There are at present only 11 pupils, but the school has not been opened long and it must inevitably be a slow business to get people to send their daughters. Mrs Littledale told us that some parents said it was too far to send their children to Chuddargath, and they could not afford to keep a carriage on purpose for the children's use. Mrs Howell thinks that the committee might arrange to keep a large carriage drawn by bullocks (of course a closed carriage) and send it every day to fetch the pupils. There was not much furniture in the rooms, but what there was was quite English in fashion. The girls sat on benches and not on the ground.

We did not stay very long, as Syed Hussein was waiting for us. He proposed that we should go on to see a Hindu school that was started about two years ago in Hyderabad. I had heard about the school from Mr Croby and I was very glad to see it. We drove on into a part of the town where the streets were narrow and crooked; we had to leave the carriage and go on foot. I had not thought of the possibility of this and had only a straw bonnet on my head, and the sun was very hot. However, we had not far to go, and soon we saw a gentleman at the entrance of a house looking out for us. We went up a few steps and through a doorway, and then we found ourselves in a large room or hall. It looked into a courtyard and on that side it was quite open; there was no wall; it was very fresh and pleasant and yet it was secluded.

There were three classes going on. The mistress is a Madrassee, a Christian; she had a very pleasing countenance and seemed to be very earnest in her work. She has several assistants; some of the teachers are men. We heard a class of elder girls sing; the teacher, a Brahmin, accompanied them on the violin. They sang a native song in Telugu; it was in praise of some goddess. It seemed rather an anomaly with a Christian schoolmistress. The singing was plaintive and pretty. Then some of the younger children sang a song in English to a native tune. They did not understand English, but they pronounced the words very fairly, and they had been told what the sense of the words was. In another part of the room there was a class of Muhammadan girls at work. They were studying Persian; it was a religious book they were reading with the professor, a book describing the various religious ceremonies and giving directions for public and private devotion. I noticed that several of the girls, although they were Muhammadans, had rings in their noses. I suppose they were already married, but it is a Hindu custom and must have been adopted from the Hindus in Hyderabad. All the pupils were not at school, it being a holiday that day. Those who were there (some 60 or 70) had been brought when the mistress heard of our intended visit. I said I was sorry the children had lost their holiday. 'They are very happy to come,' said Syed Hussein, 'they are very much pleased at your visit.' Perhaps some of the gay costumes and pretty jewels the girls wore were put on in honour of us.

This school was established about two years ago by a Hindu gentleman in the civil service. He was much impressed by the need of education for women in Hyderabad, there being absolutely no school whatever for girls, unless indeed a little ragged school started by Mr Fitzpatrick, the missionary, can be counted. He hired a room and asked some of his friends to help him. They were all engaged like himself during the day, from 10.00 to 5.00, but they gave their time before and after office hours to the school. They taught the children themselves until the school became known and more came in, when they took the present house, and engaged a headmistress and a staff of teachers. A school in which some men are teachers cannot of course supply education for *purdah* girls. The Muhammadan children leave when they reach the age of 12 or 13 and have to go into seclusion. The headmistress grieved over the necessity of losing her girls, some of them very promising, directly they reached an age when they are beginning to understand the value of education.

However, the school founded by Syed Hussein that we had just seen now affords the education for girls who are in purdah, or who, though Hindus, are so high in caste that their parents object to their attending an ordinary school. We saw some needlework done by the girls, plain work and also embroidery. It was very good considering that some of them had only learnt a short time. The writing was good as usual. Dexterity of hand, whether in writing, drawing, needlework or anything else, seems to be a power inborn in Indian children. Only the most advanced pupils learn English. The books, as far as I saw, seemed to be the same as those in use in our schools, i.e. in British India. We had a very pleasant visit and came away feeling great interest in the work going on, and a hearty respect for the founder and his little band of friends who had come forward to help womankind in Hyderabad. As we said goodbye, a tiny child came up, the youngest girl present, and shyly gave us each a little nosegay. I hope I shall see that school again and that pleasant-faced mistress.

3 August 1888

Yesterday morning it was bright and sunshiny and I was able to get on well with my sketch of the house. While I was painting I saw a carriage arrive, and a stout gentleman was presently ascending the steps, followed by a servant. The gentleman had a frock coat (what we call in Egypt a Stamboulina coat), a fez on his head, bright lilac silk trousers and a scarf round his shoulders. I wondered what he was, whether he was a Muhammadan or a Hindu. The stout gentleman disappeared in the direction of Mr Howell's office and it was a long time before he appeared again. Mr Howell told me afterwards about the visit.

This gentleman was an emissary from one of the grandest Hindu nobles in Hyderabad. With many salaams and polite speeches to the Resident he opened the interview. The object of his visit was twofold. He informed Mr Howell that his master was much troubled by the action of Her Majesty's Government in the matter of sacrifices in Hyderabad, that through the influence of the Resident, the Nizam had forbidden the offering up of sacrifices in the open streets. His master was much annoyed at not being able to have the customary sacrifices for cholera performed; that is, an animal (sheep, goat or bullock) bitten to death in the street by people. The second object of his mission was to beg Mr Howell to obtain for his master, through Lord Dufferin, a title from Her Majesty the Queen Empress, the title of KCSI. Mr Howell assured the emissary, gravely, that cholera would not be got rid of, nor any patients cured by animals being bitten to death; that if his master would give his people good water to drink, cholera would disappear.

But, (said Mr Howell,) if your master will write a letter to me asking me to obtain Lord Dufferin's consent to animals being bitten to death in the streets, and also requesting that Lord Dufferin should recommend Her Majesty's Government to confer on him the honour of a KCSI, I will forward the letter to Lord Dufferin, and you will see what the answer will be.

'Oh no,' said the alarmed ambassador, 'my master does not desire that at all,' and he fled, to carry to his master the result of his mission.

This morning we went to breakfast with an Indian lady, a half sister of Salar Jung's. Mrs Howell and I, and several other English ladies were invited, but no Muhammadan ladies, as our hostess's own brother, Nawab Munir-ool-Moolk, was to be present, and that of course would prevent any ladies excepting his near relations being present also. I did not learn the name of our hostess, her own name, I mean. She is the wife of the Nawab Muhktarool Moolk, who is out of his mind and is in an asylum. She has no children, but a little niece who lives with her.

The house was a fine building, almost a palace, the veranda supported by tall white columns with pretty capitals. There was a centre courtyard, the house being built all round it, and in this courtyard there was a fountain and some plants in pots. We were taken first into a large drawing-room furnished in the half-English style that all the Indians of rank seem to adopt; in this room there were sofas and chairs and carpets, rather gaudy in colouring, ornaments not in very good taste, and pictures on the walls, only a few of which were tolerable. The best were portraits of former Residents and some of the Salar Jung family. There was a very bad portrait of the Princess of Wales, a wretched print that one would expect to see in a very common lodging house in England. We were told that it had been sent to the family as a present by the princess herself. I hope that there had been some mistake. On one table there was a beautiful old French clock, at least 100 years old I should think from the style; it still kept good time, they told us.

Our hostess took us through the drawing-room on to the veranda where breakfast was prepared. The floor was carpeted with a soft, thick, white cloth, pleasant to sit on and very clean to look at. The table was only about a foot above the floor. The guests were invited to sit down. So down we sat, and I was proceeding to double up my feet under me as the best means of sitting close to the table, when an old *ayah* on the opposite side of the table came up to me and motioned to me to stretch my feet out under the table; '*bahut lumba*,' (very far) she said, and was not content till I had done as she told me.

The breakfast was quite Muhammadan as far as the food went, but knives and forks had been put on the table for our use. I could not eat very much, though I did my best; the dishes are so rich and sweet, or else so very hot. Our hostess had her little niece, Kareem Begum, a

211

child of five years old. Little Kareem ate everything that her aunt did with her fingers. Opposite the *begum* sat an old woman who, we guessed, was a sort of housekeeper or head of the women servants. She was evidently privileged to sit at table and eat at the same time as her mistress. She seemed to enjoy her meal thoroughly, helping herself to all the dishes she fancied, and laughing at everything that was said that amused her. The Nawab Munir-ool-Moolk was not able to be with us; the Nizam had sent for him unexpectedly that morning. At the end of breakfast finger glasses were brought to us; quite English glasses. I think the silver basin and gold embroidered towel handed to us in Cairo at the Princess Inge Hanam's were prettier.

We returned to the drawing-room for a little while before leaving, and I made a hasty sketch of little Kareem Begum. One of the English ladies asked the *begum* if she had any children of her own. I was sorry she asked the question, as I know how painful it is to an Indian lady to answer 'no' to such a question. I wondered that anyone who had lived many years in India should make such an enquiry. I should like to have drawn the *begum*, but when Mrs Howell suggested my doing so, the *begum* demurred, saying she was afraid some gentleman might see it, so of course we did not press it.

In the afternoon some elephants were sent to the Residency for me to draw. They belonged to the Nizam, but their trappings were not magnificent. They had scarlet woollen cloths on their backs, edged with dark green and gold fringe that hung down within a foot or two of the ground. Their *howdahs* were green, gilt in some parts, and surmounted with an ugly hood and footboard, quite European, added lately to the *howdahs*. A common, short wooden ladder hung at their side, fastened by ordinary ropes. The men with them, the *mahouts* and *peons*, were picturesque, but not very different to our *saises* and *peons* in Bombay. The elephant is more difficult to draw than the camel; the form is not so distinct and clearly defined, and it is a much more fidgety animal. It is said that an elephant in health is never still; if it stands motionless it is not well.

That evening a gentleman from Secunderabad dined with us, Colonel Alexander. He once made a voyage with John from Egypt to Bombay, he told me. He stayed all night at the Residency in order to go with us the next morning to the Mir Ali tank, a piece of water some seven miles from Hyderabad. Syed Hussein had planned to take us there, thinking I should like to see something of the country round Hyderabad. We were to start at seven in the morning. Mrs Howell had invited some friends to go with us, but some of them failed to appear and we were a smaller party than our host had expected. Colonel Alexander himself arrived punctually at 7.00 o'clock, bringing three carriages with him. Mr Howell could not go with us, but his son came.

We drove through the city instead of by the suburbs, the *nawab* kindly arranging it so to please me. As we crossed the bridge over the river we saw several elephants going along the bank. It was a common enough sight to my companions, but strange and romantic to me to see the huge creatures walking about, children playing on the rocks without so much as looking up at them, people passing them as indifferently as we do a carthorse at home. We soon left the city, and drove through the same kind of country as we had done the Sunday before in going to Golconda, pretty undulating ground with the grey rock showing through in great boulders, then flat marshy rice fields, then gardens and a mosque or two, and wilder and more barren land — but always a good road. At last we came down a hill and were within sight of the Mir Ali tank.

It is a large sheet of water, at least I thought it large, partly natural and partly made by a great wall that dams up the water. This *bund* (as such a wall is called in India) was built by an Italian engineer, and is a very massive construction. The great buttresses — I mean the projecting parts of the walls that break the force of the current — are round in form, which seemed to me peculiar; at least I never saw a bridge or wall built like that before. On the bank we saw some tents, and when we alighted from the carriages we found that, in one, *chota hazri* (early breakfast) was prepared for us, sent out by one of the *nawab*s. We sat down for a few minutes and some of our party managed to make a second breakfast.

The lake was very low, for the monsoon was late in reaching Hyderabad, and we had to row out in a little boat to the steamer that was lying off the shore for us. Mrs Howell, Mrs Tytler, Mr Forbes and I got into the boat with two boatmen who looked much more like coolies than sailors. They could not get the boat off for some time; we were fast aground. At last one man got up and stood in the water and pushed and shoved, and the other rowed or punted and we were off. After rowing some five minutes we found we were farther away from the steamer than when we started. However, they managed somehow, by making a circuit, to get us away from the shore and the current, and we got to the steamer at last. Then our boat went back to fetch the gentlemen who had walked along the *bund* to meet it at a nearer point.

It was a queer little steamer and a queer little voyage that we made. The captain, who was an Englishman, told us that the tank was so low that we could not go to some of the prettiest parts; in fact we had to go where we could. Syed Hussein wanted to show me the best view of the mosque on the opposite shore, and we did at last get into a position from which I could sketch it. But the little steamer *would not* keep still, but swung round and round till Mrs Howell declared she felt very ill, and just as if she was on a P & O boat, and that she would never go home to England any more! Of course she was in fun, but still I could not keep everyone swaying about in the lake for me, and so, when I had made a hasty pencil sketch, we went on to see the rest of the tank — as much as the captain could show us.

It was all very pretty; sloping banks covered with a great variety of trees, from the dark grand mango to the elegant feathery tamarind and graceful palm; the great boulders lying about as if some giant must have thrown them there one upon the top of the other; and, in front of all, the clear water of the tank — always clear I should think, for the current is very strong, setting towards the *bund*. After an hour's voyage we returned to the shore, but this time the rowing boat came quickly to the bank, carried by the current.

In the tent there was a grand breakfast prepared for us. I was sorry some of the guests had failed; there were several empty places. After breakfast we had just time to walk to the *bund* and go a little way along the thick wall. It made one feel rather giddy, as it was not more than four or five feet wide, excepting where the buttresses projected. On the land side the ground was marshy, in some parts quite under water, and some men were ploughing in the thick black mud with buffaloes. There were women working too, standing up to their knees in water, but they looked healthy, I was glad to see. They were preparing the ground for rice, probably. As we came back to the tents, we passed a gay little covered cart, blue and yellow, with a red curtain hanging out of the window. It looked very pretty. The little brown pony was tethered near, and a boy was sitting on a rock in the shade of a great pipal tree (the sacred tree). I drew the scene very hastily as the others were lingering a few minutes behind, but I do not know if I can make anything of my sketch. We had a pleasant drive home, going this time the shortest way, as the sun was hot. In the afternoon I had the elephants again to draw.

6 August

Last Friday I went to see the hospital that is under the direction of the English doctor, Dr Lowry. There is a lady doctor there also, Miss White, and I wanted to see her wards. Ellen came with me and we arrived at the hospital at about 8.00 o'clock. The hospital is a long low building running round a large courtyard. Only at the entrance, I think, there was a second storey, where the house surgeon lives. We drove under a gateway, or rather a gatehouse, into a courtyard, and there a man appeared, one of the hospital servants apparently, who took my card and went in search of Miss White. A narrow veranda runs round the hospital, the floor of which (as well as the floor of the hospital) is raised some two or three feet above the ground. Soon Miss White came out of one of the many doors opening onto the terrace, and we left the carriage and went to meet her. She proposed to show us her side of the hospital first.

One part is kept entirely for Muhammadan women and any high caste Hindus who wish to be in purdah also. After our Cama Hospital in Bombay, the accommodation appeared rough, but the doctors are hoping to get a new hospital built before very long. Miss White would like to have a separate building for the women's hospital, but I do not know if that will be achieved at present. We went first into a small ward for one patient. There was a long row of little rooms all alike. Miss White said that the women much prefer these private wards, although they are not as airy or convenient as the large ones. From the veranda a door opens into a small narrow room, with stone floor and bare walls; one bedstead of the commonest description, just four legs and a frame. There may have been a chair, certainly nothing else besides the bed, but I do not think there was even a chair. At the further end of this room there was a door that opened into a small bathroom, the doorway serving as a window to light this room. A door from the bathroom opened onto a narrow back veranda, a small portion of which, immediately adjoining the bathroom, was allotted to the patient as a place where her friends could cook her food and wash the few pots and pans. In the case of Brahmin women, it is very important that there should be provision for the food being cooked by a relation, or at least by a Brahmin cook. Light and air into these little wards were admitted only through the doorway, as far as I remember, and I think I am right.

One poor woman we saw had had a very bad attack of smallpox. Her poor bare feet were one mass of pock marks. It was only two months since she had been ill, but all fear of infection must have been over or Miss White would not have taken us to see her. In another ward a poor woman was lying on the bed with a dear little brown baby by her side. In one of the large wards, where there were several women and children, I noticed a family all sitting together on a bed. They were eating some stuff that looked like curry and were evidently enjoying their breakfast very much. They were very poor people and were thankful to have the food of the hospital.

Dr Chemeretta, the house surgeon, joined us now and showed me his part of the hospital, the general wards, and the operating room and dispensary. There were only a few private wards on his side of the hospital. Besides the men patients, women of low caste or no caste go into the women's ward on his side. One poor woman had just undergone an operation, and was recovering, but we did not see her; we did not hear about her till just as we were coming away. She had her nose cut off by her husband (a common crime in India, as I have said before). Dr Lowry had made the nose grow again, to a certain extent, by taking some skin from the woman's forehead. She will be disfigured no doubt, but not as repulsive looking as she would have been but for Dr Lowry's help. 'That poor family you saw eating their breakfast,' said Dr Chemeretta, 'were nearly starving when they came in. The very poor natives are thankful to come into the hospital to get the food. Dr Lowry calls it the poor house.'

8 August 1888 (In the train)

I am writing up my diary in the train. We saw so very much that was interesting during the last few days in Hyderabad, that it was impossible to describe everything as the events occurred.

Last Saturday Mrs Howell, her son, and Mr Forbes and I drove over to Bolarum to spend the day there, and see a paper chase in which Mrs Howell and her son were to take part. It was a long drive, but a pleasant one through open country. Bolarum is 100 or 200 feet above Hyderabad, and as we got upon higher ground the air became fresher and cooler. We arrived at the Residency at 11.00 o'clock. At some distance off we could tell which of the bungalows was the English Resident's house, for there was a flagstaff with the dear old Union Jack flying. I do not think people who always live in England can possibly realize how the sight of the English flag in a distant land affects one. Our own dear country, our own dear home, our ways, our opinions, our prejudices even — it seems to speak of them all — they are all flying up there against the sky.

We drove in at an open gateway and up a long drive with young trees planted on each side, and then we came to the house itself and the pretty garden surrounding it. Like the Hyderabad houses, there were white columns supporting the veranda, and as the house is composed of three different buildings and verandas go all round each building, there was a great show of white columns. The views at Bolarum are 'pleasing,' as my father would say, not exactly beautiful. A great common, or *maidan* as we call it here, stretches far out round the Residency and the cantonments. The ground is undulating, and here and there are groves of trees. Far in the blue distance there are low hills.

After breakfast Mr Howell went back to his work, which seems to be as unceasing at Bolarum as at Hyderabad. Mrs Howell and I went to our own rooms and wrote for the English mail. It was too hot to sit out in the garden, even if there had been any particular view to sketch. Everything was very quiet. I suppose no house in England, unless there is illness in the house, is ever so quiet as our houses here are in the heat of the day. The servants have done most of the work of the home by 11.00 o'clock and are ready to seize any opportunity of a comfortable little nap. The *peon* stationed on the veranda even dozes, and only the cry of 'boy!' or '*qui hai*' from one of the sahibs, or the sound of an approaching carriage, rouses the world again into activity. I had got through one long home letter and some other shorter letters and was just thinking that I would have a little rest before going to the sports, when I looked at my watch and found it was past 4.00 o'clock.

At 5.00 o'clock we went off to the race ground — that part of the *maidan* where the paper chase was to be run. Mrs Howell and her son were both to ride in the race; Mr Howell and I were only spectators. We found a great number of people assembled at the starting point. Indians and English both. It was a pretty gay scene as every such gathering is in India, and at Bolarum the pretty country and the fresh green of the

217

maidan added to the effect. Near the starting point, which was also the finishing point, there were some hurdles and a wide ditch — which the riders were to jump at the end of the chase. Mr Howell and I walked across the common to a little knoll where there was some shade from a few trees. The riders came galloping past us before we reached the trees, however, and by the time we got there we could only see some moving specks in the distance and presently we lost sight even of them.

While we were waiting for the riders to appear again, I employed myself picking the little wild flowers that were growing at our feet. I found four or five different kinds — none of them I had seen before. One, Mr Howell told me, was the wild indigo. It has a feathery leaf very like a very fine acacia and a flower very like the English acacia, only it is pale pink. It was a small shrub. There was another plant very like a vetch with a little red flower, much used for food for camels, or so an Indian gentleman told me. Another flower I found was yellow, something like bird's-foot trefoil, and there was another little flower which was white. But I could not learn anything about these two.

The end of the chase was very interesting to see, when the riders came galloping up over the *maidan* and one after another leapt, or tried to leap, over the hurdles — Afsar Jung, the Nizam's aide-de-camp, was the first. He leapt the hurdles and the wide ditch beautifully. It is a pleasure to see anyone ride as he does. His little son, a boy of 12 years of age, was riding also in the chase and bids fair to be as good a horseman as his father in time. Only one rider among them all had a tumble in the ditch, but several horses refused the jump. After the paper chase was over we went to the mess room of the Hyderabad contingent. A band was playing and dancing had just begun. We did not stay long, as Mrs Howell, her son and I had to return to Hyderabad, a distance of 11 miles. Mr Howell remained at Bolarum. The Nawab Afsar Jung drove us home on his four-in-hand. He drives beautifully and it was very pleasant.

We were very hungry for dinner by the time we reached the Residency at half past eight o'clock. One of the *ayahs* at the Residency was very curious about me and she asked Ellen who I was, why I had come to Hyderabad and what I was doing there. One day a *chaprassi*, one of the *peons* in scarlet and gold, came up to Ellen and asked her if she spoke Hindustani, 'No,' said Ellen, 'do you speak English?' 'No,' he replied, 'you speak English here people kill you,' and he pulled out a long knife from his belt. 'How many people have you killed?' asked Ellen, 'I not kill any. Good Nizam now, good minister, people not kill. Bad Nizam, bad minister, plenty people kill.' All the time he kept looking out round the doors to see that no one was listening. There is one small room in the Residency called the 'Nizam's room' — it is the most private room in the house. There is no terrace outside and the wall below the windows is 30 feet deep. There is only one door in the room, which opens into the great hall. Whenever the Nizam comes to see Mr Howell, or anyone else of importance, an aide-de-camp remains in the hall near this door. Mr Howell told me it was the only place in the Residency where he and the Nizam could talk freely.

Mrs Howell had kindly planned an expedition for us for Sunday afternoon. We were to go round the city on elephants. We drove down to the city — Mrs Howell, her son, a friend, Mr Forbes, Mr Marriott and I. Mr Marriott had come to India only a few months ago, and he was staying at Secunderabad working for some military examination. He sketched in pencil rather well and was as anxious as I was to get some little drawing done while we were in the city. We found the elephants waiting for us in the courtyard of a palace.

There were three of them — two of them were the same elephants that I had been painting. The great creatures kneeled down, but even then we needed ladders to mount them. The *howdah* holds two persons, the *mahout*, the man who drives, sits on the neck of the elephant. Mrs Howell and Mr Forbes went on one elephant, Mr Marriott and I on another, and Auberon Howell and his friend on the third. Even on elephants we must keep to the laws of precedence. So Mrs Howell and the *chota sahib* went first. People in Hyderabad call Mr Forbes the *chota sahib* in contradistinction to Mr Howell, who is the *burra sahib*. Mr Marriott and I followed and Auberon and his friend brought up the rear.

We came out under a gateway, into a narrow muddy street. It seemed very strange to be up so high, moving along on a level with the first floor windows of the houses. It is a queer motion, half swinging, half jolting, but not so tiring as the motion of a camel. Before we began the ride someone asked me 'if I was a good sailor,' observing that people often felt seasick on an elephant. I did not feel even giddy, but before the end of our two hours' ride I was very tired.

First we went to see the tombs of the Nizams. They are in a large courtyard, and are in a little square flat-roofed building near a mosque. The outside of this building, which is all you see, is very delicately carved. It looked very white. I suppose it is marble, but I am not sure. It is protected by a high railing, which is made of iron and is rather pretty in design. A number of beggars hung about the place, and they came round us begging for money when we went away. We threw down some small copper coins to them and they were quite satisfied.

After leaving the tombs, we rode on through the town till we came to the principal square, if you can call an open space formed by four roads meeting a square. Over each of the four streets is a tall gate, and through one you see the beautiful mosque — the Char Minar (Four Minarets). Here Mr Marriott and I came to a halt. We could not ride on past such a view. So we persuaded our companions to continue their ride while we made a sketch. It is drawing under difficulties to sketch from the top of an elephant. The great creature is never quite still, and so as you draw your view is ever changing. I do not know if Turner himself would make much of a picture if an earthquake under him were moving him and his seat, his paints and his paper, from side to side in a long seesaw. But the view was so pretty we could not help making an attempt at a sketch.

Then we saw two wedding processions pass. The first was a Muhammadan wedding. Its approach was announced by a loud report and a blazing rocket flying above us. Then another bang, another rocket, and the procession came in sight. The bridegroom and his friends all gaily dressed, and an elephant with bridal trappings; but whether the bridegroom was on the elephant or walking I could not say. I did not much like their rockets whizzing up in the air above us. However, the sticks did not fall near us. Next came some curious carriages — the Hyderabad conveyances for purdah ladies. Most of the *nawab*s and rich Muhammadans possess one or more of them. Mr Marriott drew one and kindly gave me the little sketch. There was so very much to draw; it was impossible to do more than give a very rough idea of the scene.

It was beginning to grow dark now so we shut up our sketchbooks and on we went swaying and swinging through the streets. Only once again we stopped when we saw far below us on the ground a tempting heap of brass and silver and iron ornaments and instruments, and men sitting by their wares quite ready to sell them. We tried to buy some, but it is very difficult to bargain when the buyer does not know what to offer. I would have gone on Dora's principle respecting the leg of mutton, namely that 'the butcher would know how to sell it,' but this style of business was not approved of by my companions, and so I had to hand down my pretty brass buckles and knives, and ride on without them.

It was so curious as we passed along to catch a momentary vision of the life going on in the houses. Through one open window we saw some people praying; they were probably doing *puja*, the family worship. In another house there was some festivity going on; women gaily dressed were moving about and there were sounds of music. I wished I could have seen a little of the life of the people, but I do not think that the life of the middle and lower classes differs much from that of people of the same rank in other Indian towns. It is the society of the nobles, the number of powerful *nawab*s and Hindu chiefs that make Hyderabad such a very different place to Bombay, Calcutta or Madras. We rode back to the courtyard where we had mounted, and then the great creatures kneeled down again — a great lurch forward — a great lurch backward, and then down the little ladder and we were on terra firma once more.

Khandalla, 29 October 1888

We are at Khandalla again for the October vacation, but it is only half a holiday for John. He is one of the vacation judges and has to spend half the time in Bombay. Mr Jardine is the other vacation judge and they take it by turns to do the work. But this week they must both be in Bombay for a few days as they have to sit together in appeal. The cases they have to try are criminal appeals from the *mofussil*, that means the country in distinction to the capital of the presidency — Bombay. All cases of crime occurring in Bombay are tried at sessions at the High Court, and from that there is no appeal.

Mrs Jardine came up to the Travellers' Bungalow soon after we arrived, but she was not comfortable there alone and we offered her our tent. We had no room in the house. She had intended to remain in Bombay with her husband that first week, but the heat and the mosquitoes were so intolerable that she fled from Bombay and came here. No one, not even the oldest inhabitant remembers such a visitation of mosquitoes as we have had this autumn in Bombay. We have always thought our house rather bad for mosquitoes, but in this plague of mosquitoes no one escaped. They swarmed everywhere; they were bad all day, but at dusk they increased in numbers and ferocity till it was impossible to sit anywhere for a few minutes without a *punkah* going overhead and a man standing by with a big fan, waving it vigorously.

We had a little dinner party one evening and some reading aloud afterwards. The John Jardines and Mr Birdwood and Miss Pechey were with us. It really was very funny, in spite of the annoyance, to see everyone all through dinner, whatever they were saying, keenly on the look out for the enemy. Before dinner Mr Birdwood and John had sprinkled 'phenyl' on the floor under the table and we had dishes of it on the table. Mr Birdwood and John declared there would be no mosquitoes after this, but alas! they buzzed round us all the same, settling two and three at a time on our hands or faces. Only Mr Jardine was quite happy — he does not object to it, and he let them settle on his face with perfect indifference. The next 'reading' we had was on Malabar Hill at the Jardines. They had a bonfire in the drive, and in the house, in the drawing-room and in the dining room, they had *sigarees* (earthen bowls) with incense burning. I think the smoke certainly was effective, and we had not very many mosquitoes, but then the smell of the incense was so overpowering that it made us, at least John and me, feel very tired.

Well, as Mrs Jardine did not like the bungalow, I got our tent here ready for her. She had never slept in a tent before, and enjoyed the coolness of the air and seeing the bright moonlight through the openings in the *connats* (the side pieces). I wanted to send one of the men to sleep in the outer enclosure of the tent, but she would not. Her own man, a Goanese, was very timid and she said she preferred being alone. She had her little fox terrier 'Fidget' on her bed. I did not feel very easy about her and asked her to be sure to call me if she was the least uncomfortable. Our dressing room window looks toward the tent. However, that night, Wednesday, she slept very well and the next night too.

Friday was full moon and the scene outside our house was so lovely we were loth to go in and we sat on the veranda enjoying the beauty and talking later than usual. The colonel told a story of a panther and observed that when the animal was angry it waved its long tail backwards and forwards. We went to bed at last. The Willoughbys to the little bungalow and Mrs Jardine to her tent. We were all asleep soon, I think. I had had several bad nights and was sleeping very soundly.

Suddenly John and I were awakened — Mrs Jardine was calling out, 'Mrs Scott! I've had a panther in my tent.' We jumped up and I ran out in my nightgown. There was Mrs Jardine on the veranda with 'Fidget' in her arms. In a moment we had unfastened the door and she was safe in the house. She had been calling for some time from the tent, but we had not heard her.

She told us that she had wakened partly some time ago, just enough to see something dark going out of the tent. She supposed it was a pye-dog, or at worst a jackal, and went to sleep again. But soon she woke again. She was wide awake now. There, in full view, the moonlight falling clear upon it, stood a panther within two feet of her bed. It was looking at her and the dog, its eyes shining bright, its long tail waving backwards and forwards. The mosquito curtain was down and well tucked in; no doubt that puzzled the panther. Fidget was barking furiously. Mrs Jardine shouted at it, but it did not move. She had nothing near her to serve as a weapon excepting her little travelling clock, so she caught that up, thinking she could throw it at the panther if it made a spring. Mrs Jardine struck a light presently, but the panther only moved from one opening of the tent to another. After a time it went out towards the house.

Mrs Jardine says she lay there considering what she could do. 'If I lie here much longer my hair will turn white,' I said to myself, 'so I had better go.' It was like being in the zoological gardens in one of the dens. So she tucked Fidget well into the mosquito net and ran to the edge of the tent and shouted for help. But we did not hear; there was our dressing room between our room and the side of the house near the tent, and we were sleeping soundly. Then she flew back, caught up Fidget in her arms and ran as fast as she could to the house, past the front of the tent where the panther had gone out, past the dark shrubs where it might even then be lurking, across the drive and up the steps onto the veranda.

Nellie was awake and up almost as soon as we were. John ran over to the little bungalow and called Colonel Willoughby. The colonel came directly, ready for action — but alas his gun was in Poona — and no one in this house had a gun or a weapon of any kind. John and he went prowling about with a candle, but of course the panther had made off.

Nellie offered to take Mrs Jardine into her room, and we made up a bed on a sofa. Mrs Jardine would go back to the tent with Ellen to fetch some clothes, though I would have gone of course. She handed me Fidget to hold — the cause of all the trouble. No doubt the panther came after the dog and if it had not been for the mosquito net, which puzzled him, he would have had Fidget. I think Mrs Jardine was very brave; if she had run off, as any timid person might, when she stood at the entrance calling and none of us heard her, and had not gone back for Fidget, the panther might have returned and had the dog in spite of any mosquito net. It probably only perplexed him at first sight.

The next morning we sent for the *shikarri*, but before he came the *patel* and the colonel had examined the paths near the house. The ground was so hard round the tent that it was impossible to find any footprints there, but further down the garden near the edge of the ravine they found three or four distinct marks of the panther's paws — '*pugs*' as they call them here. Even I could trace the shape. It was very interesting to see how quickly a practised eye found the faint mark. Old days when Constance and I were devoted to Cooper's novels came back to me. We lived in a world of our own, made up of chiefs and squaws, and torture and captive maidens, and I fancied how the pathfinder would have pounced upon the little indentation. We arranged that the *shikarri* and *patel* should watch for the panther that night, but unluckily they could not get a gun and did not come here, and so the first night passed without anyone being on the look out.

The next night, Sunday, they came and made proper arrangements. A goat was tied up to attract the panther, but I insisted that the men should make the poor goat safe, and it was put under a sort of hen coop. The *shikarri* and *patel* remained near, concealed by some bushes. The goat was just on the other side of the tent and it bleated loudly. We went to sleep expecting to be awakened by the report of a gun, but we slept peacefully on, and were told in the morning that the panther had not been seen. There had not been the chance of a shot. The next night the men watched again and again nothing was seen, and then I gave up trying to catch the panther. The colonel had gone, and by Monday John had gone also. Then Mrs Jardine went away to Matheran, and Marian and I and Nellie were left alone. Two or three nights running a hyena came barking and crying and laughing near the house, and one night the *dherzi*, while he was carrying a dish to the kitchen, saw an animal near him, and of course thought it was the panther, but it ran away when a stone was thrown at it. Probably it was only a pye-dog.

The same night, however, that the panther came to us, a large dog belonging to our neighbour, General La Touche, was attacked and badly hurt by a panther. At about a quarter past two o'clock Miss La Touche was awakened by hearing a sound of choking outside her room. She thought directly of her favourite bulldog that was sleeping on the veranda, and was out of bed and through the door in an instant. She just saw something running off in the darkness, and then she found her poor dog gasping for breath, his throat all torn. Her father and the servants were aroused by this time, and they brought the dog into the house with the other dogs that were also on the veranda. Eight dogs altogether they have, a tempting place for a panther. The bulldog was very ill for a week — its windpipe had been bitten through, but it is slowly recovering now and is beginning to take food again. General La Touche has had a little house of wirework made, where the dogs can sleep safely in future. Their horses and carriages, and the coachmen and *saises*, are all encamped under some trees below the little hill on which the house stands. I suppose the men keep a light burning, but I do not think they can feel quite easy in their minds.

Bombay, November 1888
I took Miss Manning to one large Muhammadan boys' school, where we heard some good recitations in Hindustani, Arabic, Persian, Gujerati and finally in English. It was curious to see the boys so different in all their ways to English boys under the same circumstances. The little boys sat down while they recited on chairs, not on the ground, the elder boys stood up. At another school — the American Mission School, where the boys are almost all either Hindus or Muhammadans — we heard capital recitations. One boy, however, forgot his poem in the middle. He tried again, and again forgot. He went back, he tried again, and finally recovered the thread and finished the long poem triumphantly amidst our applause. I think very few English boys would have had the self-possession to stand there before a room full of people trying again and again to recollect the words.

One day we went to the High Court; criminal sessions were going on and John was the judge. The case we heard was a bad case of *dacoity*. Several men had robbed a house and injured the owners who tried to defend their property. There were seven prisoners in the dock — all Hindus. The jury was just being sworn in and prisoners have the right of challenging the jury, that is they may object to any juryman they do not like. The prisoners in this case objected to every native that entered the jury box. Their counsel challenged them one by one as they took their seats, till at last the jury was composed entirely of Englishmen. One of the prisoners was thin and sickly looking, and leaned on the bar as if he were tired. After standing for some time he fainted and John ordered that he should have a chair, and he allowed all the prisoners to sit down. The robbery was distinctly proved and the prisoners were all condemned to imprisonment for varying terms — some very long. The newspapers, English and Indian, approved heartily of the sentences. There had been several bad cases of housebreaking and robberies with violence, and it was thought that these sentences would tend very much to check further crime.

That afternoon Miss Manning and I paid two visits to private houses, which were very pleasant and also interesting. One was to the house of a wealthy Hindu gentleman, not a high-caste Hindu — a plain man of business, but intelligent and kindly. Mr Ellopa Bolarum is a builder contractor and he has done good work, according to the newspaper extracts that he showed us. His wife is a little stout motherly woman, 'motherly' though she has no children — that is their trouble. Mr Ellopa told me, as he had told me before, how he and his wife had known each other from their earliest childhood. They were betrothed by their parents when they were almost babies. The wife's parents died when she was very small. They were married when they were children, 'And we are very happy my wife and I.' He added, 'Of course we ought to be, for we have been always together, since we were children.' It is an instance of a very happy child marriage. It would be difficult to convince Mr and Mrs Ellopa of the evil of early marriages.

Mr Ellopa asked us if we would like to see how a Hindu lady does her *puja*, or worship, in her own house. Of course, we said 'yes,' if Mrs Ellopa did not mind 'our seeing it'. We were taken to the other side of the house, where there was a long corridor looking onto a garden below. Here, on a carpet near the wall, was a square flat polished stone. On the stone was placed a pot with the sacred *tulsi* plant, and round it were set out the little utensils used for *puja*, all made of silver — cups, spoons, plates, a bell and a small figure of the god Krishna, I think it was; and fresh flowers were strewn about. Mrs Ellopa sat down on a low dais, a few inches above the floor. She did not cross her legs, as an Egyptian woman does, but she sat with her knees outward and her feet meeting, just as Buddha is represented. Mrs Ellopa took up a little prayer book and read a prayer, and then she repeated some words with her hands joined. Then she rang the little bell — and then she took some water in a little vase and poured it over the *tulsi* plant. Then she poured some over the little god, and after that she took up some red powder, wetted it, and made red marks, here and there, on the flower pot, on the stone and on the god. Then she took up some rice and sprinkled it over the plant and over the god, and then she read the prayer again. Then she waved the book round the plant, and then she got up and walked round and round the stone, two or three times. That was all the *puja* she could show us — the rest was not allowed to be seen by profane eyes. Mr Ellopa said the worship of the *tulsi* plant is almost confined to women. Ladies who have leisure usually perform their *puja*, four times a day. When we came away, Mrs Ellopa put two most beautiful wreaths round our necks, and poured rose water and sandalwood oil over our hands and handkerchiefs.

We went one day to a Parsee wedding. Miss Wadia, the daughter of a leading Parsee family, was to be married to a Mr Cama, a doctor in one of the Madras regiments. Generally Parsee weddings are in the afternoon, but in the Cama family, we were told, it was the custom for marriages to take place in the morning. The wedding was a very pretty one — the house, Lowjee Castle, is a fine old building, a fashionable mansion once when all the great people lived at Parel or Mazagon. There is a large garden with splendid trees — mangoes and gold mohrs, casuarina and palms. The bride's dress, with a long white sari, was more graceful than any English bride's dress I ever saw. The bridegroom did not look so easy in his attire, as he is used now to wearing the English uniform, but for this occasion was obliged to put on the costume of a Parsee bridegroom.

Another pleasant visit that we paid was to a Muhammadan family. We went one afternoon to the house and we found a very kind and very pretty welcome awaiting us. We were received at the hall door by Mr Ibrahim; he took us upstairs to the ladies' rooms. There his pretty little wife was ready for us. All across the room from wall to wall were stretched threads of cotton or silk, with little white and pink flowers

227

tied to them. These tiny garlands hung about a foot above our heads. The rooms reminded me rather of the houses in Egypt. There were comfortable divans against the walls covered with dark silky material. We sat down and the husband and wife seemed both much pleased to see Miss Manning, though the wife was very shy and would not say much.

There was one strange incident in our visit. While we were talking, we heard a queer sort of music going on — a voice, evidently singing a European air, but the accompaniment was unmistakably Indian. I asked our host what it was and he offered to have the musician brought in. He is mad, he observed casually — he always comes here to sing and have his food. He is quite harmless and he goes about from house to house, and gets a few annas or food where he can. In another minute in came the mad musician. He was rather tall, slight, with black and wandering bright eyes. He wore a short Muhammadan gaberdine and trousers, all white, and on his head a red fez with a black tassel. He carried a little old guitar. Mr Ibrahim asked him if he would sing to us and told him to sit down, and he sat down just in front of us. Then he began a pretty old French song, and he pronounced the words clearly too. Song after song he sang; I do not know how long he would have gone on. It is his one pleasure in life — his music. Many years ago he went to Europe with a gentleman, as his servant. They were a long time in France and there it was he learnt all his French songs. Now, poor fellow, that his reason is gone, he is still happy with his guitar and his songs. His whole face brightened up into a smile when I spoke to him in French. Perhaps the sound of French speech and the sight of our European clothes recalled to his poor mind the happy days he had spent in '*le beau pays de France*'.

Epilogue

A FEW lines seem to be needed to link up my diary, last written in the summer of 1889 [little remains after November 1888], with unexpected events of the following year.

During the last months of 1889, and in January and February 1890, rumours reached us of John's services being needed again in Egypt. The next reform in Egypt was to be the reform of the law, and in telegrams and letters that came from Lord Cromer and the Egyptian government, John's name was mentioned as the man most capable of planning and carrying out the reform. The years he had spent there as the English judge of appeal in the international tribunals had given him much experience; he was well known to the Egyptian government and liked by the Egyptian people.

He was very willing to go back to Egypt if the Indian government would agree to 'lend his services for a year.' So the old saying came true for us — 'If you drink the water of the Nile, you must return to it.'

We had actually been planning already for me to go home for six months; my presence was rather urgently needed and there were fresh arrangements to be made for our younger boys' schooling. It was only when our carriage was at the door to take me to the P & O boat for England that the telegram arrived with the final decision of the Indian government that, 'the services of Mr Justice Scott should be lent to Egypt.' It was too late to postpone my sailing, although it was very hard to leave my husband just when he was to take up a fresh appointment. For the children's sake we kept to the plan that had been made, and 'for a year,' as I said to myself, I bade farewell to Bombay and all our friends there, English and Indian. Our boat, the *Rome* of 5000 tons, seemed gigantic. I had not seen the list of passengers, and it was a great surprise to find that the children of TRH the Duke and Duchess of

229

Connaught were aboard with their governess and nurse. It was Saint Patrick's Day, 17 March, and the birthday of little Patricia, Princess Patsy as she was called, when we sailed.

We had calm weather and everyone was up on deck. Those long deck chairs do not attract me — one cannot write or draw in them, and I generally find something to sketch. Perhaps a passing boat, or a ship at anchor, or at least one or two of the crew. One day I sketched two Sikhs from the engine room, fine tall men, who were quite pleased to stand for me and have a reward for doing so. Another time it was the 'King of Stokers', a black man from Somaliland, who could bear the fierce heat of the furnace even in the Red Sea.

The royal children were much interested in my sketching, and little Princess Patsy sat by me day after day and loved to be allowed to put out my paints for me. Then we had games of 'shop', and many walks up and down the deck, while I told them stories of our childhood. Prince Arthur would beg me, 'Now tell us something very naughty that you did when you were children.'

There was no great heat during the voyage — indeed in the Red Sea it was rather cold with a head wind. When we got to England we found sleet and snow!

Appendix
The Scott Family: A Note
(see Plate)

This photograph may have been taken late in 1890. Despite the belief (at the end of the journal) that 'the services of Mr Justice Scott were lent to Egypt for a year,' he and the author did not return to Bombay. He worked in Egypt for many years and was made KCMG. He also received an honorary degree of DCL at Oxford University where he had studied (and gained a cricket blue) long before.

Five of the six children were to have connections with India.

Leslie, a leading King's Counsel and later Lord Justice of Appeal, was engaged by the Indian Chamber of Princes as legal adviser at the time of the Simon Commission (to recommend constitutional changes in India). He visited India in 1929 for discussions.

Arthur entered the Indian Civil Service in 1900. He served until 1909 when he unfortunately died of typhoid fever.

Jack (Johnnie), after the Boer War was posted to India with his Royal Artillery battery, and was to share a bungalow with Arthur for a time. He was killed in France in 1917.

Ranee and Mary (Baby) both married men who worked in India, the former in the Indian Civil Service, and the latter in the Education Service.

Only Lilian (Lily) missed out, but she spent some time in Cairo with her father in the 1890s.